CW00494117

PERSPECTIVE
Alphabet of Life

By

Adrian L Hawkes

Published by: Create Space

PERSPECTIVE

Copyright © by Adrian L. Hawkes

All right reserved. No part of this book may be used or reproduced by any means, graphic electron, or mechanical including photocopying, recording, taping or by any information storage retrieval system without the written permission of the publisher except in the case of brief quotations embodied in critical articles and reviews.

Create Space
4900 LaCross Road
North Charleston, SC 29406
USA
T.1-206-508-4011

Because of the dynamic nature of the Internet, any web address or links contained in this book may have changed since publication and may no longer be valid. The views expressed in this work are solely those of the author and do not necessarily reflect the views of the publisher, and the publisher herby disclaims any reasonability for them.

ISBN: 1532791925
ISBN: 9781532791925

Published in the United States of America

Publication Date: 1st December 2016

All Bible quotations are from the King James Bible or the American Standard Bible.

Thanks and Acknowledgments

To the editorial staff at Create Space
To the Rainbow Community in North London
To My Editorial help Keith Lannon
To my wife Pauline as she has inspired me in the area of helping
Refugees and Asylum seekers of which this book talks about quite a
bit
To my 3 Children and 10 Grand children and two Great
Grandchildren
And to you for reading my book.

PERSPECTIVE
By Adrian Hawkes

Contents

Foreword by Andy Smith

Preface

Foreword by Andy Smith
Co Founder and CO of Regenerate

Adrian Hawkes is at it again. Writing books that challenge, inspire and make a change in peoples lives. Adrian is a natural storyteller and the good news is that his stories are worth listening to, as his life is one incredible adventure!

I've known Adrian and Pauline for over 20 years and they have been a source of massive inspiration, friendship and support to me throughout this time. Adrian's stories and lessons learnt are worth capturing, that's why this book is important. I bet you can learn so much from his wisdom and life lessons here in this book that will give you a new perspective on things that will impact your life.

In 2004 I said to Adrian and Pauline that I'd love to learn from them and was interested to learn how they get alongside people who are starting projects abroad. I have seen what they have done in London with running a foster care agency, a school, a church, their incredible work with asylum seekers and heard stories about how they have helped set up projects in places as far off as Sri Lanka! I had heard to that they were going to Kenya to start another adventure helping people there. I wanted to learn from these guys. They invited me to go with them to Kenya to hatch plans with a guy they had met called Sammy in Kenya. Sammy used to be a street kid in a town called Nakuru and Adrian and Pauline had met him and wanted to support his vision to reach out to the next generation of street kids. Sammy wanted to help others in the same way that he had been helped. Adrian and Pauline very kindly invited me onto this Kenyan adventure and it changed my life.

We stood on some empty fields on the outskirts of Nakuru and listened to Sammy's vision of building a school, medical centre and housing to bring hope to some of the children that had had a really tough start in life, kids that were orphaned, living on the streets and addicted to glue. To cut a long story short, Adrian and Pauline set about sending teams over to Kenya, raising money to buy those fields for Sammy and his team and now in 2016 there is housing for over 170 children who have been rescued from the streets and dump sites, many orphans and kids being looked after, housed, educated, fed, loved and cared for. These were kids that were forgotten and now are thriving. There is a school there now on those very same fields with around 350 children getting an award winning education and there is a medical centre, a car mechanics garage, a water pump for the whole community and other employment generating schemes for the young adults who are passed school age. I've had the privilege of going back out there dozens of times and watched the dream grow and it was Adrian the story teller and his remarkable wife Pauline that behind the scenes have are the rock of support and a launch pad for lives being changed through Sammy's projects there.

Enjoy the book, get inspired by Adrian's perspectives and go and do some of the types of things Adrian does and the world will be a better place.

Cheers

Andy

http://www.regenerateuk.co.uk

PREFACE

Having written five books with a subject in mind, and a sixth that is fiction, this one is a bit different. I hope you will find it a sort of, "dip in," book where, from the chapter headings, you will see something that, "gets you,' and you will want to take a read and have a think.

Much of this book comes from my Blogs. I suppose that people write for different reasons. I usually write because I want to persuade people, change things, and even alter people's mindsets. I think a lot, and have discovered perspectives on important issues that I believe are important. You may think that is somewhat inflated and that they are not so. Whatever! However, perhaps I can change some things.

Sometimes just small changes bring about large benefits. Big doors swing on little hinges.

So. read on and tell me if I got it wrong!

A is for Asylum Seekers

The Long Road to Discovering the Presence and Plight of Asylum Seekers

Gaining perspective on Social Care on the way from Middlesbrough to London

I lived in Middlesbrough, a large town situated on the South bank of the River Tees in north east England, for five years (1969-1974) and during that time I got very involved with the students in the local college. Gradually the number of students coming to our church community increased substantially. A number of the students were doing degrees in social work and we often had long conversations about this issue. Some of them had reached the conclusion that pastoral care was their area of expertise and anything that I did out of care and concern was, in their opinion, outdated and in need of replacing, and I should not be crossing over into their perceived domain.

I thought a lot about these discussions; I did not feel intimidated by their attitudes, but I did believe I should give it some consideration. Since that time I have developed my knowledge considerably in the area of social care, and advanced my perspective on its broad issues, some of which I will share in these pages.

It struck me that "followers of Jesus," while seeking to bring to reality the Kingdom of God, were the main instigators of much good in the societal areas that I now refer to as the four pillars that hold up, influence and effect change in culture and ultimately His world. These four pillars, I would argue, are what people of, "The Way," need to be active in for strategy and influence as they pull down from heaven kingdom values and bring them into effect on earth. These are values required to effect change for good in society.

It seems obvious to me that Paul, in the scripture, understood the powerful effect of Rome and hence wanted to bring in the values of the kingdom of God where Roman culture would be impacted!

What are these four pillars?

Education.
Media, including TV, radio, advertising, hoardings, the web, books, newspapers, magazines, theatre, film and art.
Politics
Business

Let me enlarge a little more. These pillars holding up the table of culture are to some extent fluid and interchangeable.

So let us have a brief look as to how it works. First of all EDUCATION we should never really stop learning, but those early years at school are actually moulding our future thinking and actions. Of course, family too is an educator and a very powerful one. However, have you heard young children arguing with parents because teacher said something different? Have you also listened as school educators say loudly, "We do not push children in any particular direction. We have an unbiased approach'. Sorry, but that is just silly. Travel and life are also educators.

The second table leg is BUSINESS; this really does mould culture, thinking and action. If you don't have money for food it will affect you. If you have no roof over your head, you will think a certain way. If you are rich, be careful as to what colour that gives to your speech and thinking, as mother Theresa said, "You could end up being poor in what matters."

Leg three, that would be MEDIA and by that I would mean newspapers, hoardings TV, Theatre, Cinema, the web in fact all we see as "the arts and entertainment world."
It really is a powerful moulder of culture. Have you heard

people say, "I am not influenced by advertising?"
How very funny. Of course we all are. That is why people spend so much money on it to persuade us to part with ours.

Last leg, which would be POLITICS. Many young people turn up their nose at this point and often say, "Boring!" Trouble is that those politics end up moulding the culture, so things that once were wrong become legal and therefore normal and *right.*

As an obvious instance of what I am referring to, let us take a brief look back on **education,** especially in the UK, and consider Robert Raikes from the eighteenth century. (A statue of Raikes was erected on the Victoria Embankment, London in 1880, sculpted by Sir Thomas Brock, R.A., to celebrate the centenary of the Sunday School movement. A statue of Raikes was also erected in Gloucester Park fifty years later, in 1930. It is a copy of the Brock statue.) Raikes founded Sunday School, and let us be clear; the origins of Sunday School were not as many know it or imagine it today. It was in fact a comprehensive educational programme that taught children to read and write. Sunday was the only day the students could attend. Of course he wanted them to understand the bible, but primarily it was an all-round educational programme. The change in society that was instigated by this man was extensive.

In **politics,** who could forget William Wilberforce who, in 1805, achieved, after many years of effort, the parliamentary abolition of slavery in the UK? This is another societal trend setting, ground breaking, kingdom value being put in place. Wilberforce was a man of "The Way," that is, he was a Christian.

In **media,** there has been, historically, a tendency in Christian thinking to discourage young Christians from getting involved. What a tragedy! The media is a powerful moulder of our culture, influencing far beyond what we give it credit for. People of the Way need to get involved in the media - and stay involved.

I take my hat off to people like Dan Wooding and Assist News who constantly disseminate good honest information for the whole of the press world.

In **business,** there has been numerous fantastic trend setters; people who were ahead of their time, seeking justice and presenting a value system that hadn't been seen before in their respective generations. Take the Cadbury brothers for example. Originally, they constructed their factory in a huge garden to enhance their workers well-being and invited their staff to have a voice on the board. This was utterly unheard of and radical at the time. Where did such ideas come from? I would argue that it all came about from the kingdom values that the Cadbury family held.

When the new factory was built at Bourneville it had many facilities which were unknown in Victorian times - properly heated dressing rooms; kitchens for heating food; separate gardens for men and women as well as extensive sports fields and women's and men's swimming pools. Sports facilities included football, hockey and cricket pitches, tennis and squash courts and a bowling green. Country outings and summer camps were organised. Special workers' fares were negotiated with the railway company and 16 houses were built for senior employees.

Morning prayers and daily bible readings, first started in 1866 to preserve a family atmosphere, were not abandoned until 50 years later, when the size of the workforce was too large for such an assembly. George Cadbury was a housing reformer interested in improving the living conditions of working people. In 1895 he bought 120 acres near the factory and began to build houses in line with the ideals of the Embryo Garden City movement. The motivation for building the Bourneville Village was that George Cadbury wanted to provide affordable housing in pleasant surroundings for wage earners.
(See http://www.cadbury.co.nz/About-Cadbury/The-Story-

[11]

of-Cadbury/The-Story-of-Cadbury---Continued.aspx)

What has all this to do with my chats with social care students in Middleborough? A great deal. Those discussions were, I believe, a catalyst for shaping much of my thinking since then. It actually contributed to shaping the direction of my future.

I remember, when I was moving to London, driving down the M1 and talking to God. I said "I would really like a million pounds or so, Lord. I would like to see those early things re-established, I want your followers to move into those influential areas that change our culture, I want to be, "salt and light," seeking to influence and show new directions in some or all of these important strategic areas."

I had a passion to be involved in these four cultural areas, and I wanted to encourage people who knew God and had similar passions, to seek to draw down God's kingdom into these areas. I had almost forgotten that conversation with God on the motorway, but He listened and He answered and the millions came and we spent it on buildings, employment, business start-ups, housing and schools. How the money came in is another story - many stories in fact - but I am still seeing the influence in the areas of the four pillars. I want to see others catch the vision, and realize that that is where we need to seek the kingdom.

The move to north London in 1974, was to take up the responsibility of leading two local church communities in the area.

While I was pasturing these two churches in north London. My wife, Pauline, and I were shocked as we began to discover the plight of asylum seekers who were flooding into London from war zones like Sri Lanka, Bosnia, Herzegovina, Kosovo, Congo, Afghanistan, Iran and Iraq, to name just a few. These were men, women and children who had escaped the violence of their homelands to make the long and dangerous journey to the British capital.

We were now settled in the Metropolis, and through a long series of events, we had taken the local authority's training course and began to foster children on the council's behalf. As a couple, we had fostered children for the local authority for 15 years, giving homes to around 30 children. After many years of doing this, and getting somewhat older, we decided that bringing up teenagers should be for others. We began wondering what we should do with our hard learned experience.

While considering what to do with what we knew of fostering, we passed through a sad occasion as Pauline and I visited a good friend named Alan Pavey in hospital. We knew he was very ill. In fact, he was dying. He passed away not long after our visit. But while we were there, he turned to us both and said, "You need to be helping refugees." We both asked, "What do you mean by that?" "You just need to do something about them," He replied. I guess we both saw this as some kind of prophetic word. The problem with prophecy is that you don't always know how to react or what to do. And at that time we didn't have a clue what to do about it. So, we put it on the shelf, as it were. It was a word from a friend that seemingly had no relevance to where we were.

A few weeks later in August 2001 while watching the news together on BBC TV, Pauline and I were horrified to witness the story of a Norwegian freighter that had picked up a group of refugees in international waters from a troubled fishing vessel. The ship was on its way to Australia with 20 million Australian dollars worth of cargo. The Captain of the ship tried to help them to find asylum in Australia. The Prime Minister of Australia, however, refused to allow the refugees ashore and I think some of them subsequently died.

Some were injured and I believe others died in the incident.. As we watched the news item, we thought, "How awful to risk one's life in such a way simply to escape from where one lives and go to an unknown land and culture!"

The crew of Tampa received the Nansen refugee award for 2002 from UN high commissioner for refugees for their efforts to follow international principals for saving people in distress at sea.

The John Howard Government of Australia had refused permission for the Norwegian freighter MV Tampa, carrying 438 rescued refugees from a distressed fishing vessel in international waters, to enter Australian waters. The people were predominantly Hazaras of Afghanistan. (The Hazaras are a Hazaragi speaking people who mainly live in central Afghanistan, Hazara Town in Balochistan, Pakistan and Karachi. They are overwhelmingly Shia Muslims and make up the third largest ethnic group in Afghanistan.) This triggered an Australian political controversy in the lead up to a federal election, and a diplomatic dispute between Australia and Norway.

When the Tampa entered Australian waters, the Prime Minister ordered the ship to be boarded by Australian special forces. This brought an official censure from the government of Norway who said the Australian Government had failed to meet obligations to distressed mariners under international law at the United Nations.

Within a few days the Australian government introduced the Border Protection Bill into the Australian House of Representatives, saying that it would confirm Australian sovereignty to, "Determine who will enter and reside in Australia." The government introduced the so-called "Pacific Solution," whereby the asylum seekers were taken to Nauru while their refugee status was considered, rather than in Australia. Nauru is a tiny island state in the middle of the Pacific. It is the third smallest state by square metres in the world, the Vatican and Monaco being the only smaller sovereign states.

[14]

This news item ultimately became a life changing catalyst for us both.

When the report ended, I had to protect our TV from being attacked by Pauline, who was, by now, boiling with anger. I explained that the TV itself was, "not guilty," and that the reporter was just reporting the facts of the story. This single piece of information had a major impact on my wife. She wanted to catch a plane and punch the Australian Prime Minister for his inhumanity and lack of human concern. While she was angrily jumping up and down, I was shielding our TV from being damaged and trying to diffuse the emotive situation. I said to her, "Pauline, there are many refugees in the UK, why don't you start there rather than spend the air fare going to deal with the Australian Prime Minister, who might not even see you? Why don't you start by phoning Social Services, they know us and perhaps they have some kind of refugee department?"

After she had calmed down a little, I told her that there were, "loads" of refugees coming to the UK because of wars in their countries. We had observed this fact over the years that we had lived in London. So, why should we not try and help them instead of those on the other side of the world?

Pauline agreed to ring the local authority and talk to them about this, especially as we were quite well known to Social Services, having fostered for them and even led their foster team for many years.

The next morning, I listened to Pauline talking to the Social Services telephone operator. She asked, "Do you have a department that deals with refugees?" By her smile. I assumed they did have such a department. I was surprised, though, when listening-in to the conversation, as I heard a man at the other end say, "Yes, I am the manager of the authority's asylum service. Is that Pauline Hawkes I am talking to?"
It turned out that Pauline had worked on training other

foster parents for the department, together with this man, who had now been promoted to manager of this service.

"We have so much need in this area, I am now managing the authority's refugee department and if there is anything you can do to help, we will be more than happy to have you on board."

I also, importantly, heard him say, "If you want to help in this area, tell us how you plan to do it and we will fund you. We will have you on board tomorrow." Wow! What a response! That is what started us on a most incredible journey.

What to do? How to help? We did our research and discovered that the Muslim community in our area had already stood up to the plate and were meeting the need with many homes. We turned to them for help and advice on to how to start and what was needed. They suggested people who would advise us and we ended up using much of their expertise. We were somewhat sad that there seemed to be no Christians on the block doing anything to help. For that reason, as we moved into this new arena with our offer of help, we did not come with a, "Christian," agenda, or a church based view; rather we came simply as willing helpers. By this means, Phoenix Community Care organisation came into being. But more of PCC later.

The refugee department was very happy with our suggestions to help, but the programme we envisaged needed to be accommodation based. We were perplexed about how this could be accomplished. Out of the blue, our daughter Carla, her husband and three sons said, "We want to help. I'll tell you what we will do. We shall redecorate our house, and then move out, and you can use that." To cut a long story short, that's exactly what happened. My youngest daughter magnanimously donated her house to the vision and moved out, and that house became our first property in which we housed-refugees. There were, however, months of jumping through fiery bureaucratic hoops and endless regulations, which often make it very hard to help folks, but, jumping ahead for a moment, we soldiered on and at the time of writing we have ten houses and can accommodate over thirty people.

Back to the commencement of the whole project, following Pauline's telephone conversation, we put together a programme to help asylum seekers. It involved housing, support and care, and just being there, especially for the young people. So we set up a "Not for Profit" company called, "Phoenix Community Care." (PCC)

As a "By the way," the company name came about after a man I did not know made a cold approach to me at a conference I attended and confronted me with, "I am calling you "Phoenix," because you are about to lose everything. But God will restore it to you many fold." Hence the company name, "Phoenix." He was right. I did lose everything I had, and God restored it back to us. However, that's a story for another day.

Bureaucracy and Pedants

As I mentioned above PCC was originally formed as a, "Not for Profit," company, in June 1999. During those first few months after Pauline's conversation with the local authorities, making connections and moving forward was *not* at all easy. As already stated, our youngest daughter had donated her home for the first clients. Once she and her family had moved out, we then took on their mortgage. This was in October of that year. The local authorities kept telling us, "There are lots of young girls we will want to place with you." But then we began to encounter the vast and sometimes overwhelming bureaucracy. And one of the top priorities of the bureaucracy was to inspect the prospective homes for the clients, to ensure they were safe. We are talking, in particular, of a certain "Mr Sniffy." Pauline kept me away from contacting this man, due to his remarkably pedantic approach to checking the buildings. I am not a violent man at all, but Pauline feared I might thump him for his pedantry. I nicked-named him 'Mr Sniffy,' because every time we felt we had met their requirements, he would say, with a sniff, "Not good enough!"

To say it was a frustration is an understatement.

Although the house was supposed to be homely, and feel "just like an ordinary, normal home," the list of requirements was long. For example, "Door closers should be fixed to every door in all rooms," … just like everyone has in their home? I think not!

The way Mr Sniffy tested the doors was to place a piece of thin paper between the door jamb and the top of the door, and then close it. If the paper slid down, Mr Sniffy would give a prolonged sniff and say, "failed!" with a subtle hint of glee in his tone of voice.

I am sure my readers can imagine the cost of doing every aspect of the work as Mr Sniffy prescribed. Secondary lighting, door closers, interactive fire alarm system, and on and on went the list. Mr Sniffy had a field day. After much expense and many "sniffy" failures, we finally got our certificate. It was now late November 1999. We were rather swamped with the bills and monthly mortgage repayments, but at least we were ready to help. We contacted the local authority and said, "OK! We are ready!" Their response was;

"It's nearly December and we don't do much in December."

"Are there no refugees in need in December?" we asked with just the slightest tone of sarcasm.

"Yes there are, but it's the processing," they said, "And December is a holiday month."

Finally, January came. But then, apparently, the December

holiday continued well into January. No one in the department answered the phones, or responded to us at all. Eventually, towards the end of January we had a phone call and the department asked us to take the first young lady. The placement was made on 1st February 2000.

Pauline said, "I don't know how we will pay the bills, the mortgage is due and the bank account is bare. It's great we are helping, but how do we survive financially?" The department would be paying us for the work with the young lady, but we had no idea when – and thereby we discovered the next hurdle that needed to be jumped.

We contacted the department and they explained the system for payment. "You give us an invoice at the end of February for the people we place in that month, however you will have to give us thirty days credit, so we will pay you on the last day of March. As it happened, we were not paid until the second week of April. Incredibly, we survived, but I still am not sure how we did it.

On February the first, we started off with our first client, a young Muslim girl from the Congo. She had been raped and was terribly frightened and desperately looking for help. We still remember the trauma and our first meeting, and actually, we are still good friends with her.

The process, which has become a regular routine nowadays, works like this: Our Company gets a call from Social Services saying, "We have such and such a person. Can you help?' If we have space, we usually say, "Yes." We then arrange a collection, usually from a Social Services office, occasionally a Police Station. On this first occasion, Pauline went herself. These days, one of our key workers would usually go.
On this initial experience, when Pauline arrived at their office, the Social Worker pointed to a young lady huddled and slumped over in a chair. On her knee she clutched at a solitary plastic carrier bag. That was all she had to her name. She was pale and drawn. In fact she looked totally

drained. Once introductions had taken place, Pauline drove the young lady to the house. We have a policy of trying to make the accommodation as welcoming as possible, which we define as, "Having the, "wow" factor." Pauline showed the young lady the bedrooms, and the food in the kitchen, and said, "As you are our first ever guest, you can choose your room from the whole house."

The young lady chose her room and simply said, "May I sleep now?" She then climbed into bed, coat and all and immediately dropped into a deep sleep. She did not wake up for a couple of days.

Pauline, having finished the, "I'm a professional Placement Manager," part and seen the first client into her room securely, drove the car around the corner, parked up, and wept bitterly about the terrible situation of the refugees. She then mopped her face, dried her eyes, pulled her mobile out of her handbag and called me. "Quick!" she said, "Get another house. We need to be helping these people!" She wept as she simply said further, "Get more houses. There is a great need here."

Momentum began to pick up, and soon we received a call for another placement of a sixteen year old young lady, she also came to us as a frightened and confused teenager. But several years on, she has a degree in modern languages, speaking four of them fluently and is still our friend; her husband and baby are an integral part of our community.

The process continued, until the house was full and we saw the urgent need for another house. My daughter purchased another house, renovated it and then moved herself and the family yet again to another home, and as before, we took over, ready to expand and help more people.

One of the things that sticks in my mind through the passing of time was Mr Sniffy's continuous on-going attitude even as the work developed. While the first house was full and the second one had not yet passed the expensive inspection process, the department called up and said, "We have a young lady, she is sleeping on a park bench and is very vulnerable, can you help us? We cannot find any other accommodation."

We explained our position. "The problem is we only have a box room available in the house and it does not meet your inspection standards for size. We have a bed in it, a chest of draws, a TV, and a bedside cabinet, but I think its six inches smaller than Mr Sniffy's regulations." (I hasten to inform you that I didn't ever refer to him as Mr Sniffy when talking to the department.)

"But this is an emergency!" They said. Hence we agreed to get the room ready to receive the new placement.

The young lady was pleased to have her own room, with a bed, TV, and a place to eat which was out of danger and away from the park bench. Mr. Sniffy, however, had other ideas. He did a spot check in the middle of the second week she was there. He phoned us straight away, "Get that girl out of that illegal room or I will close you down!" As per usual, he sniffed before he added, "I will be back at the end of next week to check you have moved her."

We had people working like mad on house number two and we managed to re-accommodate the young lady in a regulation sized room. However, it still strikes me that in these situations the bullying bureaucratic regime had - and still has - no compassion, no common sense, and takes no account of a very real and urgent need.

I am reminded of what the Bible says in Galatians chapter 5 verse 22, "...*that there is no law against 'kindness, goodness (benevolence)*" (Amplified Bible).
I do wonder to myself if Paul, the writer of Galatians, ever met a first century version of Mr Sniffy!

We have expanded considerably since those early days. Not only do we accommodate young people who are refugees.

but now we also have our own foster care agency. This was initially conceived because, although the refugees we deal with are aged 16 and over, there are in fact many who find their way to the UK who are much younger.

Alongside that, we formed another company, London Training Consortium, (LTC) which handles the youngster's educational requirements, particularly ESOL, speaking English as a second language.

There is still a great need for people to help in this area, despite the fact that the government is always trying to discourage refugees from entering the UK. As we watch the news and see the wars and dangers that people are in, we can see that people are going to run somewhere, and undoubtedly some will make it to the UK. Often we can tell by the clients who come to us, where the latest, "hot spot,"or war area is in the world.

Incidentally although we did not announce that underneath it all we have the love of Christ constraining us, nevertheless Social Services did latch on to the fact that we were people who were, "Followers of the way," and they often said of Phoenix Community Care and its placements, "You people seem to go the extra mile," which seems to us like a good Scriptural principle as spoken of by Christ in Matthew 5:41. We hope we still do deliver more than is legally required. (Find out more about us by going to our website at www.pheonixcommunity.org.) I ask anybody who reads this story, to pray for us as we bring the love of God to these very many needy people who have seen so much hate and violence in their lives.

Ten years on we can house 30+ in our own properties with support workers caring for both 16 and 17 year old unaccompanied minors (young people in the UK without parents or guardians).
We also care for 18+ year olds who are considered vulnerable, often, young ladies escaping from war and rape situations. Alongside this we have added the housing and support care of those who have been in the

care system but whom the authority deem not quite ready for total self-support.

Some years ago we recognised that foster care was also needed for youngsters in the country who were without parents. After being registered as a foster care agency, a status which was another long, complex and difficult process, we began by fostering a young person of around 9 years old, who could not speak English and had been found by the Police after wandering around in a Supermarket for many hours, and who is now happily placed with good foster parents by the PCC agency.

What Value Refugees and Asylum Seekers?

It is amazing how much we misunderstand the process of why there are refugees and asylum seekers, be it in the UK or anywhere else in the world.

As explained above, I work for a company called Phoenix Community Care. This is a, "Not for Profit company," that works with people in need. We work with refugee young people aged 16 and 17 years old, who are in the UK but have no parents or guardians here. These young people actually come under the care system as looked after, "children." One is considered a child by UK law until one reaches the age of 18 years. The problem for the care system in the UK is that, in real terms, most local authority agencies for foster care were overstretched before the wars in so many areas all over the world.

Where do asylum seekers across Europe mainly come from?

[23]

The four main countries of origin of asylum seekers in Europe according to a recent report were Iraq with 50,058 applications, Federal Republic of Yugoslavia with 32,656 applications, Turkey with 28,455 applications and Afghanistan with 25,470 applications. (UNHCR Asylum Applications)

Refugees have been precipitated from war zones all over the world. Places like Afghanistan, Kosovo, Darfur, Somalia, and Iraq had huge numbers fleeing for their lives. On top of that there are localised wars like in Congo. In addition to that, there are internal wars in Sri Lanka. Add to those problems the issue of persecution, which still exists in countries like Vietnam and Cambodia.

If your life was threatened would you run away? Would you try and protect your family and loved ones?

As a company we are housing young people from most of the above countries. We also have young people from China and Iran. "Why Iran?" You may ask. "No war in these countries!" No! However, if you are a Christian or a Jehovah's Witness, then life is almost impossible there. There are those from Ethiopia. Why do they come? Many say to me, "My father speaks Amharic, but my mother is from Eritrea. And so, no one wants you."

I am sure there are bad apples. I have met a few of them. However, most of the stories I hear would make you wonder how some of these people have not gone insane with their personal situations. Some, it has to be said, because of the extreme pressure, are actually in need of prolonged psychiatric care.

Nutty Newspaper Nonsense

Sadly, I often hear from people, it is not fair that these people are stealing our houses and jobs and being paid large amounts of money in government benefits. I work in the sector and what I see definitely does not fit those newspaper "nonsense" headlines. I see youngster's just about surviving with a roof over their heads, a small amount of food money and some help with language.

Many of these people are ambitious and keen to work and contribute to the country that has given them refuge. Often the law actually does not allow them to do that.

I reached the ultimate in surprise recently when I was asked if I knew that black people are able to receive a free oyster card(bus and tube pass) if they live in London. Come on! All my black friends, if you did not know this – go and get one. The problem is; I do not know where from. The young lady who was telling me this story went on to tell me that the person who had told her this great piece of news, when told, "No, that is not true", looked at her with that knowing look that says "Oh, that's what you think!"

It really is nutty nonsense from people who read certain types of newspapers that come out with this stuff, and then when you tell them, "No! It's not true," they prefer to believe their fairy tale rubbish rather than any real facts.

Some of the other apocryphal stories I have been told are as follows, usually by wide eyed people who, when, like my friend who told me the story of free travel, are told, "No! It's nonsense", and look at you as though *you* are the stupid one:

"Did you know that they now give foreigner's free cars?"

"It's terrible that one can only get a house on the council if you are not English."

"Did you know that immigrants get £120.00 per week unemployment allowances?" and so on. I have heard lots more. I must admit that I had not heard the one about black people getting free travel until recently. Is that nutty stuff or what?

The problem is that if you read certain newspapers, so called, then even though you tell me you don't believe everything you read in the press, you will nevertheless not take note of these facts because it does not fit with what you want to think for whatever strange reason, or, '*because you read it in the press*'! However the facts are:

▪ A single, adult, asylum seeker receives £36.62 a week – that's just £5.23 per day.
▪ A single unemployed UK citizen of the same age would receive £67.50, plus other benefits they may be able to receive.

- Asylum seekers cannot claim mainstream benefits.
- Asylum seekers do not qualify for council housing tenancy or housing benefit. The government is currently increasing those restrictions.

My big problem concerning these nutty things, wrong as they are, is not so much the people who put them into my face - as though this was the truth about life and the universe.
It is bad enough that people think these things, but worse because they fail to check it out. It's even worse that papers produce stories with very little factual material around them that beguile such gullible people, and stirs up strong feelings against refugees and asylum seekers, and all immigrants as a whole.

The most frustrating thing of all, however, is when government responses to this nonsense popularise the lies by trying to pass legislation that says such things as, "We won't allow asylum seekers or refugees to get driving licences in this country." "We won't allow them to get any health care for free," and of course, "We won't allow them to work." What is that about? They already cannot work.

So when, we put in that law of unforeseen consequences, what are desperate people to do, who have run away from danger in their own countries, have tried to feed their families and themselves? What should they now do? Steal? Become criminals? Come on! Let us be reasonable and look again at those facts and figures. Most up to date true facts and figures can be obtained from
http://www.refugeecouncil.org.uk

We are only a small Island. Other larger countries should help!

And who else helps? Of course the UK does, and many Brits think we are doing more than anyone else. However, which European countries have the highest number of asylum applications?

Glance at these statistics which are based on the population for the country per 1,000, and see who in Europe does take the most refugees per head of population.

When the number of asylum applications are compared with the total population of the state in which the applications are made (i.e. applications per 1000 inhabitants), in 2002, out of 25 European countries, Austria was the European country with the highest ratio of applications to population with 4.6 applications per 1000. Austria was followed by Norway (3.9), Sweden (3.7), Switzerland (3.7), Ireland (3.1) and Liechtenstein (2.8). The UK was behind them all with 1.9 per thousand permanent inhabitants. Germany, at that time, had 0.9 applications per 1000 inhabitants. (Source: Table 1: UNHCR Asylum Applications Lodged in Industrialised Countries: Levels and Trends, 2000-2002).

When questioned about what percentage of immigrants there are that go to make up the UK; people hold wildly wrong numbers, usually way too high. In fact out of the 15.4 million refugees in the world currently, due to war, bad government and the like, in 2012, the UK only had 193,510 of these people in the countries that go to make up the union and that represents just 0.33% of our population. Did you know that?

In 2011 UK did not feature in even the top ten of receiving countries for refugees, in fact the country that had the most in 2011 was. surprisingly. Pakistan. Jordan with its own population of around 6 million hosted something like 550,000. How does that compare with UK population of 70 million or thereabouts and the figure above?

My major point is, however, that the UK can use asylum seekers to the economic and social benefit of the nation, as well as simultaneously helping some very needy people. The UK has an ageing population. Many have paid into private pensions as well as the national Insurance for all their working life. Pension funds, of course, rely on the working population paying into the fund, which then pays out to those who retire and are no longer in work. Of course if the number of people working falls to a smaller and smaller total, the ability to continue to pay those who are no longer in work becomes increasingly difficult. This is the very reason, of course that the UK is constantly taking steps to increase the statutory retirement age.

At the time of writing, the British Work and Pensions Secretary has stated that "The state pension age is set to increase to 68 by 2050, with anyone aged less than 47 facing a longer working life. Only those born before 1959 will be unaffected by plans to phase in a higher retirement age over the next three decades." This has been outlined in a recent government white paper on pension reforms.

From my perspective, the most interesting issue is that the vast majority of the refugees/asylum seekers coming to the UK are of working age. Possibly a hard working refugee and Asylum seeking population could help your pension status!

Asylum seekers and refugees will often, when given the opportunity, create jobs for others, and even become entrepreneur's that will benefit the economy and indirectly comprehensively benefit all of the current population. We need to open our eyes to the benefits as well as the perceived problems of the refugee's and asylum seeking people. They bring benefits in our hospitals, in our transport system and in our building programs.

My view is that some of these young people with tragic stories and terrible life experience can be of great blessing to all of us. We need the forward vision to see it and help them to achieve it. My cry is can you do something as well?

Since the events surrounding "Baby P" and the latest child death recorded by Birmingham Social Services, Social Workers are unwilling to take any risks. At the time of writing there are some 4,000 children who need foster carers but for whom there is no foster carer. Could you volunteer? Could you be a foster carer?

Many people want to, but think they couldn't do it. Well, you just might be able to. Usually our first question, as an agency, to a prospective foster carer is, "Have you got a spare room?" That isn't a hard question is it? Well can you help? Please phone us on 020 8887 6888 and if not us, there is probably another local agency or your local authority. To get a lot done all it needs is for a lot of good people do a little.

Actions Speak Louder than Words

The Bible talks about rewarding people for the simple giving of a cup of cold water. Isn't that amazing!

When we come to the New Testament, we find that the rewards and the commands are very definite things, like looking after widows and orphans, visiting prisoners, and generally being there for those who have not received justice. The scripture actually talks about the fact that if we really love Jesus, it will be demonstrated in practical ways, such as keeping his commandments. I think so many Christians and church communities miss this.

Many of us are selective in what bits of scripture we see as important and those things we would like to skip over. One person said, "There are some parts of Scripture I don't want to read. It makes me feel too guilty." I wonder how selective our understanding of Scripture, of Jesus the Word is and what being a Christian, and being part of the church community, really means.

Did you know that in the UK each year usually around 40,000 babies, toddlers and young teens end up in the care of Social Services?

These youngsters, usually through no fault of the own, end up without the normal parents who can nurture, care, love and take note of their welfare. The reasons they are in this position are multitude, in fact, too many to mention in a short chapter like this. However, to name a few: death of parents, debilitating sickness of a parent and/or wrong use of chemical substances, like alcohol. Some are in the care system for short periods. I have seen some come into the system because a parent is in hospital, the other parent is at work all day to pay the bills, and there is no close relative with whom the child could stay.

On top of the 40,000-plus that do come into the system there are usually around another 40,000 on the 'At Risk Register,' that is, youngsters whom are at risk of abuse or neglect and may end up in the care system.

When I first became aware of the need of these children, while at the time also leading a church, I went along with my wife and learnt how to become a Foster Carer. At the time I had no intention of doing the job, I just wanted to understand it. To cut a long story short, we ended up fostering for the borough and have had many young people pass through our hands in the 15 years or so that we worked with them.

Many Social Service departments are looking for Foster Carers and I believe that such an appeal is being made in various areas across the nation at present. For around ten of the years, during which I was fostering for the local Authority, I held the position of Chair for the borough's Foster Care Association. I was aware that as each year passed we were always short on the amount of Foster Carers we needed. Sometimes we needed about an extra 12; sometimes as many as 40. This then meant that some children ended up in a fairly impersonal children's home while overworked Social Workers tried to find a better placement for them.

In the midst of our own initial training programme, I began to think of all the people in our church that had a spare room and who, if they understood the need, could and maybe would be excellent Foster Carers. Actually, over the years, many of them ended up doing just that, however, I also began to think about how many Christians there would be in the wider UK Church Communities.

Our population in the UK is over 60 Million. If just 5% of those are Christians, and it's probably a lot more than that, it means that there is likely to be around 3 million Christians in the UK, subscribing to all those scriptural things that I mentioned earlier. There are 40,000 children in need, like orphans, that we are supposed to care for. So it seemed to me that if we really thought about it, believed the scriptures and became a doer of the word and obedient to His commandments, surely there wouldn't be any shortage of Foster Carers, would there?

In my area we also had a problem of, "strangers," in the community ("Strangers," meaning as the Old Testament Bible Word is intended, i.e. people who are not native to the land in which they live); refugees might be your word, or asylum seekers. Again we decided that Christians should do something about it. When we began our research, we discovered that our local Muslim Community had opened some fourteen homes to help these people. I enquired if there were any Christian homes. No-one knew of any. So, we started our own. The people of the Muslim community were very helpful and advised us where to go for this and that, and who to approach to get advice. Now we have some 14 homes operating in the area: looking after some 30+ young people, but I did wonder why the Christians hadn't picked up on this obvious need.

So what to do? Really we as Christians, as a Church Community, could do something about fostering couldn't we? We have people and the resources. Why don't you and your Church Community contact your local Social Service Fostering Department and take it to the next step. Let's be obedient, and if we are, there surely won't be any shortage in the UK for Foster Carers will there? Let's help with those young people's lives. Let's care!

Refugees: The current issues - is there a solution?

I was privileged to have been able to speak at the United Nations on the subject recently. The reality is that the present situation of refugee displacement around the globe is the worst refugee crisis since World War Two. Actually, in regards of displacement and movement of people, it's worse. According to UNHCR there are currently 59.5 million displaced people in the world at the moment.

In the UK there is a lot of anti-immigration press, telling us how many, "illegal people," there are and the fact that they are taking jobs, school places, and homes. This has created a great deal of tension and distrust. Many of the figures quoted are not true, and when you look at real figures from reliable sources you find that the story is very different.

There is another story also that is not being talked about much, and that is one that needs to be brought to Europe's attention. In Europe, UK, Germany, and Italy particularly, there is a need for young workers who pay tax. The reason being that in the UK and other European countries the indigenous populations are getting older. Most of us have things like state pensions, paid from taxes.

When these were originally introduced with a male retirement age of 65 and female retirement age of 60, life expectancy was between 68 and 69, very different to today's predictions. The current life expectancy in the UK is heading towards 100 years. Who is going to pay for all those retired people? Whose taxes will fund it? We need the refugee's help to do that. Politicians don't have very much to say about this.

There is a lot of nonsense being spread around too, that the refugees are just economic migrants. *Really*? The millions from Syria are just after better jobs are they? I don't think so!

We also talk about how many are coming to Europe, but in real terms it is only a small percentage of those displaced. In fact, in 2014 the UK took in 31,945 refugees compared with, say, Turkey's 1 8 million or the 69,540 at March 2016 in Jordan. Tiny Lebanon, with a population of just 4 million of its own people, took in 1 million refugees. We need to be talking about the millions in places like Jordan, the overwhelming number in Lebanon and the massive camps in Turkey. Some politicians tell us, "We are doing our fair share; we are taking a big slice of the cake." Really?

We also need to be asking the questions as to why the rich countries like Qatar, Kuwait, Saudi Arabia etc., at the moment, seem to have no refugees from the war areas of Syria, yet they speak the same language.

Note also that in the Middle East those calling themselves Muslims have killed more people who are also calling themselves Muslims than any other group has.

I note that a friend of mine in Poland has come under quite a bit of flak for persuading the government there to give refugee status to people from these areas that have some kind of Christian background. It needs to be noted that Christians are in fact under huge pressure at the moment. I think that we should just take all comers but I do note the need for the Christian community and the real danger they are in.

I think we should, as countries, be taking in those in need, but we should note that in many areas it is the minority groups like Christians and the Yazidis who have come under the most pressure. Some have even been thrown overboard and drowned from the boats that they were escaping on, by others who did not like their Christianity. Many Christian groups also are saying that even in the refugee camps the discrimination against them is too hard to bear.

I recently wrote to the UK prime minister with my suggestions for dealing with the problem. My solution would not deal with the short term issues; for that we have to take in refugees. However, these problems are not going away any time soon. The prime minister's answer to me and others is that we have to deal with the source.

 Maybe, but who is going to do that, and in the meantime, what do we do? My mad suggestion is that we lease land for 99 years and start a new big city; like a new Hong Kong. We put it under the laws and administration of a country like the UK. We use aid budget to fund jobs in the new land, creating new housing, roads, schools, hospitals and general infrastructure, charging a levy to the EU for asylum seekers that they did not take.

The country setting it up has first bite of infrastructure contracts, thus benefiting its GDP. The new occupants are given passports, possibly stamped and not allowed to work or receive benefits in Europe, a bit like the stamp on Channel Island passports, who, of course, hold UK passports.

Mad? Of course it is, but we need a mad answer to such a mad situation. I am glad as I watch the global response to such madness, that there are other mad people out there that think this is a possibility. Recently an Egyptian multi-millionaire offered to buy an island to do just what I am suggesting. Another rich philanthropist in the USA also wants to buy an island, and then in the UK Lord David Alton recently put the whole idea to the British House of Lords. (http://davidalton.net/2015/07/10/2015-the-year-of-the-refugees-just-put-yourself-in-their-shoes-full-house-of-lords-debate-and-government-response-and-a-reply-from-a-north-korean-refugee/)

I said earlier how I was privileged to have been able to put this problem to a UN audience recently, but talking is not enough. We have to do something. I am glad that the pressure being put on the government by the ordinary person is having some effect, and I note that, at the time of writing, the UK will now take 20,000 refugees. Even Iceland has offered places for 10,000.

In terms of the pressure being put on governments by their populace to do more, at a recent march to put on the pressure in London, I was amused by some of the posters. One youngster carried one that said, "A refugee can come and stay at my house and play minecraft." Though I thought the best was one that said, "We need to be more German," especially as the UK had just agreed to take 20,000 people over five years on the day that Germany took in 40,000.

B is for Blogs and Books

Blogs

Saying Hello

Well! Everyone says to me, "Have a blog! Write a book!" So I started both. I hope those that are reading this book may have enjoyed my blogs and/or my other books also, at some time or other. I hope you have even commented on what I have had to say on the blogs. Hopefully it's still there at www.adrianhawkes.blogspot.com. But seriously, why write a blog? Why write a book for that matter? For me, I want to influence people, bring about change and see the world get better. It's as simple as that.

I do come from the perspective of a follower of Jesus. I use that phrase rather than epithets like, "Christian," as one of my frustrations is that the world we live in so wants to put people in boxes. That allows them, in their boxed perspective, to dismiss, "Christians," or keep them, "in their place." I don't want to stay in a, "place," or even be put, "in a place." I believe God has given us a mandate to look after His world; that we are all created, "in His image," and therefore have dignity and respect given us from Him, and that similarly we should have the same respect to and from each other.

The reality is though, life is not like that, and we should ask the question, "Why not?" Why is there such inhumanity from mankind to mankind? Why so much injustice? Why so much suffering? Why so much domestic abuse? And being a follower of Jesus, I would want to say, "Hello! There is another way, a better value system, another way to live, a way of living that seeks righteousness and goodness, one that attempts to bring the Kingdom of God to the earth - not sometime in the future, but now. Sometimes we succeed and making some aspect of some people's life better. Sometimes we fail. However, as Nelson Mandela said, "Do not judge me by my success. Judge me by how many times I fell over, and got back up again." Yes! The world can be changed.

[35]

This book is, to some extent, all about my attempt to do what Jesus commanded you and I to do: "Seek first the Kingdom of God." And that doesn't mean looking forward to Heaven. It means bringing about rightness now!

My Writings so far – Some Background

I just thought you might find it interesting to know a little more about my blogs and books that you may like to read.

Why do I write books? I guess that people do it for all sorts of reasons;
- to tell friends,
- to advertise their wares,
- to just put their thoughts out there.

I guess for some people it's almost therapeutic.

For me; yes, I would like to put my wares out there. I have six books published that I would like the world to read. I guess my real reason for writing is that I want to see change in certain issues and things. I also think that I would like to use the words I write to make the world a better place. I also, actually, like to introduce lots of people to, "the Word," because I know, having met the Word, that it – and He - changes one's life, one's outlook, one's culture perspective, and one's value system. In fact, the Word changes everything for the better.

I also think it is interesting to discover who reads my blogs and books. This is quite fascinating to me. I am sure you know that these days with the internet one can track and analyse all sorts of things, and my blogs and books are no exception. Here is some of the interesting data to date. (I think it's interesting anyway and I hope you might too.)

The country from which I have the most readers is the United States. This probably isn't such a surprise as we speak the same language and I do have many friends there. I suppose what does surprise me is how many. As of the time of writing the stats tell me that 3,138 have taken a peek.

[36]

I live in the UK. One would expect that as I live here most of my readers would come from that part of the world. As I write, according to the current statistics, 3,018 people in the UK have had a look at my blogs.

What really does surprise me are countries number three and four, a long way behind in terms of numbers, but "Hey! Welcome to all of you from Russia, and South Korea who have had a look." South Korea is 658 and Russia is 450.

I would really love all readers of these pages to click their way to my blogs, find the comment button and just tell me what you think.

I will, of course, say, "Thank you!" to those of you who have joined my journey and discussions in my blogs, who hail from Germany, Brazil, Slovenia, Slovakia, Kenya, Taiwan, Netherlands, Norway, France and Switzerland. Thank you all for joining me and for taking the time to read my perspective. Now all I need is for YOU to join the discussions. So far, more than 10,000 have joined me at some point. Thank you to all who have joined in the fray. I appreciate it.

It is also interesting to see what you are all reading, and the stats tell me that the most read Blog that I have written is the one put up in October 2009 on the subject of, "Women." And I didn't even write that one. Bah! It was actually written by my good friend Dan Wooding of Assist News Service. He is a professional news hound, so I guess I am happy that you like to read his stuff. For those who like trivia, he was also my Best Man when my wife, Pauline, and I were married. Check out his news service at www.assistnews.com. It will be worth your while.

It's also fun to note that my second most read blog is the one entitled "Beer and Bandits," which I posted in May 2010. Does that tell me something of my readers, or about what I write about? Mmmm! Send your answers on a postcard please.

I like the fact that people are still reading Blogs that I posted some time ago. If that is you, thanks again for that.

[37]

I could go on and tell which search engines and what referring sites my readers use - but I won't. Enough already! Just to say again, thank you, hope you continue reading and enjoy, and most of all I hope that together we can affect change for the better.

Don't forget, I would love to hear from you, so please add your comments and join the discussion on any of my blogs or comment on my books, you can do it.

Books and especially Fiction

Talking of my friend Dan Wooding, here is something he wrote:

From The Rainbow, to Icejacked, to Red Dagger
The fascinating story of Adrian Hawkes and how our lives have collided once again
By Dan Wooding; Founder of ASSIST Ministries.

I first met Adrian back in the mid-sixties in Birmingham, England, when he brought his Ribbons of Faith outreach team to my father's little church, the Sparkbrook Mission, in Birmingham, England.

The female members of his team from the Sparkbrook Elim Church seemed rather glamorous for this rather dour area of England's second city, wearing colourful sashes and singing modern songs, and then Adrian brought a challenge for our church to start going out into the community with the Gospel.

We were so stirred up by his sermon, that soon my sister Ruth and myself, and my wife Norma, started The Messengers, which grew very quickly to about 60 members. We would go out each Saturday night to the local pubs and coffee bars with the Good News of Jesus Christ, and soon we partnered with the Ribbons of Faith, and other groups in Birmingham, to start the Late Night Special in the huge but empty Lloyds Bank Building each Saturday night.

Then Canon Bryan Green, a liberal evangelical who was sometimes described as "the Anglican Billy Graham," invited us to start a Sunday night outreach in St. Martin's Church in the Bull Ring, Birmingham called "The Late Night Special."

[38]

When Adrian married Pauline, his lovely wife, he asked me to be best man at his wedding and, of course, I agreed. Not long afterwards, Norma and I had become involved in working with drug addicts at All Saints Hospital in Winson Green, and this developed, with the help of some local businessmen, into the start of Hill Farm, Europe's first drug rehabilitation farm. We were Hill Farm's first wardens.

After we left the farm, our family moved to London in 1968 where I became the chief reporter with, "The Christian," Billy Graham's newspaper there and shortly afterwards, Adrian and Pauline moved to Middlesbrough to run an Elim Church there.

Then, in 1974 he and Pauline moved to north London where they took over the famous rock venue, The Rainbow, to establish a unique church there. The Rainbow had hosted hundreds of shows, including several of the Beatles Christmas concerts, and also had David Bowie performing as Ziggy Stardust, as well as Queen, Cat Stevens and Jimi Hendrix, to name just a few of scores of rock luminaries who performed there.

In June, 1982, Norma, myself and our two boys, Andrew and Peter, moved to Southern California, but Adrian stayed in North London to pioneer a unique series of ministries, including those to asylum seekers in the capital city. He has also planted multi-racial churches all over the world. Having travelled extensively -- he has just returned from Venezuela - he has started many schools, vocational training centres, orphanages and support for vulnerable people. He has ongoing work in Africa and Sri Lanka as well as working with leaders in many other countries.

Adrian is the author of five other books, but now our lives have collided again as both of us have recently released our first novels. Mine is called Red Dagger (www.lulu.com/product/11050174?cid=060610_en_email_SUMME RREAD305) and Adrian's is called Icejacked, which you can get at his website --www.adrianhawkes.co.uk.

So why did he write it?

"I am fascinated at the way that things are changing in our world with items like mobile phones and the Internet, and how they quickly have become part of our normal world as if they had always been there and always will be," he said.

"In my travels I was captivated by how those who have not seen new technology, or young people who have lived in third world situations and never been to a big city or flown on a plane, nevertheless when they do get the opportunity within days they are using it all like it was normal.
"I often see refugees in their first two days after coming into the UK with nothing, being absorbed by everything they see, and in one week their whole dress style has changed a mobile phone is on hand and they want to learn to access the Internet.

"I am very aware that sometime fiction is more persuasive in changing things and I remember that some books have had powerful effect on nations and cultures. Take 'Uncle Tom's Cabin' for starters; that fiction book had a powerful effect."

So bearing that in mind, Adrian told me about the plot:

"An Iceman is found, and he is thrown into a new environment; a world that he does not understand; and he finds everything very strange," he said. "But alongside that, he is holding onto values that do not change because of technology and advancement. They are his real and lasting values.

"Also alongside that is the hidden plot that asks the question: Have some things really changed as much as we think they have, such as slavery? Where are we with that today? One of the central characters is trying to work it out in the middle of that are those who seem so genuine, but are they really cheats?"

Our novels are both very different, as mine is partly based in Gaza, but I am delighted that Adrian has also been able to try his hand at fiction. So again, if you would like to get a copy of Icejacked, just go to: www.adrianhawkes.co.uk

C is for Coincidences

Another coincidence?

Those of you who read my blogs and books will know that for a while now I have been going on about the perceived difference between answers to prayer and coincidences.

More recently I have been checking through my memory banks to bring to mind some of those "answered prayers"/"coincidences" that happen to those who pray and follow Jesus. Looking back, I regret not keeping mementos of some of those incidents -perhaps in future I will. However, in life I often just say, "Thank you God,' and move on. Though, I hope I am grateful and really thankful and have regard for these specific answers.

The memento I could have kept of the story I am about to tell you, was a genuine response to prayer and a true account.

This answer to prayer (or coincidence, depending on your perspective) took place before UK decimalisation, so young readers might struggle with the figures, not understanding the notion of 240 pence making one pound.

Anyway, at this time I was living in the North of England, my salary was the grand total of £8.10s (that is eight pounds and ten shillings) or, for younger readers: £8.50p in today's currency. My wife was the full time secretary for a local school and earned a grand total of £5.00 per week. To put these amounts into perspective my rent was £5.10s per week (£5.50p). As you can see there was not a great deal of financial elbow room. There was very little money left over for frivolities.

Unfortunately for us we had somehow run up a deficit at the bank to the tune of £31.12s 2d (that is thirty one pounds twelve shillings and two pence) and the bank, sadly, had allowed us to go overdrawn by this amount without any permission given. Now, however, they had called me in and wanted their money back. I, of course, had said, "Yes! I would sort it out."

When I arrived home I told my wife that I had no idea what to do and that we had no chance of funding the deficit.

Pauline suggested writing them a cheque. I explained that this would not work as that was where the money came from in the first place. We agreed that we needed to pray for God to help us, we needed a £31.12s 2d miracle, and frankly, I had no idea where such a miracle amount could come from.

In these situations, I find, that one always wants to provide God with the answer that you have trusted him, in prayer, to sort out. I hope you know what I mean.

Later that week, I had a letter from an old friend, he wrote to me enclosing a cheque made out to myself and Pauline; the letter went something like this:

As you know some years ago I had a serious motor accident, it's taken years for the insurance company to make a settlement to us, but finally it has come. I wanted at this time to say thank you to friends who helped me and my wife during this awful time, and so now I have the financial settlement I thought I would like to send you all a monetary thank you. So enclosed is a cheque. I know you will think that this is a funny amount £31.12s.2p but just to explain that for you, I had quite a few friends who helped us at that time so what I have done is taken the amount of our settlement, deducted 10%, I then divided that 10% between all the friends who helped me at the time and so that is why it is such a funny thank you amount.

Well of course my friend wanted to explain his reasoning behind the division of the "Thank you!" money, but what my friend did not know was that that cheque was to the exact £sd (pounds, shillings and pence for younger readers) amount of my unofficial overdraft.

When I think about this, it's totally mind boggling, how everything came together in such perfect sync; the accident years before, the insurance company taking its time, the amount of friends my friend felt had helped them at the time, the long period of time it took to sort the settlement, that my friend was writing out the cheques during the week that I was concerned about my overdraft, the prayer my wife and I prayed that week, and that very week the letter arrived containing a cheque for the exact amount. "It's all just coincidence," I hear some say. Well how about a Father God who loves his children, knows their need and answers prayer. How about that for an answer?

Here's another "answered prayer"/"coincidence."

The answer, my friend, is blowing in the wind

Many years ago, when my children were only 7 and 8 years old, talking about "coincidences" was in vogue. It seemed that every other conversation was about this subject. Then, as now, I would find that my coincidences' seemed to come in answer to prayer. With both these elements in mind, I thought I would tell you a true story.

I am reminded of when I lived in the North of England, a 14 year old would constantly come and talk to me about eternal things. He was puzzled and sometimes annoyed with my answers, particularly any that involved prayer and its results. One day he knocked on my door at 36 Wilton Way. When I answered the door and he looked at me with great confidence, he said he had dropped in on his way home from school and had been thinking all day about my so called answers to prayer, "so called" is how young "Langy" described it. I smiled at his enthusiasm as I looked at him though the open door, observing his obvious new found confidence. I said, "Oh! And what is the answer then?" He said with delight, "They're just coincidences!" "Well," I said, "Thank you for that, but it seems funny to my mind that when I pray I get a coincidence, which seems like an answer to prayer to me."

Now, I am sure that there is a much more complex discussion needed than what I said to that 14 year old, however, there isn't the space here.

[43]

But I have tried in other places to discuss this further, what I really wanted to do this time is to just tell you one of those *coincidence* stories, and let you make up your own mind.

As I was saying, this is a story about my two young children aged 7 and 8 at the time. I had signed a form to say that they could go on a school trip. The terrible thing was that "today" was the day I had to send the money with the children to the school. It was breakfast time, and both girls where looking into my face imploring me for £5.00 each for the school trip. This was £10.00 which I genuinely did not have and did not know where to find it from. I was regretting that I had signed the form in the distant hope that by the time came when I needed to pay the money I would have the required tenner!

It hadn't materialised.

What was worse, I now had two strident little girls nagging at me, demanding to know what I was going to do about it, and they, let me tell you, were worse than facing the school authorities or the teacher.

I tried some suggestions. How about if I came and talked to the teacher. They remonstrated with me; that, apparently was far too embarrassing. "Everyone else," so they said, "had already paid!" "I tell you what," I said humbly, "I will come and see the school secretary, perhaps I can pay a little off each week." That, it seemed, to the two little girls, was an even worse idea, loud cries of, "Oh Dad! How could you!" Where echoing throughout our breakfast time.

Breakfast now over, and the time for them to leave for school had arrived. We stood ready to go, with the girls still firing off angry comments at me. I interrupted them as they stood there, angry and forlorn, coats and scarves on, school bags on their shoulders, faced with telling the teacher they had no money and could not go on the trip. I said,"Why don't we stop right now, pray and ask God to do something, as I really don't know what else to do as you obviously don't like my suggestions?" They reluctantly agreed. We bowed our heads and I explained to the Father that I did not have £10.00 even though I had said I would pay £10.00 for the children's school trip, and I said,

"I don't know what to do for my children, so will you please, please help me!" I think you can see that my prayer was heartfelt, whatever the children's position was.

So that the discussion did not re-start, I immediately said, "Okay let's get to school!" I opened our kitchen door to walk through our side entrance to our front door. We still live in the same house and it's a bit strange in that we have two front doors, the main door is accessed through a corridor. When it's blustery, this corridor turns into a wind tunnel. It was one of those windy November days, and as I opened the door a gush of powerful wind blew in, bringing with it all the leaves of the neighbourhood. I didn't go out, instead I moved the children back out of the way and asked my wife for a dust pan and brush, deciding I needed to get this mess cleared up before I take the children to school. I began sweeping up the leaves, and to my amazement, and I have to say wonderment, in the middle of the great pile of leaves was a ten pound note, swept in by the wind with the leaves. The children were impressed, I was Impressed we stopped and said, "Thank you, Lord!" I don't know if someone lost it, or if it was a special delivery from God. However it seemed to me a very, very immediate answer to prayer. Needless to say, they went on the school trip.

Well I don't know how well my children remember that happening all those years ago, but what is your take on the story? Another coincidence? Or does God answer prayer?

And yet another true story. Was this a coincidence or an answer to prayer?

Is God into fashion?

A few years ago we were visiting some friends in a small church in the Cheltenham Area of the UK. On the way home I remarked to my wife, Pauline, that the couple leading the church community appeared to be very hard up financially.

My wife agreed and told me she had left them an envelope on their mantelpiece containing some money, to help them out a little. My reaction was very godly.

[45]

"Where on earth did you get the money to leave them a gift? We are broke too!" Pauline explained that she had been saving up to purchase a jump-suit she had seen in a local boutique. She had been squirreling the money away into an envelope at the bottom of her handbag. It had taken her a while, but finally she had saved up enough and was all set to go and purchase it. This is the money that she had left on the mantelpiece. So, no jump-suit for Pauline!

I congratulated her and commiserated. It was rare for her to have any new clothes. Pauline explained, "It's not as bad as all that, I saw two jump-suits one was really nice but very expensive, one was okay and cheaper. I had just saved up enough for the cheaper one, but it was really a compromise, because the expensive one was the one I really wanted, so I haven't lost that much by leaving them the money." This kind of feminine logic does not always make sense to the male species.

We arrived home, unlocked the door, and walked into our London home. To our surprise, hanging over the door to our lounge area was a piece of clothing in a cellophane cover. My wife hastily pulled off the cellophane and held it against her. There was a catch in her voice as she explained, "This is the jump-suit I was telling you about, the more expensive one, and it's the exact colour I wanted, and it's my size!"

There are always other people living with us, so we rounded them up and asked them why a jump-suit was hanging in our lounge. They explained that a man had delivered it earlier in the day, he said that Pauline had done him a favour a couple of years ago and he had never said "Thank you." The jump-suit was his way of showing his appreciation. He also said that if it was the wrong colour, the wrong size, or the wrong item, that it could be changed. But it was perfect in every way.

I know there are those of you who will want to say that this was a strange coincidence, but that is one word I am extremely sceptical about.

Rather I think that Father God does care about and love his children. He cares about every detail of our life, and he loves us passionately and profusely. But I know some of you will prefer to cling to that doubtful explanation of "coincidence."

Surely, the stranger to coincidence, the more likely it is to be an answer to prayer. Here is another personal experience of what happened after a very desperate prayer.

Do Angels Smoke Pipes?

Some years ago Pauline and I were on a visit to Nigeria. I have a rule: don't carry too much cash. We had £30.00 between us. We had flown into Lagos from Accra, Ghana. We presented ourselves at passport control and one of the officers said, "I need to see the £200.00 that you will change into Naira as you enter the country." I explained that between us we only had £30.00, but I had a credit card.

This made no difference whatsoever, he insisted that I was lying and demanded to see the £200.00 or, he said, "We will return you to where you came from." What could I do? The answer to this question was made for me by the officer; he lifted his rifle, stuck it in my ribs, and marched me and Pauline down the long corridor back to the aeroplane on which we had arrived. It had taken a long time to queue to get to passport control and our incoming plane had already departed. The soldier then decided that I would have to go to prison and, he said, "Your wife will go to the women's prison." Neither Pauline or I were impressed with this idea so I said, "can I try something?" He looked at me suspiciously, pushed the gun a little harder into my ribs, and growled "what are you going to try?" "Well," I said, "I thought I might ask someone to give me some money." He pulled the gun out of my ribs and slung it up onto his shoulder, looked at me steely eyed and said, "Are you mad?"

"Not really," I replied, "but anything is better than going to prison. So, will you let me try?" "Who will you ask?" he said. I looked around for a friendly face in the myriads of people waiting to fly out, which is what Pauline wanted to do right there and then. I spotted a man leaning against a wall smoking a pipe, I said to my gun totting guard, "Him over there."

He shrugged and said, "This should be fun. I am coming with you." Our party of three made their way over to the pipe smoker. I opened the conversation. "Excuse me. Do you speak English?" The man replied, "Just a little." I explained that the gun wielding soldier was inclined to put me in prison as I did not have the required £200.00 to change into Naira. Could he help? Much to my guard's amazement the man said, "Of course, I will go to the bank outside and get it for you." A few moments later he was back with £200.00 Sterling. "There you are," he said. I thanked him profusely and said, "I need to pay you back, when I get back to the UK where should I send it?" He laughed and at my insistence wrote something on a piece of paper which I carefully stowed in my wallet. We said our farewells and my now, somewhat quieter, guard escorted us back to passport control.

At the counter he announced, "They have the £200.00!" "Oh! They've found it have they!" The man in the booth responded. "No," the guard said, "I have just seen the most amazing thing; a man gave them the money." I chipped in, "Well I did pray to God before I spoke to him." A hush descended. They stamped our passports, and we were waved through.

While in Nigeria, I took names, addresses and business cards of many people, all of which I tucked into the same place that I had put pipe-smoking-man's piece of paper. My intention was to write to everyone with whom I had made contact on my return to the UK, including writing to and repaying "Mr Pipe-smoker."

On my return to the UK every piece of paper was still safely stowed, and I started and succeeded in writing to every person - all except "Mr Pipe-smoker." His piece of paper was missing, and even though I turned out my wallet and luggage, it was nowhere to be found. All the other address details to all the other people I had met were there.

I wanted to pay back my friend, but as his details had disappeared I was not able to do this. Who was he? Where is he? Why he gave me the money I have no idea. Perhaps if he reads this volume, he will let me know. My thoughts about it? Perhaps, maybe, it was no ordinary man. How extraordinary that he gave me £200.00 very quickly, very easily, without any argument or debate, and with very little forethought.

At the time, because I was so stressed, I did not think these elements through. If angels smoke pipes I want to say "Thank you!" to God for sending that particular pipe-smoker at the perfect moment.

Really, Do Angels smoke pipes?

I thought you would like to know what happened next, the sequel to the story immediately above about the pipe smoking angel who gave me £200. A friend was supposed to meet Pauline and I in Lagos airport but he did not turn up. We made our way through passport control and customs; then found ourselves stuck in the airport not knowing where to go or what to do next.

While I was sorting the final paperwork, my wife was standing by a barrier just inside the country, feeling traumatised by the few hours that we had just gone through of being marched up and down by a rather, in our opinion, unstable gun-toting border guard. I think Pauline had been crying a little due to the intense pressure and was still feeling stressed and wanting to immediately fly home to the UK. As she waited for me a young Nigerian man came up to her and said, "You seem to be in trouble. Can I help?" Going on her very recent experience she was unwilling to trust any stranger, in what was to her a strange country. As she was responding, "No thank you! I do not need help." I arrived back at her side with cases and completed paperwork. The young man said to me, "I'm not sure what has happened to you but obviously you have been through some kind of difficult time. Can I show you where the airport restaurant is? I'm sure you would be glad of a coffee." It had taken a great deal of time up to this point, due to the gun happy guard and the stringent passport control, so I said, "Yes! Okay. It would be a good idea to sit down with coffee to sort out our next move." Plus, I now had lots of Naira in my pocket and it was a long time since our last meal. The young man escorted us to the restaurant and the staff seated us. He said "Let me leave you to it. You have obviously had a hard time. I will come back in an hour or so see if you are ok." We thanked him, ordered food and coffee, and tried to unwind a little.

We decided to go and find a room for the night. Just before the hour was up I signalled to the waiter that we wanted to pay the bill. "What bill sir?" he asked.

"For the food and drinks," I replied.

"Well sir," the waiter replied, "Your friend who brought you in has already settled the bill."

To say I was surprised is an understatement. This stranger who knew nothing about us had paid for us to have a meal, in a place that was quite expensive for locals. Just as Pauline and I were discussing this strange turn of events the young stranger appeared again, and asked if we felt better. We thanked him and said that we felt much better and began to talk to him about our story, and the fact that we believed that God had been looking after us and that knowing Jesus and being in touch with the Father was great at times like this. We then asked him why he had come to help us and why he had paid our bill.

He said, "I travelled a long way today, from up country, to meet a friend who was supposed to come in on a flight at the same time as you came through customs, but he did not arrive. I was feeling a little fed up, thinking I have come such a long way, for no purpose and I prayed, "Father God, why have I come all this way for nothing?" and I distinctly heard God say to me, "You are here today to help that couple over there. They have had a hard time." Many years ago I went to study in the USA. At that time I did not know God. Yet, just like you, when I got off the plane, the person who was going to meet me and help me did not arrive. I was standing in the airport totally bemused as to what to do and a man came up to me and said, "You are in trouble. Can I help you?" To cut a long story short, this man really knew God. He ended up taking me to his home, where I lived for two years. He even helped me pay my college fees. I found God in his home and it has changed my life. I want to at least put some of that experience of God's favour back into someone else's life."

The young man settled us into a hotel. He looked after us for three days, until we finally made contact with our friend who was supposed to meet us and who somehow had the dates mixed up.

And "No!" I did not lose his address, so perhaps he was not an angel. I rather think he was a young man listening to God and being a great help to us in our need.

I still don't know what to think about my pipe smoking angel, but I am convinced that in times of need God is with us and cares for us. Sometimes I don't understand his answers.

Sometimes I am puzzled by events. But I am confident that God cares, loves and is listening to those who know Him as Father God, and "Yes!" from time to time, he sends his messengers both angelic and human, to assist in time of need. What do you think?

D is for Dying

A Pioneer and a dear friend Dies

George Canty 1911 to 2010

I was sitting with friends celebrating the end of 2010 when my mobile rang. It was around 9.30p.m. The voice at the other end said, "I'm sorry to tell you but George Canty 'went home' at 9.00p.m." I was upset. I knew he was 99, but I wanted him to make it to 100. I wanted him to finish the autobiography that I knew he was half way through. I also knew he had been ghost writing another important book for Christ for all Nations (CFAN) and wondered if he had finished the work. I phoned one of his relatives the next morning to get more details.

"What happened about the CFAN book?" I asked.
"I took in the finished script early in the week." they replied.
"Why didn't he stay until 2011?" I asked,
"Well," they told me, "He was in pain, and kept saying he wasn't worried about being around to make the 100 and was happy to go home. However, I know he was in the middle of some legal stuff and was waiting to sign some documents. The lawyer came into the hospital that morning and George signed everything off. I think he was happy then." The relative then told me, "I went to see him later in the day and he told me off for walking around, and said, "For goodness sake, rest, sit down, and relax." Then, at 9:00p.m., he went!"

What and who was George Canty? Well, like most human beings he was different things to different people. Father to some, Pastor to others. For me personally, he was a friend, although I did not see him often. The last time I saw him was just over a year before his passing. I asked him how he was doing. His reply was typical; "Still working full time. So I am a little tired." He went on; "Still praying for you every day." And I believed him. He also told me that he had taught himself to use a computer, set up a web site, www.canty.org.uk and now I could email him." Not bad for a 98 year old as he was at that time!

He was born in Hull, in Yorkshire, England. He used to say to me; "I can say this because I am a Yorkshire man, but you can't say it. "From Hull, strong in the arm thick in the head."" He wasn't that strong, being small in stature, but he certainly was *not* thick in the head. What was he like? What will be missed? Well! My perspective again. He was an awkward, sometimes difficult to work with, highly intelligent mind, a man who - when I met him as a youngster - was already ahead of his time, thinking in new ways, understanding things others did not, unwilling to be boxed in by the past or the establishment and therefore not often fitting in with the establishment's expectations. As usual people like that fall foul of the establishment who of course want them to conform and be the company man. He did become president for a while of the Elim Churches in the UK, probably because he connected as he would have said, 'with the ordinary folk'.

I worked with him as a youngster, along with my friend Mark Drew, at a series of meetings in Port Talbot, where Mark and I spent many weeks living in a marquee, underneath a motorway slip road. George Canty's approach was different to say the least. He would sit with us and go through the advertising for the meetings. He would ask, "Are there any religious or spiritual words in this advertising?" If we came up with anything, those words would come out of the text. People who were completely non-religious, not church goers and often not interested in God, would flock to the meetings. They came because he said he could heal the sick. That caused problems amongst the establishment, they said, 'Only God can do that!" I said to him, "Why don't you change your language? You are upsetting the establishment figures." His answer was interesting, he said, "For years I could give you a thousand theological reasons why the sick would not be healed by praying for them. Guess what? I never prayed for any to be healed and no one ever was. Then God did something in my life and I changed. I started to pray for people and guess what? Some of them were healed. Sure; it's God's power! But I need to do it and act on it. So, I heal the sick - and that's what Jesus told us to go and do!"

I saw amazing things in those meetings and many other meeting like them as I worked with George. The deaf *did* hear and the lame *did* walk. Was everyone healed? No! I asked him about that too.

[53]

"Why are some not healed?" He responded in his usual nonchalant way. "Some are!" he said, "and guess what - I don't know why they are." When those who were not healed asked him the same question in a more personal way, he would always respond in the same way; "Have faith in God." "For how long?" they would sometimes ask, "Until the end!" was his response.

Another reason people came to the meetings was because he would paint scenic views in oils. He painted whilst talking to the audience, then he would give the painting away to the person who brought the most people to the meeting each night. What a nightmare that was for Mark and I. Sometimes the people would want to fight and argue about who really had brought the most friends disagree over who should get the picture.

Later in life I bumped into that same nonchalant approach when I was in college. George turned up as one of the lecturers. His subject was church History, and, as usual, he made those who wanted things 'Normal,' mad! There were hardly any dates given in his lectures. For example: "Which pope ruled when?" and, "Who killed who?" and, "When was Luther or Calvin born?" That was what people expected from church History. Instead, what the were given was, "This is the history of the church," and "This is how it has moulded us," and "This is where we went wrong," and "This is what you should now do to change things, and to move on." As always, his passion was to introduce a hurting world to Jesus, to the God who really does care and who loves ordinary people. "The good News is that the word has become flesh. Now, go and let people know." It was inspiring stuff rather than dead dates.

However, there are always those who don't want the boat rocked. I remember one student confronting him angrily over a practical issue and saying to him, "But if you take that to its logical conclusion then...." I would walk away laughing as I heard George say, "Oh! I wouldn't do that!" "Do what?" the angry student responded. "... Take it to its logical conclusion" George said, walking away.

I also heard him in discussion with a theologian on the subject of Pentecostals and charismatic's.

Again his answer to the critic made me laugh. He said, "I am trying to work out some theology for us all on this subject. Don't blame me if the church hasn't had a good one for centuries on how the Holy Spirit works." George Canty certainly did not fit in the box. I love people who don't fit into conformist boxes. I hate the boxes that people want to put others into. Church boxes. Christian boxes. They even want to put God in a box too. I love it that He never lets us put Him in a box – God, that is.

George was the author of many books, my favourite being, "In My Father's House". Unbeknown to many, he wrote a weekly column for a Yorkshire newspaper under the pseudonym of Jack Yorkshire. Using the same pseudonym he compiled a joke book that was sold at railway station bookshops entitled "Jack Yorkshire's weekend book", it was full of cartoons, political comments, and just plain common sense fun. A couple of times I came across articles in magazines, under his pseudonyms, even in the denominational magazine of which he was a part. I knew George's writing style, so I recognised them as his work. One I remember was under the pseudonym of Jack Pullford. I asked him, "Did you write this?" I didn't get a straight answer. He said to me, "The thing is, as you get older people put you in a box and they say "Oh! That's the sort of thing George Canty *would say* isn't it?" So, magazines I sometime write for won't take articles that have my name on." So I asked again, "Did you write this one?" No answer!

I know that in recent years George has been doing a huge amount of work for Reinhard Bonnke of CFAN, and that was the book I was referring to at the beginning of this tribute to him. I am sure he was working full-time right to the last. To quote what I think really sums up his approach I have stolen some words from his own web site which is still out there at the time of writing. Here they are:

Standards are written across the pages of Scripture, but not in express commands. Issues of music, dress, hair, jewelry, entertainment are peripheral matters decided by the major principles of wisdom and love. Our rule book is love.
The New Testament is not a law book like the Koran, nor does it give us the right to legislate.

Christianity is not routine religious performances but action and love to please God, that is the God who sets us free.

God planted a garden, and the devil led Adam out of it. A young Scottish minister one morning found the roads too frozen so he skated to church. Afterward, called by the Kirk elders to give account of his Sabbath sin, they were in a dilemma. If he skated he broke the Sabbath and if he did not turn up at church it was worse. Then clarity inspired one leader. He demanded of the young man "It amounts to this – did you enjoy it or not?" "Well, I've known people refuse ice-cream because they might 'enjoy it'. I have no such conscience." I hope there is ice-cream in heaven!

I know he was 99, and some will say he has had a good innings, personally I would have liked him to stay a little longer, make the 100, and I will miss a radical friend. I had only just opened his Christmas card on which he had painted the front picture written the verse and had it printed up. I will miss him, even though I know I will see him again.

Some of the Books by George Canty:
1. Practice of Pentecost by George Canty (**Paperback** - Apr 1987)
2. Evangelism by Fire: An Initiative for Revival by Reinhard Bonnke and George Canty (**Paperback** - 3 Nov 1989)
3. What's going on?; The George Canty Viewpoint. by George Canty (**Paperback** - Apr 1977)
4. In My Father's House: Pentecostal Exposition of the Major Christian Truths by George Canty (**Paperback** - Dec 1972)
5. The Hallmarks of Pentecost by George Canty (**Paperback** - 18 May 1989)

E is for Education

EDUCATION

Why Christian Education?
A little bit of history

We need to remember that Education in Britain was originally not a State or secular idea but rather one that those who were followers of Jesus thought of. As mentioned earlier, the invention of the so called Sunday School (1736 to 1811) was thought of by Robert Rakes whose statues stand in such places as Victoria Embankment in London, Gloucester Town Centre and Queens Park Toronto in Canada.

I say "so called" Sunday school because this was not in the format that we often think of today. It was really what Robert Rakes was thinking of whilst seeking to educate young people to read, write and do maths - and because Sunday was the only day that children in those days did not work. It was therefore called "Sunday School." By 1831, Sunday Schools in Great Britain were teaching weekly 1,250,000 children, which was approximately 25 per cent of the entire population.

One needs to remember that there was at that time no such thing as, "State Education." The gradual take over by the British State probably began in August 1833 when Parliament voted to allocate sums of money each year for the construction of schools for poor children. That was the first time the State had become involved with education in England and Wales. A meeting in Manchester in 1837, chaired by Mark Philips, led to the creation of the Lancashire Public Schools Association. This association proposed that non-denominational schools should be funded from local taxes.

What I am saying is that education was the prerogative and the initiative of people of faith long before the State thought of universal education. Gradually the State takes over these things and we have to ask: Does it always do a better job?

I am glad that there is education for all, but I am not convinced at all that it carries the value system and character development that I would want for all children.

I hope my readers also want that same high character building for their children. Interestingly, Martin Luther of Reformation fame (1483 to 1546), way back then, said of public schools, "I am afraid that the schools will prove the very gates of hell, unless they diligently labour in explaining the Holy Scriptures and engrave them in the heart of the youth." Not much has changed, has it?

Raison d'être

So why did I implement a Christian School in North London some 30 plus years ago, not by myself of course, but with the help of so many other 'believers?' Really, it was because of the opinions of people like Martin Luther, and of course other more modern proponents of Christian Education, and because I know that we have, as parents, real concern that we need to protect our children from all sorts of thing as they grow up. Things like, not letting them cross the road without holding hands, not letting them go off on their own at too young an age. In other words we need to protect them while developing their character. And why not?

Why not also protect what is put into their heads? Why not protect the knowledge element? Is this not sensible for the children we care about and love? Sometimes parents say things to me like, "Well! Our children need to know the real world; the good the bad and the ugly. They need to know what is evil as well as what is good." They will get that in school - for sure they will.

I cannot help thinking about what the Bible says about such things. It says things like, "I want you to be wise in what is good, and **simple** concerning evil." Romans 16:19. , or what the devil said to those in the Garden which sounds much the same to me as we need to understand good and evil; "For God knows that in the day you eat of it your eyes will be opened, **and** you will be like God, knowing **good and evil**." Funny ending to the story though isn't there? Genesis 3:4-6.

Disappointment

At the beginning of opening our first Christian School in North London in the early 1980's, as there were very few such things in those days, especially the kind we were operating, I got invited to all sorts of places in the UK to talk about education. Many, who came to such talks, usually put on by local church groups, were people involved in education or interested enough and broad minded enough to look at another way of "doing" it – education that is.

After many such events, and I do mean many, I got used to the standard questions. Questions like: "Aren't you just running a Christian hot house?" My answer would be, "You usually keep your flowers that you want to grow well in a hot house until you know they are hardy enough to survive outside!" Another common question is; "Are you not brain-washing the children?" I am usually careful not to say that some brains need washing, however, I do think it amazing that we think that any education system does not have an agenda embedded in the curriculum and is putting what the curriculum writers think into children's heads whether it is for good or evil. It is frightening to think that anybody could be so naive as to be unaware of that fact.

Nonetheless, on my travels, the greatest disappointment came as I talked with those who would tell me that they were followers of Jesus and that knowing God was the most important thing in all of life to them *and not education*! As if education was not relevant at all to the building of Christian character and knowing Christ! When I persistently heard that mindset, my conclusion was, that for all their words about the importance of knowing God, if push came to shove and it was a single choice of either knowing God or going to university, then the university would win every time. It was a double standard. They saw their Christian life and education as unrelated, separate, and neither of them having any impact on the other. I do not think that University or knowing God *is ever* the single choice, as I will demonstrate shortly, however, to think it may be the only choice for children at school is somewhat frightening when you hear what people confess about the importance of knowing God.

I suppose the disappointment of hearing that particular response is sort of tinged with the story that Jesus told as recorded in Luke 14:16-24. It's the story of the great party, probably the best party ever held, but those who were at the top of the invitation list found "good" reason not to come. One had got married and "could not" attend, another had bought land and so "had to" give it a miss, and still another had bought a new car – eh, sorry! – a yoke of oxen - and that stopped him from attending. University also was a better option for another. Oops! Sorry again. My slip! They had what they considered, "good reasons," not to take up the offer to be at the great party and so, "The master of the house said in wrath to his servant, "Go quickly into the great streets and the small streets of the city and bring in here the poor and the disabled and the blind and the lame. Maybe those who are not the top of the list can be persuaded to see the advantages of attending."", and I have to say, my experience so far is that they can be. Those who do not claim to be followers of Jesus, my Muslim friends for example, seem too often be more aware of what is on offer than those who should know better.

Advertising an Independent Sector School

We are so persuaded by the, "normal," and what is perceived to be, "the right approach," that those of us who do things differently always expect to have to swim upstream, to move against the odds, to climb the mountain, or whatever other metaphor one can think of to demonstrate an alternative.

When going against the norm, to persuade people to join is difficult. I always find the story of Moses and the release of the Israelites from slavery interesting. The Old Testament gives us a clue to some of their mass thinking. They were all slaves. Their next door neighbours were slaves. Their friends were slaves. Their wives and children were slaves. Slavery was the norm. When you have been brought up like that, it's very hard to convince people of the radical concept of "freedom," or, for my purpose in what I am saying about education, any other way of doing or thinking. The Old Testament Scriptures tell us that the people of Israel were angry with Moses for trying to set them free.
"What did you have in your slavery?" is the Moses question. They responded with the ludicrous answer of, "We had leeks, onions and cucumbers back in Egypt!" The problem was they were not looking for freedom, they were looking for bigger onions!

So when people consider putting their children into our school, many aspects of the cultural, the expected, and the, "norm," is simply not there! "How many classes do you have?" they say. "We don't have class rooms, or classes, it's an individualised method of education!" "What GCSE's do they take?" This is often the next question. "We don't do that either. Our students enter the ICCE certification." More problems. All people really want is a bigger onions. "Does the system work?" "What does the school deliver?" should be the next questions. From my point of view maybe these two should be the first questions.

We are interested, as an educational establishment, in not only good education for our students, but also good character development. We want the students to know God. We want them to become leaders in whatever area of life they end up in. We want them to become the best that they can possibly be. So, the big question should be: "Do we succeed in those aims?" My plain answer is, "not always!" but let me tell you about our recent school leavers. At the moment the school is around 40 students and growing. So, I thought that what I would do is look at some recent leavers and tell you their results, hoping that this will help you to assess us and decided if we are successful or not?

In recent years, of all the students that left our school, we have, with relational concern and follow-up been surprised and extremely pleased at the reports from the leavers. These students entered the university with their ICCE (International Certificate of Christian Education) certification which is the qualification that our students obtain. They later succeeded in the world of academia, each one of them telling me that it was the character training, the learned disciplines, and the thorough comprehensive nature of the learning process put into them at our Christian Schools that they insist facilitated their success. We are talking of University Degrees in English, Accounts, Business and Accounts, Music, IT, Photography, and Medicine. These achievements were all gained at established University's like London, Kingston, Canterbury and others. They were all warmly welcomed and received at later School Banquets with stories that make strong arguments for the validity and value of the system and curriculum we have implemented in our schools.

Here are some of those comments from students who have left us:

Recently, in interviews prior to the School Banquets, I had the pleasure of meeting these older students who had graduated from our schools and since studied at college and university. It was so good to chat with them and to ask some pertinent questions. This anecdotal information needs to be shared with a wider audience.

I asked one student how his first year at Canterbury University had gone. He responded, "I missed my London friends, but the studies were fine." I asked him for his opinion of our school system after having been at University," here are some of his comments: "One of my University' modules is Accounting. I had already done that subject for my Intermediate exam with International Certificate of Christian Education (ICCE), so of course, I had that down as one of my options from the advanced level course. However, when I saw the stuff at University I had to laugh. I said, "I wish my school studies had been this easy!"

I asked the same student if there was anything else he had noticed about his University' studies. He said, "The Algebra, as with accounts, was simple. I wish that the school stuff had been as easy as the University material." His final comment was; "When you have been to a school using the ACE (Accelerated Christian Education) system, a fundamental element that you learn is how to manage your study time and how to complete work within a given period. I am finding that my stuff gets done, whereas lots of other students seem to have problems completing work and bringing it in on time. We all have the same amount of time, and I think some of them are possibly brighter than me, but what they lack is the discipline that has been put into me over the years to complete work on time."

I also had the chance to talk with one of the lads who had completed his General Certificate at ICCE level, and asked him how his college studies were progressing.
"Great!" he said, "But what is funny is how the other students don't seem to be able to complete work on time. I have just handed in one of my first essays. The lecturer asked for 1,000 words. I was about 400 over so I went to him and asked how critical the word count was?

"Oh," he replied, "I only ask for 1,000 words as most of the students cannot get anywhere near that number. I am happy with anything up to 2000 words. However, I would be surprised if many can even achieve 800."

I asked him if he had made any other observations since he had left school. He said, "A friend asked me if I could help her with her GCSE material as she had to take an exam in Maths. So, I said I would come around and try. I was very surprised at the level, and helped her to complete the work, showing her how to work out the material. I then asked if I could take a copy of the paper with me. She agreed and explained that it was an old exam paper used for practice. I took it home to my younger sister who attends the same School I attended, she is just 13 years old, and asked her, "Can you do these maths?" She said, "Oh crumbs! Yes of course! I am doing that stuff now.""

For those who are au fait with the Accelerated Christian Education system, this girl was on PACE 1083 which, according to ICCE, is two units below where we would say a student is who has begun General certificate work.

There was another young lady at one of our New Year's Eve parties who had also been to a school using the ACE system, but not at one of the schools that I run. She is currently reading English at Liverpool Hope University. I asked how she had found it, and if there was anything she had learnt from the system that was useful in ongoing university studies. Her reply was amusing. "Well!" she said, "I am the only student in my group who knows how to break down an English language sentence into its component parts. The whole class were saying, "We don't even understand what we are being asked to do." So, I ran my own tutorial group for my friends. They asked me how I knew how to do this. I told them that I did it all when I was quite young in my Christian School and that it was standard practice. I am just surprised that such basic things are part of this English course at university."

Flack or no flack, the results speak for themselves. You might say to me, "Are you trying to sell your system to us?" My answer to that is; "You bet I am!"

Even if you are one of those in the highways and byways of life who believe that the state educational system is morally and philosophically neutral, we have great possibility for students, both educationally and in terms of life values!

Running an Independent sector school

I have been running independent sector schools for over 30 years. We are still small. If I had more money I would have bigger buildings and more students. Why do I do it? I believe in it. It works. It is value for money. Most importantly, it gives young people a head start in their lifelong educational journey.

Over the many years that I have been managing Christian schools I have received plenty of flack, partly because of the system that we use: Accelerated Christian Education (ACE). I am well aware that this system is not perfect. Has the perfect educational system been devised yet? To quote the inventors of the curriculum, "ACE is a system of education. It's a tool, and one has to make it work," which is what we do. We adapt and tailor the system to meet the requirements of our students. It is a system of education which in my opinion is better than most.

I have keenly watched the success of our students as they go into their chosen pathways of life. I know and they know, that some of the success they enjoy is down to the hard work of our school staff as they have guided the students through their early educational journey.

Faith Schools

I noted that the atheist "religious evangelist" Richard Dawkins was on Channel 4, again, complaining about faith schools and telling us all in superior and somewhat condescending tones, how divisive they are to the community.

I also noted that in these presentations and debates there are underlying assumptions that are never mentioned, and I therefore suppose, do not exist to the debating fraternity on the box. At least that is the conclusion towards which I am expected to be drawn into by the programme producers.

But think about it for a moment; not about the premise of whether Richard Dawkins might be right or wrong. Consider what he does not tell us in his programme, or does not allow us to ask. He simply makes the bold statement, "Faith schools cause community division," as if that is the root cause of all social division. Where I live, post codes cause community division. There are young people I know that won't move from one post code area to another as they fear they will be beaten up. Then there are people who live in "posh areas", who divide themselves from those live in the "not so posh" areas. Isn't that community division?

I did not go to a faith school, I went to an ordinary secondary school. We wore green blazers. The school up the road wore red blazers. The two groups had fights and thus divided the community. There are many things that divide communities; money, housing, blazers, music, clothes, skin colour, accent, language, post codes, and I'm sure you could add to my list. Whilst it suits Mr. Dawkins's spurious agenda to highlight faith schools as divisive, the division of community is a deep and highly complex problem, and his opposition to faith schools is, of course, deeper and more complex. If his proposed atheist schools go ahead, will they not also be divisive?

During his Channel 4 programme he states, "These faith schools indoctrinate children." He makes it sound like a wicked thing, to indoctrinate children. It is implied that we have no right to give children a view on the world, to tell them things are right or wrong. The manner in which he says it leaves us with the impression that we have all agreed that indoctrinating children is wrong.

On the subject of indoctrination, which I have thought about and addressed myself to deeply because people like Mr. Dawkins would always accuse me of practicing it: Are you really convinced that "non-faith schools" don't indoctrinate children, about anything? Does anybody really believe that all teachers have no world view, no opinions, or that they pass on to the children pure, unadulterated, unbiased teaching on every subject? Please! Whatever areas of learning children are exposed to, there will always be an element of indoctrination of some sort. It is truly unavoidable. And none of us have the privilege (or misfortune) of being a totally blank sheet.

[65]

In schools, one often hears the phrase, "…The Hidden Curriculum…" This refers to things that are not mentioned, nevertheless are subliminally present and real, and apply to the ethos, values and world view of the staff and administration who are presenting the teaching material, and will be evident in all they say and do, and be filtered down to the children.

I'll give you a couple of examples. These are from my own experience with my own children, from two of the schools they attended. Both of these examples were English grammar exercises, with the request to, "Re-write this sentence correcting grammar, spelling and punctuation."

Sentence one – *jesus went around doing good and healing the sick in israel for around 3 years.*

Sentence two - *when i got home from school i found my boyfriend john in bed with another girl*

No hidden curriculum there then? No indoctrination?

In my opinion, Richard Dawkins is a religious, atheistic, fundamentalist who wants to indoctrinate us all to his point of view. I strongly believe that he **should** have the right to try. However, I know from my email post bag that there are those who share his view, who, if they had the power, would not want to extend that *same* right to me. They would, as one of them put it, "Silence me," if they could. I wonder why they do not want me to have the same right to speak out, indoctrinate and influence as they would want for themselves? A freedom I, of course, want them to retain.

Asking the wrong questions

When one asks the wrong question, of course one will not get the right answer. How can the question be wrong, I hear you say?
Sometimes people just don't think. Let me show you what I mean.

London Evening Standard, Tuesday, twenty-seventh of July 2010. Pippa Crerar writes, "I don't want to find God to find a good school?" It is, perhaps, a rhetorical question.

[66]

She goes on to say that she doesn't want to go to church in order to get her child into a good school. However, she is obviously worried about the local schooling.

Here is a question that she doesn't ask, and maybe she should: "Why are Christian schools, or Church schools better than the others?' Answers could include issues like; selection, size, and parental involvement. Here, however, are some other answers - things that perhaps we don't so easily come up with in our sound-bite, cynical age. How about a comprehensive world view, an understanding of a moral base, an insight into good and evil, an awareness of the essentials of not just, "knowledge," but, "character," and even more than that, 'wisdom'- where does that come from?

Interestingly, plans to set up atheist schools in the United Kingdom could soon be given the green light by the British government, or so it seems according to a report by Assist News July 29th 2010. It says:

Education Secretary Michael Gove says he is open to the idea as part of reforms to his department.

The move comes after high profile anti-faith campaigner Professor Richard Dawkins suggested the idea, Premier Radio said. Ann Widdecombe, the Former Home Secretary who is also a believer, said, "It is not something that should be opposed."

She told Premier Radio: "If you can set up faith schools, then I think quite obviously you must also be allowed to set up a school that will cater for people whose parents are bringing them up specifically to have no faith."

Widdecombe added: "I think it is a great pity if somebody is brought up that way, but our job is to win those people over, not to look to the law to do it for us."

It is interesting to think of atheists setting up schools. I am not aware of many hospitals, orphanages, opposition to injustice groups that they have set up so far.

Perhaps they do not understand the nature of thought.

What we think is ultimately how we act. If I think I am an animal, does it surprise anyone that I might act like one? If I think there is no point to life, why should I care, why should I not be depressed and suicidal? If I think it's just all mechanical like one great machine, why not treat my fellow human beings like a cog in the wheel? On the other hand, if I think there is a law-giver, an ultimate reckoning day and a purpose to my being here, that will affect my thinking and my dealings with the rest of humanity.

John Newton, the famous reformed slave trader, preacher and hymn writer and of fairly recent film fame, captured the elemental truths of transformation when he penned, "Amazing Grace." The International teacher and author, Ravi Zacharias (www.rzim.org) hits the nail on the head when he describes man as "lost and dead." He explained, "Jesus did not come to make bad people good; He came to make DEAD people LIVE."

I have met modern people like John Newton. I have a friend who was once a rebel fighter. He could list all the women, children and men he had killed. When I met him, I thought he was a mad man. Then he found God. It may be a bit of an easy cliché to say that, but when you see a messy life changed, new thinking found and actual death into life discovered, one knows the difference. The cynic and atheist can say all they like, but I say, "Show me!" When you see their new concern for others, good citizenship, and a life that is progressive and enriched, one knows something special has taken place. There is this new passion for the life they now have.

Richard Dawkins said to me that he was more moral than me as I needed a God not to pillage and rape, kill and burn, murder and so on. My answer was "Good for you. You need to watch the news more."

So maybe Pippa Crerar, in her future journalism, could ask some more questions as to why these schools that have God seem to have better education. Ask the right questions!

Back in 1980, a couple of Educational Doctors, one from Texas and one from Fleetwood in Lancashire, asked if they could hire our building to put on a conference to explain to local church leaders about Christian Education.

We hired them the building, and I got the job of unlocking, putting out the 100 or so chairs for those who came and making sure that, as we had hired them our building, it was all "OK." So I stayed for a meeting that I otherwise would not have gone to.

I think that probably would have been the end of it, except that many of our parents in the church in North London at the time, were having problems with their children in secondary schools. These parents came to me and pleaded, "Please don't dismiss this! This may be an answer to our needs."

At that time however, I had seen and heard about Christian schools in the USA. I was certain it would not work in the UK. I was surprised, therefore, to discover that one had already started in Fleetwood Lancashire. Because of pressure from the parents in the church, we arranged to visit the only English ACE Christian School and see for ourselves what it was all about. I didn't want to be, but I *was* impressed, mostly by the children. Two years later we opened our own Christian School in Finsbury Park, Islington. We have moved many times since then to various sites, but have never stopped functioning at any time. I believe we have progressed with good success, seen in the lives and success of former students, both in careers and college success.

We have quite a few students who are 12, 13 and 14 years old but look like completing the equivalent of high grade GCE's. This is with the ICCE Board.

We have in the past had students who were years behind academically, then having studied with us they were able to go on to University. One such student sent word via his mother to say "I am here because those people (our staff) were the only people that ever believed in me."

One of our past students, now married with children and a mortgage, says "I use the life skills I learnt in the Christian school every day of my life. How to set goals, how to finish things and how to break things down so that I accomplish good things." She is now a qualified lawyer.

Currently we have around 15 children in our Islington Primary school 20 children in our Islington Nursery, 20 students in our Enfield Senior school and 3 students in our 6th form college.

Three years ago, with European funding, we started a college for ESOL Asylum/Refugees and currently have around 30+ students studying with us.

This recent addition to our education programme is really important to me. I like to see what we have been able to do for those most marginalised of people, asylum/refugee young people who really have nothing.

Banquets to celebrate and discover

At a recent banquet, a joint one between our Christian school and our small college that teaches English, the audience were surprised and pleased when one of the students stepped forward and in good English thanked the teachers and all other staff, for providing such a resource for them as students of English. In clearly pronounced English, she explained that she had come to the college not understanding the language and was now standing here to deliver a speech on behalf of all the students to say, "Thank you," for the possibilities that had been given them. This student has already been accepted at a Further Education college for further training.

This was the first time the rest of the students were able to hear one of their number making a speech in English to say. It is great knowing that 6 months previous to making the speech, she had no English knowledge at all. That, I think, is very rewarding.

These students come from most of the war torn areas of the world, making our school banquet, (numbers climbing to around 100 this year) in the Wood Green Indian restaurant, almost like the United Nations, with students from Afghanistan, Angola, Albania Congo, Ethiopia,

Eritrea, Gabon, Guinea, Kosovo, Mauritania, Romania, Sierra Leon, Iraq and Iran, to name just a few.

At the Banquet this writer gave a speech explaining that we are all important people, and how it only takes one person to change History, and one person with a God element changes the negative to a positive and makes us look self-confident, although in reality it is really God confidence. And even if one had come to this country from a frightening situation, feeling really at the bottom of the pile, nevertheless, one can make a difference. Be somebody that makes an effect on the world for Good.

Our banquet evening was rounded off for us all with an exciting mini concert by Tekiva, a well known local recording artist who not only presented the certificates to all the successful students but gave us some great music too.

It is exciting to see people that others have written off becoming potential future leaders and history makers.

The independent schools we run always hold an annual end of year banquet. Recently it was held in late October. Is that very late or very early? A few of the staff had been on maternity leave, and in order that they could attend we avoided June. There were approximately 120 people there, staff, students and friends. We enjoyed a wonderful meal supplied by the Curry Leaf Sri Lankan restaurant in Turnpike Lane in London. The Nursery and ABCs class presented their Space Programme. The Beehive Junior School sang songs they had composed; which they will shortly be recording to a CD, supported by Alex Greg, their Supervisor, their teachers and their music entrepreneur!

After almost 40 years of running Christian schools, today, I am more convinced than ever of their value. The banquet this year was especially pleasing to me, alongside the usual awards for, "Most Work Done," "Best Athlete," and, "Students with Highest Marks." I also had the privilege of presenting ICCE certificates for successful completion of examinations to seven students in the 11-16 age range.

The General Certificate was awarded to six students, one of whom was only 15.

Usually it takes students to 17 or even 18 to get to this level one student completed the Intermediate Certificate giving her passage to her chosen university. The other successful students chose a variety of options including continuing their studies at "A" Level or remaining at our sixth form further education unit, "Base 6." One has decided to work for us and is now employed by us.

The ICCE Examination Board issues qualifications that match the General level of the Cambridge International Certificates, according to NARIC (Nation Agency Responsible for providing Information advice and expert opinion on vocational and, academic and professional skills).

 As the National Agency, managed on behalf of the UK Government, they provide the only official source of information on international qualifications to organisations), the Government body that quality checks alternatives to GCSEs and other examinations.

The reasons for my comments here are multiple. First and foremost it is because I thoroughly enjoyed the banquet. The whole thing was superbly organised by our top flight administrator, Angela Kelly. I must also mention our senior students, who set to with a vengeance and successfully set up all the technical requirements. One of the banquet attendees, who is not part of the school, said, "It's so encouraging to see your students taking on responsibility with such reliability and integrity." That was good to hear, a fundamental aspect of the curriculum is character development.

It was an excellent day; I spent time with some great students and we all shared in the joy of rewarding them for the completion of a year of hard work. Our schools and nurseries are almost at capacity, and we would love to expand to enable more of you to entrust us with your children's education. Then perhaps next year, you will also join us at our year end Banquet.

If I'm totally honest, a key reason for my reference to the banquet is to redress comments that people make about our school. Firstly the often heard comment that states, "It's a nice school. But of course, the children can't go on to university as the qualifications are not good enough!" Here is solid, proof that such comments hold no weight.

F is for Funny

Getting your hair done

Black people in my church community, well to be more specific, the black girls, tell me that I need to understand that getting their hair done is (a.) Expensive and (b.) It takes a very long time to do.

For years I took this on board as a fact and sympathised with the money they shelled out and the hours they spent sitting in the hairdressers. One morning I woke up and thought, "Today I'm going test this fact out. I am going to take my white man's hair to a black person's hairdresser."

Lunch time came around and I left the office and headed to the local black hair salon. Now, I must confess that it was a ladies salon, but that did not seem to bother the hair stylist when I popped my head round the door and asked, "Can you fit me in for a haircut?" "Yes, darling, come in and take a seat,' was the willing reply.

It was 1pm

I was ushered to a seat by the basin and my hair was washed quite quickly. Then, with a towel wrapped round my head, I was offered tea, then cake. Other goodies appeared and after quite some time I was placed in a chair in front of the stylist who began to scrutinize my hair. She pulled it this way and that, and then back to how it had been. Then it started all over again. All the while chatting away and telling me the local news. The music soothed me, and the cutting and styling went on. And on and on. And on. Eventually it was done, and done very well I must admit. The cost was not that high considering all the food and drink and time spent based on an hourly rate. Being of the male species I'm not sure I want to spend so much time on getting my hair done, I gave her a generous tip and went on my way.

It was 5pm.

Now, when the girls say, we are black and our hair takes time and money. I reply, 'You can't kid me, I know all about your hairdressers!'

[73]

Yes or No?

Our sound bite age is impatient with answers that take more than two minutes. We want it simple and we want it quick and we want it to be correct and all encompassing. Our culture may be in that 'want' position, but it's unrealistic, unhelpful, untruthful, unfulfilling and just does not work.

I am reminded of the story of the old farmer with a horse and cart riding through the country lanes with his dog by his side and a load of hay on the back. A sports car came around a bend far too fast and crashed into the old farmer, causing considerable damage and loss. Eventually the farmer and the driver had their day in court, and of course the farmer was trying to get compensation for his loss. On the other side, the defence for the insurance company were trying to settle for as little as possible.

The lawyer defending the insurance company against the farmers claim had a last chance to cross examine the farmer in the witness box. He started by asking, "Now, please sir, please just answer my question with a, "Yes," or "No," answer. It very simple. Did you, or did you not, when questioned" by the police officer at the scene of the crime, answer the constable's question; "Are you alright?" with "Yes, thank you. I am fine?"

The farmer did not want to answer, "Yes" or, "No," and began to say, "Well, my Lord, it was like this …" He got no further as the lawyer interrupted with, "Now please just answer the question, "Yes," or, "No!"

Again the farmer tried. "I was lying in …" Again the lawyer stopped him. "Please sir! As I have already said, "I require a "Yes," or, "No!" answer.

The farmer tried a third time. "When my horse …" Yet again, the lawyer interrupted. "Please sir! What is it that you don't understand about "Yes!" or, "No!"?

Fortunately, at this point of the proceedings, the judge intervened and stopped the defence lawyer and said,

"I know counsel wants a simple answer. However, I am going to rule that we let the farmer answer the question in his own way. Please do not interrupt him again. We will hear what he has to say." The Farmer thanked the judge and proceeded with his story.

"When the car came round the bend very fast, it hit my horse and cart. My horse was knocked to the ground, my dog was flung over the hedge on one side of the road, and the impact threw me over the hedge on the other side of the Road. I was lying in the ditch groaning with pain when the police quickly arrived. Being in a farming community, they looked at my poor horse lying on the ground and I heard them say, "This horse is in great pain. He definitely cannot be helped." As I say, being in a country area, the police are used to animal problems and one of them went back to their car, brought out a gun. I heard them say, "This animal is really injured. We need to put it out of its misery. Then they shot my horse. They then found my little dog who was whimpering in the ditch on the other side of the road from me. I heard them say again, "This dog is so badly hurt we need to put it out of its misery. Then they shot my dog. Finally the policeman carrying the gun found me in the ditch where I lay, and looking at me with his gun in his hand he asked, "Are you alright?" To which I anxiously replied, "I am fine thank you"!!!

So what am I going on about? I have just watched one of those question type programmes on TV with all its discussions, trying to track the big issues of the day, but expecting people to give good summaries of complex issues in sound bite answers in an attempt to reach helpful conclusions? They never do reach sound conclusions because the sound bite, answer does not really give us the depth and breadth of the understanding that often these questions require. So what do you want? The easy "Yes" – "No", or something that is more meaty, accurate and really addresses the issue.

There was a large yellow dancing duck

My new wife, Pauline, and I moved to Middlesbrough. New area, new situation, new problems, but the same need for people to hear the good news, and the same challenge of how it should be communicated. I am always willing to try something new, but one has to have the idea in the first place before one can try it. At that stage of our lives I didn't have any new ideas, so I forged ahead with my tried and tested methods.

Grangetown, where we were living, did not have much for young people to do, or places for them to go to. So, I revisited the "60's" coffee and chat idea. We had a church hall that we could use, attached to the main building. We set it up as a coffee bar. We had no singers as there was only Pauline and me. We dished out the invites and waited to see if anything would happen. We used taped music and made the coffee. Youngsters came, but it was hard to have one to one conversations as we were outnumbered 30 to 1. So, instead a talk from a central point seemed the way forward.

In this part of town they also had the tendency to throw things if they didn't like what was happening. Quite similar to my experiences in Birmingham at St Martins where they occasionally threw vegetables at us. Here, in Grangetown, it was rather more aggressive and destructive. Bricks through windows were a regular occurrence.

It was a rough and tumble type of town, but ever so many of the youngsters that we met wanted - truly wanted - to know God. In fact I have heard from a few of them recently and it is now over 30 years ago.

I was puzzled by the fact that many of the local kids managed to find the hall where we were holding the coffee bar. It was not located anywhere obvious, being right at the extremities of the town. One evening, I was chatting to one of the youngsters. I asked him how he had managed to find us and why he had come to listen to me. He told me that the local vicar had been going round the schools with a stern warning to all the young people. "Stay away from those new people in the church at the end of town," he told them.
"They are weird! Americans! And they will corrupt you!" We could not have had better publicity. Telling youth *not* to do something is guaranteed to ensure they will!

Gradually, many of these young people became part of our church community, although they took great pleasure in playing tricks on me. We also had to deal with gangs of them invading our house night after night. In that area, at that time, the culture was "open door - come right on in" If we forgot to lock the front door, we would be washing up in the kitchen, and then return back to the living room only to discover 6 to 8 young people had appeared.

This was quite a pressure for a newly married couple just starting out in their first leadership role. However, they wanted questions answered. They really wanted to understand the meaning of their existence.

One day, we had a very special speaker who was visiting the church building. They all turned up and were on their best behaviour. (This was often not the case. I was regularly getting complaints from the "established churches" that these youngsters were too noisy, too young or did not observe religious etiquette.) As I stood at the front, leading the meeting, I was pleased that they were all so well behaved. There would not be any complaints about them this evening. Then, to my surprise, I noticed that some of the older ladies were looking decidedly wobbly and flustered. So much so that one or two of them left the building half-way through the meeting. I also noticed that there was suppressed laughter rippling through the rows of youngsters.

At the end of the formal part of the meeting, I found some of the ladies sitting in the side room looking quite ill and sipping water. "What's the problem?" I asked. They all spoke at once, but I eventually gathered that they had all been having hallucinations which had made them feel faint. The hallucination, it turned out, was a large yellow duck behind me and the speaker. It was obviously a very spiritual duck because it danced in time with the music. It had deeply disturbed them and sent them scurrying out as they just couldn't take it any longer.

I smelled something fishy, and quizzed the teens in order to try and get to the bottom of the mystery. It turned out that they had stolen my own daughter's bath time toy, a large yellow plastic duck, broken into the building where we were meeting and placed it on the top of the large unused organ situated at the back of the platform. They had then tied an almost invisible nylon cord around its neck, which they threaded along the ceiling and dropped down into the rows where the youngsters were sitting. By sleight of hand they made it dance in time with the music of each song.

I feigned great disappointment at their actions. However, deep down, I was hoping that over time their creativeness and hard work would be turned to more constructive use as their passion for Jesus grew.

A yellow duck dancing – Again.

In November 2011 I published my sixth book, my first fiction book, and as part of the publicity I sent out a picture of the book via email. Imagine my surprise when the book cover came back somewhat adjusted. I just thought you would all like to see it.

Here is the link to the original story...
http://www.adrianhawkes.blogspot.co.uk/2010_05_01_archive.html

My Pope stories…..

I have lots of stories about my wife. Her antics are a mine of interest and humor. Let me share a couple with you.

Story One - Who is he?

Some years ago I had a friend. Let's call him Scott (not his real name). He was South African. When we were in South Africa we stayed at his home and consequently got to know him very well. He even used to lend me his car so that we could explore the country. Some years later, my rather famous friend was appointed as a special representative to the Vatican, speaking on behalf of his religious denomination.

As Scott was attending many meetings in Rome on behalf of his denomination, it became very newsworthy. One day, on the front cover of an international magazine, a photograph was published of Scott with the man who was Pope at the time. Inside was a large spread all about the work he was doing.

My wife and I, with a group of friends, were in Central London. We walked past a certain newsagent. The window display was of this same magazine, along with the photograph of Scott and the Pope. Pauline scrutinised the picture. She then turned to our friends and said, "We know him. That's our friend Scott. But who is that man with him - the one in the funny dress?"

Story Two - Ignorance is bliss

A couple of years ago my wife kindly treated me to a trip to Rome, as part of my birthday celebrations. If one is doing the sights in Rome, one must, or course, visit the tiny nearby country called, "Vatican City," which, as it happens, is the smallest country in the world. We wandered around taking in the sights and sounds and inspected the Swiss Guard. Pauline noticed that there was a meeting of some kind taking place in the chapel. She was keen to go in.

I was not. However, as she had treated me to this trip, I thought it best to tag along. It was obviously some sort of celebratory mass (not that I understand much about Catholic ecclesiology). There was a crowd of people at the front of the chapel and we watched as a procession of men moved down the aisle. One of them had on a very large pointed hat. Pauline asked, "Is that the Pope?" "No," I replied, "But he might be one day. I think he's an archbishop judging by the special hat."

We found a couple of empty seats and sat down. Pauline then decided that, if they were doing communion then she was going to join in at the front. I told her, "it's for Catholics!" But she was having none of it, saying "I follow Jesus. So I'm sure I must be included." She headed off to the front. I sat tight.

There was a large multi-national crowd at the front. The man in the big hat was moving along the rows of people with a container of wafers, which he was placing on outstretched tongues.

As he placed each one he said, "Bless you my child!" Pauline wanted to return the favour, so she put her hand on him, in order that she could bless him back. In a trice, the plain clothes security squad was at his side, to protect him from perceived danger.

Once the members of the crowd had received communion, they began returning to their seats, whereupon, I found that Catholic love and grace does not extend to someone who has pinched their seat in church. I was swiftly ejected from my perch and was made to feel I had committed a heinous crime. I managed to squeeze in at the end of the row just as Pauline returned. The procession now weaved its way out of the chapel. Pauline noticed that the man in the big hat was waving at her, or so she thought. He was, in fact, pronouncing a blessing on the assembled crowd. She began waving back, frantically, at her new found friend.

I perceived rapid, shadowy movements out of the corner of my eye, so I put my hand in the small of her back and began propelling her to the exit and hissed, "It's time to leave, NOW! Quick, before it's too late and the plain clothes security squad arrest you as a trouble-maker."

A funny thing happened to me on the way to the theatre

I thought you would enjoy this true story. If I turn it into a short story and stick it on Amazon, perhaps they will pay me commission when you buy it. But I am running ahead of myself. Let me start at the beginning.

In the early 1970's after my family and I had moved to London to lead two congregations for a particular denomination, Samantha, one of the young ladies in the church, said to my wife, "I've got two tickets for "Godspell." will you come with me to see it?" Pauline is never one to say no to a freebie, so whilst I stayed at home to baby-sit, they headed off to London's West End.

During the show the audience was invited to join the cast on stage in an "on-stage Communion Service." Pauline and Samantha were sitting far away up in the balcony. A steward explained that to get to the stage they would have to leave the theatre and re-enter by the stage door. Both of them were keen to join in the fun and left the theatre in search of the stage door. In the West End, the theatres are huddled together cheek to jowl.

As they tried to enter the stage door they found themselves confronted by two burly bouncers who would not let them in. Pauline got into a heated and noisy debate with these men, to no avail. The ladies eventually discovered they were trying to enter the wrong theatre. They had been attempting to join Diana Rigg on stage in Pygmalion.

The following evening we were out to dinner with my old friends Dan and Norma Wooding of ASSIST News. During the evening Pauline told Dan what had happened to her and Samantha at the theatre the previous evening. Dan, being the eternal journalist and at the time freelancing for the London press, asked permission to create some copy from their escapade. Pauline shrugged and said, "Why not? Go for it!" Neither of us thought any more about it.

The following week the daily papers began carrying the story, and many of our friends called us when they saw it in their newspaper of choice. The largest spread was in the Daily Express and it even appeared in the notorious Private Eye.

There is a small detail you need to be aware of. In the opinion of the denomination for which I was working, going to the theatre was frowned upon as a "worldly experience," and to be avoided at all cost, *especially by the wives of ministers*. Not, I should add, a view that I personally have ever subscribed to.

Two weeks later, I had a phone call from the denomination headquarters. The "big boss" wanted to meet with me. I received no explanation as to why, only the summons. I headed off to HQ and received a dressing down for not keeping my wife under control. I was informed that my potential as a future "world leader" was being jeopardised by such "lax behavior." I was then given a generous payment to cover my expenses before I headed home.

At that time, in the early seventies, the role of women was blurred and unformed. However, one thing was clear, the woman's place was at home, and my job, as the minister was not to be doing the baby sitting. Unfortunately, this attitude still lingers in some areas. Pauline was exceedingly miffed at not being invited to put her side of the story.

To soften it, I took the family out for dinner with the expenses I was given.

Six months later I had a call from my good friend Dr. Phil Moor. Prior to a recent train journey he had purchased a book by Stephen Pile entitled "Heroic Failures." The author, who classes himself as a "failed writer" had decided to compile a list of failures and turn it into a book. This volume went on to become a best seller, and made him a lot of money. Phil told me that Pauline's failed attempt to get onto the stage of Godspell was one of the stories in the book.

Thanks Dan, someone made some money from Pauline's story. All I got was a reprimand!

Here is how Dan presented it:

A funny thing happened to my wife on the way to the stage of 'Godspell' in London's West End

And it resulted in her story being widely featured in the British press, 'The Book of Heroic Failures' and a telling off from my denomination.

It started out as a bit of innocent fun for my wife Pauline, but it ended up in a reprimand for me from my boss at the headquarters of my then denomination.

It was in the early 1970's when my family moved from Birmingham, in the English Midlands, to North London in the British capital, to lead two congregations for this particular denomination.

Samantha, one of the young ladies at one of the churches, told my wife one day, "I've got two tickets for 'Godspell.' Would you like to come with me to see it?"

For your interest, Godspell is an archaic spelling of the word gospel, and was a hit 1970 musical by Stephen Schwartz and John-Michael Tebelak and was playing at that time in a well-known London theatre.

Pauline is never one to say no to a freebie so, while I stayed at home to babysit, they headed off to the bright lights of the West End for an enjoyable evening.

Just before the interval, the audience was invited to join the cast on stage for a communion service. Pauline and Samantha were sitting in seats far away from the stage -- up in the balcony in fact -- and so they asked a steward how they could get to the stage and he told them that they would have to "leave the theatre and re-enter by the stage door."

So, both of them, keen to join in the on stage celebrations, left the theatre in search of the stage door. I need to explain here that, in the West End, the theatres huddle together, cheek by jowl, and so as they tried to enter the stage door they found themselves confronted by two burly bouncers who would not let them in.

Pauline is not a person who gives in easily and she got into a heated and noisy debate with the men, but to no avail. It was only then that the ladies discovered they were trying to enter the wrong theatre; they had been attempting to join Diana Rigg on stage in "Pygmalion."

The following evening, we went out for dinner with our old friends Dan and Norma Wooding. (Dan had been the best-man at our wedding.) During the evening, Pauline told Dan what had happened to her and Samantha at the theatre, and Dan, being the eternal journalist, asked permission to create some copy about their escapade.

Pauline shrugged and said, "Why not; go for it!" Neither of us thought anymore about it, but soon afterwards problems began to arise.

The following week, the British daily papers began carrying Dan's story and many of our friends called us when they saw it in the paper of their choice. The largest spread was in the Daily Express and it even appeared in the notorious Private Eye magazine, the country's top satirical publication.

What made things worse that the opinion of the denomination for which I was working for at that time, viewed going to the theatre as something to be frowned upon as a "worldly experience" and they believed that it should be "avoided at all cost," especially by the wives of their ministers.

I should add here that this was not a view that I personally subscribed to.

Two weeks later, I received a phone call from the denomination's headquarters and was told that the big boss wanted to meet with me. I was given no explanation as to why, only the summons. So, in some trepidation, I headed off to the HQ and there received a dressing down for not keeping my wife under control, and was informed that my potential as a future "world leader" was being jeopardized by such "lax behaviour."

However, to reduce the impact of telling off, I was given a generous payment to cover my expenses and I headed home.

At that time, women's roles were blurred and unformed, but one thing was clear, and that was their place was meant to be at home, and my job, as a minister, was certainly not to be doing the baby sitting. Unfortunately, the attitude still lingers in some areas even today.

Pauline was exceedingly miffed at not being able to put her side of the story. To soften the situation, I took the family out for dinner with the expenses.

It seemed that things had died down -- until six months later -- when I received a call from my good friend, Dr. Phil Moor, who told me that, prior to a recent train journey, he had purchased "The Book of Heroic Failures" by Stephen Pile, who founded the short-lived "Not Terribly Good Club of Great Britain." (To join Pile's club, you had to be "Not Terribly Good" at something, and preferably awful.)

The author, who classed himself as a failed writer, had decided to compile a list of failures and turn it into a book, which went on to become a best seller, and made him a lot of money, but because he was now a success, had was forced to disband his club.

Phil told me that Pauline's failed attempt to get onto the stage of "Godspell" was one of the stories that was featured in the book, which became an overnight sensation - we Brits love failures -- and led to a sequel, "The Return of Heroic Failures."

Pauline said at the time, "The only blessing was that the book missed out my name, not that it made much difference as all these people already knew the story from the press reports. They had great fun with me about it.

"And to add salt to the wound -- I never got a penny for the story. I realized that I had well and truly become an 'heroic failure.'"

At least someone made some money from Pauline's story. All I got was a reprimand!

When Funny Is Not Funny...

Some years ago I was with a white friend who was marrying a black African girl. It was great fun. They had an English/African wedding which was full of dancing and laughter.

Later, in conversation with the young man, he asked, "Would you like to see what the African Elders have given me as a wedding present?" Of course I was interested. The Newly wed groom showed me an ornate stick. "What is it?" I asked. I could plainly see it was a stick, but I didn't know what you were supposed to do with it. He laughed and said, "It's presented to all young men who get married. It is a stick to beat your wife with to keep her in order." Then he laughed. I did not! He then said, "I of course would not use it, I just think it's funny." I replied, "Personally, I don't think it's funny at all. I cannot laugh at such a gift, such an action or such a thought."

The problem with such an action is that it implied that within the particular African culture of the bride's origin such an attitude was right, acceptable and permissible. The thinking that created the gift that he had thought a bit of fun, actually represented an attitude to life where beating the wife was a godly thing to do.
I do not think that it was any of those things. I think it is wrong thinking. It was and is wrong culturally, wrong humorously, and in fact just plain wrong. It should not be given space.

More recently I listened to a conversation between a young couple. They were discussing the fact that a young African child had been taken into the UK care system. The young man, a white African asked, "Why has that happened?" "Well," was the response, "he has been badly abused, in fact often beaten." The 2015 answer was, "That is normal, surely. He is black. That is their culture!" So, in that case, it is not wrong?

I like culture. I have lectured degree students on the subject. I have also conducted courses with students as part of a Continual Professional Development on the subject. I have even written a book on the topic. I love different cultural expressions, different food, fashion, greetings and ways of being. However, sometimes we have to identify when people use the cultural "get out." Excuses like, "This is just a cultural way that is different to yours." Sorry, but culture needs to change when it condones what is morally wrong. Personally, in those situations, one's country of origin, one's skin colour, one's language group, one's answers such as, "In my culture we beat our wives," are unacceptable.

On the same theme, some years ago I got talking with a Pastor of a particular ethnic group. We agreed to have coffee together. In the course of conversation he said, "I am having such problems with the people in my church, the husbands beat their wives too much." (By the way, maybe I need to say that here; the skin colour of this particular ethnic group was not black.) I replied, "I don't understand. What do you mean? "They beat their wives *too* much?" Are you saying that it's acceptable to beat them some, but not too much?" "Oh yes!" he replied. "From where they come from it's the culture (there is that word again) for men to beat their wives. However, the village makes sure it is not too much. My fear, here in the UK, is they might kill their wives." I interrupted and said, "I'm sorry, but I think that beating your wife is unacceptable. Full stop. Any beating is unacceptable!"

He got very angry with me and left. He did not even finish his coffee.

"How could one be so naive and narrow minded and not pay attention to other people's culture?" he shouted over his shoulder as he walked out.

Frankly, I want to stay naïve and narrow minded. I will do all in my power to make sure there are laws, and/or whatever else it takes to

[86]

change such wrong-minded cultures or "otherwise thinking." It is not funny. It is wrong! Can I say that any louder?

Fences on Cliff Tops

Often times when we make new laws or change old ones, we are not thinking of the consequences unseen up the road. We would do well to do so; even when those decisions or laws are made with the best intentions in mind.

Early on in the UK, a law was brought in to make tenancy of rented housing more secure. The good reason for it was that some people were being put out of their rented house for very little good reason. However, the unforeseen consequences were that for a period it actually created homelessness. People were reluctant to give others a room in their house if they thought they would turn out to be a bad tenant. That of course was not the intention, but that was what happened.

I wonder, as I look at recent changes in legislation in the USA and the UK, if we are heading for unforeseen circumstances that we will not like. Of course, from a legislation point of view it may have been done for good reasons like equality and freedom, but are we really sure of the outcomes?

I don't know, but I do wonder what our new freedom so called, our new equality so called, the removal of fences if you will, are going to bring *up the road.* I wonder if they will have good or bad effects on our society.

It is a bit like that fence on the cliff top, the very low one with the sign that says it is dangerous to step over the fence.
Then of course, in the name of freedom and equality someone questions why it is dangerous, and they step over the fence and walk around on the wrong side of the fence. Then they shout, "Look I am okay! Nothing has happened to me! Who said it was dangerous?"

This sort of incident is then followed by a great furore and complaints to the local authority about taking away our freedom to walk on the cliff top and putting up wrong signs and questions as to who made this rule anyway. Eventually, even though the powers that be, know that the cliff in question has erosion at its edge, the fence is removed and the signs are taken down.

Of course the first fence crossers were just dancing around very near the said fence, they were only interested in challenging the fence, they were not interested in getting a better view, their wailing, running, and dancing was close to where they crossed over. They had disobeyed the instruction, but were still safe.

But now we are all free to walk where we like. We can go to the cliff edge. It may take time but it will come, when one or two will stand right on the edge of the cliff to admire the view. There is nothing to stop them, no fence, no danger signs; they are just expressing their freedom to be there.

The cliff gives way and they are plunged to their death on the rocks below.

Maybe the fence had a purpose after all?

G is for Grandparents

Grandparents: What were we made for?

When I was a little boy, not so long ago, I regularly visited my Grandparents house together with my sisters and cousins. The house was big. And so was the garden.

There were many trees in the large garden. In the Spring lots of birds made their nests in them. Occasionally there would be a family tragedy in one of the feathered families. A small bird would fall out of a tree and could not get back to its nest, or a bird would end up with a damaged wing and be unable to fly.

My cousins, siblings and I, loved this situation. We would rescue such a bird and take it to my Grandfather. He knew about these things. He would disappear into his Tardis like garage, and reappear with an old cage, into which he gently placed the lost or wounded bird. We would then add some water to the cage and find some way of feeding the bird - usually with bread soaked in milk, the occasional worm. They also seemed to like cat food! We kids learned to feed the bird using a match stick with tiny morsels of food on the end.
Obviously we got very attached to the bird in the cage. It became a family pet. We enjoyed watching it grow, and get stronger. We loved feeding it. Often the bird would become quite tame and sit on our hand in order to take food from us. We carried out similar bird rescues many times. The trouble was, it always ended the same way. There would come a day when my Grandfather would say, "OK! This bird is now strong and well. It's time to set it free."

As usual, us kids would all cry out, "No Grandpa! This bird likes us. It wants to stay with us. It doesn't want to be free!" Grandfather never listened. He would take the cage to the top of the garden, together with a bunch of kids in tow, and putting the cage down on the grass, he would then open the cage door.

Often, at this stage, a funny thing would happen.

The bird would hop out of the cage, as it had done before on many occasions onto our hands. Then the bird would hop around the lawn for a few moments and, to our surprise, go back into the cage. It's funny how we are drawn back to familiar things - even a prison or a cage.

Grandfather would then give us a lecture on what birds were made for. "Birds are made to fly. Birds are made to be free. And birds are not made to be in cages." And so on. We kids, of course, responded with, "But this bird likes us. This bird wants to stay with us. Please let us keep it Grandpa."

As I remember those birds, it does set me thinking about what we humans are here for? What are we made for? What things we should be free from? What should we be leaving behind, but find that we still return to? What is the environment that we should fly in?

Grandfather would then do something that would make us kids cringe, and cry out, "No Grandpa! That's too cruel!" He would cup the bird gently in his very big hands, move to the centre of the garden, swing his arms low, then as hard as he could he would swing his arms forward and up into the air, opening his hands at the highest point, throwing the little bird as high as possible into the air. The little bird would often flutter down, catch the air in its wings, and then begin to fly. Sometimes it would fly around the garden a couple of times, perhaps sitting for a few moments on one of the branches in our apple tree. Then, to our utter dismay, it would fly off to join the other birds, gone, as far as we kids were concerned, forever. Grandfather would console us by saying, "It's where it should be. Free to fly. Free to be a bird. And birds are not meant for cages." Neither are we!

H is for How

How to have a Vision - and make it work

Fleas

If you take a jam-jar and fill it with fleas (the jumping kind), placing the lid firmly on for your own protection, you should note that the fleas will jump up and down until they bang their heads on the lid. At that point they will reduce the height of their jump to a point just below the rim. Fleas, apparently, don't like bumping their heads. I am told that if you later remove the lid, the fleas will continue to stay in the jar because they are conditioned to believe in a lid.

I have not done this experiment myself, but you are welcome to try it. The point is they are conditioned. Most of us are conditioned by what is around us. It encloses us, it limits us, it controls us. If we understood what a big God we have, we would understand that he has taken the limits off and we can jump out.

Breaking the vicious circle

People come to look at the work that has been achieved in our church here in North London and often say things like, "If only I had . . . then I could. . ." It is foolish to look at what is and assume that it has always been, or that everything floated down from heaven, ready-made, just for that pastor, team, leader, music director or whatever, to take charge of and enjoy the fruits.

In every situation there is always the vicious circle. It goes something like this. We do not have enough people; if we had the right money we could get the people; we also lack resources. To some extent that is often a correct conclusion, but somewhere those circles must be broken. We have some choices to make, and the key to those choices is vision--not looking at what is, but at what could be. Not looking at who you have with you, but at what they are going to become. Not looking at the money you don't have, but at knowing how much you need to spend.

It takes vision plus faith to break the circle.

You might break it at the financial point; you might break it at the resources point; you might well break it at the point of people whom you do have and know and who are willing to be with you to help.

Most people have what I call tunnel vision: they see what they want to see. They see what they are conditioned to see, what logic tells them they should see. The mind fills in the details. Almost like the fact that the action of the mind prefers to compensate for the blind spot in the eye, filling in the details from past experiences. We need to jump out of that mind-set. We need new thinking lateral thinking. 'Put on the mind of Christ,' the Bible says. Dream dreams! Have a vision!

Chickens

Chickens could tell us a lot. A farmer once told me that, as a child, he would take a hen, firmly push its beak to the ground and then, with his finger, draw a line in the farmyard dirt. The hen would watch from its right eye the line being drawn nearer and nearer to its head. When the finger got to the head, he would run the finger firmly across the chicken's head so that it really felt it, and then down the other side of the head. He then continued the line along the dirt, which the hen watched with great suspicion with its left eye. The hen could see a line with the right eye and a line with the left eye, and it surely felt it go across its head. Then he would gently release his hold on the chicken which would stay right there, tied to the floor. It could see the "rope" with both eyes. The chicken had felt the "rope" over its head. It knew it was tied down.

Some of us can see what we see, but we see it only with our human eyes. We fail to see with vision that is clear. We can only see the reason why we have not succeeded, the reason why we have been tied down, the reason why we did not get the breaks.

You are not too old. It is not too late to have a dream, to have a vision and to plan the first steps. You will then discover that the things that tied you down were actually illusions, and were only there to limit you in what you need to do for the kingdom.

Elephants

They tell me that the way to train an elephant is very simple. Again, I have not tried it, but will be glad to receive the results of your research. I am told that you find a sturdy tree stump and tie the elephant's leg to it with a strong chain. You then put food for the elephant just out of reach so that as he moves towards it, the chain cuts harder into his leg, creating considerable pain. After a few days, the elephant learns that to try and reach the food simply causes tremendous pain and is unachievable. You can then feed the elephant. You can change the chain for a light rope that normally the elephant would snap, but the light rope will now be sufficient to restrain him.

The elephant has been conditioned to believe that moving his leg, if it is tied, would cause him pain. So he has learned to move only in the area where the slack would allow. Conditioned, controlled and tamed, the mighty elephant is now limited. There is one thing, however, that will spoil the training of an elephant. Should you have completed your training and then be unfortunate enough to suffer a fire (one that comes towards your elephant), the fire would enable the elephant to overcome the conditioning, overcome the pain, overcome the fact that he knows he is tied, and he would break loose. The breaking loose would mean that never again could you train him or condition him. You have lost your elephant!

Changing our thinking

It is very obvious that the way God changes people is by changing their thinking. 'As a man thinks, so he is,' says Proverbs 23:7. 'Be transformed by the renewing of your mind' (Romans 12:2). What we think about ourselves, our situation, our upbringing, our God, is all-important. "I am unable to," means you will not be able to. "I can," means you will. Paul says, "I can do everything through him who gives me strength" (Philippians 4:13), and he could!

The fire changes the elephant and makes him free once again.

The fire of the Holy Spirit should burn into our minds and set us free. Maybe some of us speak in tongues, but we somehow need the fire of the Holy Spirit to burn up the old negatives - the disillusionment, conditioning, upbringing, old hurts, laziness, worldliness, wrong conceptions of God etc - and free us to be visionaries who will take action and change the world.

This is how it happened in the Bible. I am not trying out a new doctrine. Danny Moe, a Canadian friend of mine, takes seminars for sales representatives for some very large companies. He told me once that fewer than 1% of all groups (and he does seminars for Secular as well as Christian organisations) have any goals, plan or vision of where they are going or what they plan to be or do.

A pastor of a church in North London spoke to me at a Minister's Fraternal. When I asked him what his goals and aims were, his answer was, "I am just waiting to be led. I do not plan anything. I just want to see what God does." That sort of nonsense showed in the life, or non-life, of his church! I am sure that God is still willing to speak with us, guide us and redirect us, but there is a broad-based plan in Scripture that offers scope for us to change the situation. God is with us to do just that.

How do we get started?

How do we change if we are visionless at the moment? Where do you get dreams from?

I believe the first place we ought to go is to the word of God in order to gain understanding of who God is and what he is able to do. Fill your mind with it. Fill your mind with the fact that he is a mighty God, a God of miracles, a God of power, a God who is love. Know that he is with you, for you, and plans for your success. He is just waiting to be involved with your work, and for you to be involved with his plans.

Secondly, start to dream – and not necessarily while you are asleep! Dreams without inhibition. Unlimited dreams. Do not limit your dreams by what your qualifications are, or what you don't have, or what you may or may not need, or what resources you lack. Dream as if you have them all.

Thirdly, begin to have a vision of the dreams fulfilment. See it, taste it, walk round it, hear from God, tell him what you see.

Fourthly, set goals—real goals, long-term goals, short-term goals, medium-term goals -and say: "My goals take me there. My long-term goal is to arrive." The goals must interlink. It is not usually sensible to go south if your ultimate plan is to end up in the North. Write the goals down. Review them regularly. Life is made up of choices and some things have to be rejected in favour of others. Don't get side-tracked and channelled into the wrong direction from your goal. God is for you, so go for it! Remember that destiny is a matter of choice not circumstance.

Fifthly, and here is where many people get frozen in their tracks (where dreams and visions may die), have a plan of where you are going. You must have bite-size, achievable objectives. To put it another way, the goal must be broken down into small pieces. What will you do tomorrow? These composite part of your vision must have time limits. They must be measurable. You might miss the time or not quite make the measurement, but if it is not stated, then it is not measurable and you will hit nothing and go nowhere. (Unless of course you are like the farmer who hit a bull's eye every time on his barn door. The only problem was, he painted the targets after he had fired the bullets.)

Sixthly, we need a philosophy of ministry. We need to be reminded at this point that we are kingdom people, children of the heavenly Father. We cannot regard what we do as simply employment, even though we may be employed. We cannot see it as just work, though we may have to work very hard.

Ministry

The best way of describing what we do to accomplish the vision, is ministry. That means you and your vision are not only working something out, you are a gift to the church. Not a cheap copy that will break down after a couple of uses, but a real valuable genuine article. What is ministry? Where do we minister? It seems that many definitions of ministry have a very narrow band of preaching, visiting and studying.

There are some who would tag other gifts to the church with that, such as teacher or pastor. From my own perspective, it has been a great tragedy that many denominations see the pastoral role as the main ministry and only pay lip service to the other ministries. We need a philosophy of ministry that is broad based, enabling, involving and one that will allow us to be inclusive of the whole church community.

I have tried to work out a philosophy of ministry as follows:

1. To be an enabler - which usually means getting out of the way to let the church work.
2. To have the broadest possible vision. I would see that as the local church being involved in every angle and aspect of human happening - worship, praise, evangelism, education, business, and medicine. Politics and social concern.
3. To have a vision broad enough to allow me to incorporate other people's vision into my vision making it "our" vision, and to help them exercise their ministry in the widest possible way.
4. To seek to obey the biblical injunction to pass on to faithful men that which I have learned, that they in turn would pass it on (2 Tim 2:2), and to allow that participation across the whole ministry. I do not imagine that I will always be the preacher, teacher or whatever, or that the team around me will always be doing what they are doing. They must be passers-on and developers of others. To seek to have structures that teach the church and then the community at large to bring forth facets of ministry, so that care takes place for the whole church.
5. To seek to be expansionist in every area of church activity. Remember that evil is expansionist and therefore the kingdom needs to be as well.
6. To continually find other people's ministries and develop them. I do not mean that you must adopt my philosophy of ministry, but you do need one. Many do not have one.
  They are going through the motions of a tradition, or they have a job, or they have never taken the trouble to define what they are about. Think it through, define it and go for it! If you are not planning to hit something, then most likely you won't! This may put some off because of the 'hard work' factor.

Reaction

We had quite a substantial work in North London and God blessed us in many ways. We spent   considerable time showing people around the numerous facilities. Most of the people we showed around were church leaders of various ilk. The reaction concerning what God had done usually came in three forms:

(a)   Those who regarded me, or the team, or both, as something unique, specially used of God. As if we were a "one-off." This is not a compliment. We are very ordinary people. Usually visitors said, 'If I had your . . . and named some aspect of our church's talents, ministry or plant, as if it had fallen down from heaven. It did not. It took battles, disappointments, despondency, misunderstandings, stickability, faith in God and sheer hard work.

(b)   The second group, who perhaps were a little more honest, looked around and said, "Oh! It's great! But it looks like hard work to me. I would not want to cope with so much." Sadly, this group seemed to be the largest.

(c)   The third group, and by far the smallest, looked and said, "I can see what God has done for you. He can do similar things in my church town/area. I am going to become the catalyst for change in my sphere of influence."

7. I believe in models. I believe in setting trends, in challenging what is. It is only as some do, in God, what has not been done before that others will follow. I don't think it is wrong to want some of the good things God has done for others. They are my chance to know him more, to enter into a deeper relationship and to experience His working. I noticed that Jesus called busy people in the New Testament to follow him. He did not call those who were sitting around doing nothing. I think work can be great fun, especially when it is Kingdom work.

8. I do believe leadership must set goals so that visions do not become a one-man show, or just personal vision. Their vision must be something the whole church can see and go for. I often go into other churches and I am told what the vision of the church is. Sadly many times there isn't one.

Worse still, people often say to me, "Tell our pastor what is going on in your fellowship so some of it can go on here." It is not as simple as that. Many pastors don't want to hear or know! It is possible to have a people-led revolution, but it is usually bloody, hurtful and often does not succeed. Much better if leadership has vision, translates it into goals and persuades others to own those goals.

Some years ago I came back from a Pastor's School with what I believe was a vision from God, or "Word from the Lord." A goal. It was a vision to become a church that is an effective visible voice for him in our area of North East London, with at least 3,000 people coming together for celebrations. We have not arrived there yet, but if you had asked people in our fellowship, one year later, "What is the goal of the church?" 10% would have said, "A congregation of 3,000." If you ask that question now, 90% would give you the same answer.

9. You have to start somewhere and the best thing to start with is what you have got. Too many people claim they are going to do "so and so" when God sends the person with "such and such" a gift or talent to the church. They will do it when finances are right, or, worse still, when the church is right.

God gives the increase
We need to learn from the two little ones who were late for school. One said, "Let's stop and pray that the bus will be late." The other one said, "No, let's run and pray." It seems to me that God wants to do a great deal with the little that we have. We need to see and be willing to use the little we have if we want God to move for us. God's miracles always seem to have a human element in the Bible. Here are three examples to demonstrate what I mean.

(a) 'What have you got?' asked the starving Elijah of the starving widow. 'Nothing,' was the first reply. The second reply was, 'Except some oil and meal.' 'Bake it and give it to God,' was the answer. God gives the increase (see 1 Kings 17:7-16).
(b) 'What have you got?' the man of God asked of the widow who says her children will be sold into slavery. 'Nothing,' was the first reply. The second reply was, 'Except a little oil.'

'Go and collect vessels and use your oil,' said Elisha. God gives the increase (see 2 Kings 4:1-7).

(c) 'Feed the people,' Jesus commanded the disciples. 'How?' they asked. 'What have you got?' asked Jesus. 'Nothing,' was the first reply. 'Five loaves and two fishes,' was the second reply. God gives the increase (see Matthew 14:1S—21).

I ask many leaders, 'What have you got?' The reply is often that they have nothing. Because my eyes are adjusted to seeing, I go to their churches and see talents of music, witnessing, service and caring, and I long to have them say to God, "I have these and I give them to you. I will use them. I will start." Then they will see God give the increase.

Having started - continue. So often we want to give up because it is hard. It is not what we expected. We were misunderstood. It is a pressure. "Those we trusted have left." But the end is not just yet. The story is not finished. The climb is not over. Stay with it. Don't cancel. Don't close. Don't sell. Invest instead. Don't call it a day. Don't give up. Stay in there, and God will give you the increase. Sow liberally and reap the harvest. There are lots of great starters, a few good continuers, even fewer finishers. Be one of the few finishers. Finish what God has called you to do.

10. When you start to go forward, you will need an essential ingredient -real friends. Friends who will support you. Friends who will understand you when you are hard to understand. Friends who are real enough to tell you when you are wrong. Friends who will be with you when nothing particular is happening. Friends who will stand with you when it seems the sky has caved in. It will take time to earn such friends. They will need cultivating. Enjoy meals together. Work together. Play together. They will help you and you will help them become all that you both need to be in the body of Christ.

11. The eleventh thing we need on our way forward is a lack of neatness. Yes, I did say 'lack'. People who have everything sewn up have usually stopped church. Those who have everything in neat tidy committees are not going anywhere. People who want every 'i' dotted and every 't' crossed before they start out will probably never leave home.

Our Western minds like the tidy approach, with everything in its place. We think structures, and of course we need structures to make us function, but they don't always have to be as tidy as we think!

One pastor visiting my church one day said, 'It is so untidy, more like a circus.'

'I like circuses,' was my reply.

'What is your leadership structure?' some say to me. I know what it is at the moment, but it is also like a kaleidoscope, continually changing.. We change things around to meet the changing needs and doors of opportunity. I am very suspicious of neat answers and/or neat churches. Long live the ragged edge! Long live anomalies! Long live exceptions!

12. It is dangerous to become too introspective. When I was a little boy my mother allowed me to plant some seeds in the garden. Every day I went along and dug them up to see how they were doing. They didn't do very well! We must not do that with ourselves, nor with that part of the work that God has entrusted to us. However, we do need to look back.

We need to look back to what we were before God saved us. We need to look back at what has been done. We need to remember the rough diamond that we were and observe some of the polish now beginning to show – no matter how little. We need to remind ourselves that a life once wasted is now bringing forth fruit. We can go forward. We can conquer.
 We can be more than conquerors - never mind the toil, never mind the hard work, God is worth it! When you do look back and see those things, it will make you want to rejoice. I believe that God wants us to rejoice in him. Be glad in the Lord, even if there is nothing else to be glad in. But there is, for we can be glad in what we have accomplished.

(Written by Adrian Hawkes. Taken from the book: Breaking the Mould. Published by Kingsway. 1993 ISBN 0-86065-699-3 Editor Gerald Coates.)

NB Life is a journey. Life in knowing God and learning His ways is also a journey of developing relationships. Some of what I wrote in 1993 are still principals that I would find useful and would want to encourage. In terms of the way I would now use the word, 'church' and other areas like, "Kingdom" and what that means then I would have to say that my relationship with God has developed me and changed my thinking. If you want to know how and more, you would need to ask me. My email is adrianhawkes@phoenixcommunity.co.uk

Negative - Lukewarm – Self Obsessed

I don't like to be negative but is it my imagination that in the UK there are lots of people who are living in a small bubble?

Isn't it great to be with passionate people? People who have vision, enthusiasm, Mission, concern for the big things? Such people are attractive to be around, they draw like magnets they are not boring they are challenging, inspiring, and usually "full of life," and often fulfilled people. None of that is negative is it!

Yet around me I see lots of the alternative. Conversation, both in person and on FB is of the small talk kind. Latest dress, shoes, entertainment; usually fairly inconsequential, never going to change the world, much less the small, space where they dwell. Often the pressure of life is the things that affect them personally, the things that they believe will bring them happiness. Joy would not be something understood here. Sadly the things they want are usually the, "me," kind. I guess that is the spirit of the age. "I am number one!"

The trouble is that this is not true. You are not number one. Those things you aspire for are really not important. The trouble also is that if you get them and hold them, usually they, like soap bubbles, will quickly leave you with just a wet palm. You will be left asking, "What is the point of it all? Why? Where? How? What is it for?" So sad!

It is quite interesting how much God does not like lukewarmness. Listen to this from the book of Revelation 3:16:

[101]

"So, because you are lukewarm and neither cold nor hot, I will spew you out of My mouth!" In other words God does not want that "mediocrity stuff." God likes passion!

The reality is that God comes to give 'real life.' That is not a boring, self-obsessed, lukewarm, negative life, but real life. John 10:10 says "I have come that you may have life and life to the full."

What those who live just for the "me," or are content with the lukewarm and the selfish life do not understand is that to really live, have life, we need to be followers. Not only that, but when we follow the Son, we find that love, meaning, reason to live, purpose in life, lack of boredom, lack of the question "what is the point?" is replaced by care and concern for others. We discover that love is expansive (as of course is Evil). In fact we tap in to love to receive the very reason we are here, the love of God, flamed out and expanded to you and me.

It's very strange that parents often say, "I can love my child. But how would I love another one if I had one? That's the funny thing: Love expands. Where there is need of it, there is more of it, especially for the followers.

Being loved is satisfying, purposeful, meaningful and joyful. I want life. I guess I want others to have it too. And when I observe those around me who opt for the "me" life, I am angry at the robbery I know they are about to experience and be victims of. My observations are that they do experience it. It is such a cul-de-sac. The only way out is to turn around from dead ends - they are just that: Dead ends! Turn around and follow the Son. He will allow you to participate in the Father's purposes, and even empower you to see it happen. Why stay in such a self-obsessed, rut.

Pick 'n' Mix followers of Jesus

I am slightly puzzled by various people I meet up with of late, and some I hear speaking publically, who seem to want to stress to me that they are, "people of faith," that they, "love God", that they are "Christians," or that they are "followers of Jesus." I suppose some of those statements could be understandable, but "follower of Jesus," seems a bit harder for me to swallow.

Is it the Jesus who says, "Do whatever you like. I don't mind?" I don't know that one. Is it the Jesus who says "Whatever values you think fit you, that's ok, as long as you say you are following me, that's fine?" I don't know Him either. Is it the one who says, "We are all going in the same direction and it does not matter what you believe?" I've never met Him.

You see the Jesus I follow says, "I am the way." He says, "Take up your cross and follow me." He says, "If you love me, then keep my commandments." He is the One who says of some, especially those with power, and especially the religious, "Don't expect that if they have hated me that they won't hate you because they will."

We love the "Pick 'n' Mix" that our culture wants to persuade us is the norm. A bit like the old Woolworths sweet model, "I would like to choose this, but exclude that." It seems OK when we are choosing sweets, so why not when we say we are choosing to follow Jesus? 'Oh! I am happy to follow you down that path Jesus. But you want me to follow you down the next one too? Sorry! I don't like that direction so we will connect later." Is that really how it works? I don't think so.

Becoming a follower of Jesus requires repentance first of all, and that word suggests a turnaround of direction. In other words, we go in a new direction, the, "Jesus direction," if you will. And this new direction is very contrary to much of the world we live in. It has a whole new set of values to start with, such as, "Love your enemies" and, "Do good to those who use you badly." There are other things that give us problems too in this following of Jesus, such as, "Deny yourself." Oh dear! I thought my happiness and what I want, my emotions, my feelings, my particular leanings or desires, i.e. I/ME/MINE, was the most important thing in the world.

Actually, following Jesus includes that difficult part of dying to self and living to Him.

Oh dear! This "Pick 'n' Mix" is such a problem. And this, "I am a follower of Jesus," is such a problem too. Let's be honest. I like the idea of following Jesus, but not giving up on my wants, my personal desires, what I think is best for me and my choices.

[103]

That's a bit hard. Maybe I will give it a miss and be a bit more honest in future, and not say I am one of those people. Maybe I will just say, "I like them, but am not, "following." A bit like some of those people right at the start 2,000 years ago - this is what happened then.

On the other hand, those who put their trust in the Master were added right and left, men and women both. Perhaps those admirers where just a bit more honest, what do you think?

Persuaders - Influencers

I was at a wedding recently in Kenya. Two men came up to me. Old friends of mine. They said "Hi," and then asked me if I had realised that I had been coming to Kenya for 11 years. I hadn't realised.
They reminded me of the first time we met, which was on my first visit to Kenya 11 years previous. I remember and laughed, they had turned up to a seminar that I was running, but one that people needed to have pre-booked. They hadn't done so, because they didn't know it was on. We made special arrangements to include them anyway.

The two guys went on to ask, "Do you realise that 11years ago you changed our lives?" I laughed. After all, it did sound a little over the top, I thought. They said to me "You don't understand do you?" I admitted that I didn't quite think I was on the same wave length.

These two friends of mine went on to explain that by coming to what I had been doing 11years previously it had changed their thinking. Because of their changed thinking, they had changed their actions, and because of changed action they had gone back to their village and the village had changed. Because their village had changed, they were able to help the village next to them to change. I felt very humbled, realising that actually what had happened was that I had been able to be a catalyst or conduit introducing many others to these friends who had provided water, business enterprise and opportunities that had ultimately changed the way their village worked all for the better, providing water storage, education, and greater food security, as well as a different way of thinking.

Most of us, like me, underestimate the power of influence. Yet actually that is often the most valuable thing that we can contribute to this world.

At least we could be a *good* influencer, persuader and world changer, or we could be a *bad* one.

The thing about good persuading, is not just the words but the, "Who you are." Do your words match your actions? Are you acting with integrity? Does the way you speak influence, persuade and match the medium that you use to do it.

It was Marshall McLuhan in the 60's who coined the phrase '**The medium is the message,**' …

> …*"meaning that the form of a medium imbeds itself in the message, creating a symbiotic relationship by which the medium influences how the message is perceived, creating subtle change over time. The phrase was introduced in his most widely known book, Understanding Media: The Extensions of Man, published in 1964. McLuhan proposes that media themselves, not the content they carry, should be the focus of study. He said that a medium affects the society in which it plays a role not only by the content delivered over the medium, but by the characteristics of the medium itself. (Winipeg the free online Encyclopedia)*

So what does that mean in practise? In real terms, if I say I believe the Bible when it instructs us to love strangers amongst us, but then I were to constantly quote Daily Mail articles that tell people that "Asylum Seekers and refugees are really crooks and scroungers," what is happening is that my actions drown out my words and the message conveyed is the one that the Daily Mail delivered. Certainly not the Bible one.

Again in Kenya. A young man came to me one day, after I had delivered a talk in a church meeting. He asked me, "Are you telling me that you can be a Christian and not have to wear a suit?" I looked surprised. This had nothing to do with what I had been talking about. Being my usual casual self, I had turned up in blue jeans and a tee shirt to do this particular talk and had not really considered my bad dress sense. I thought the question was some sort of joke, but then looking around I realised that all the men where in suits. I am sure no one had told him to wear a suit to be a Christian.

However, the culture of the medium of church there in Kenya made sure that one conformed to this particular social requirement, unless, of course, you are as insensitive as I had been.

I have often had discussions with people concerning style. Style, or the way of being or doing things, can often be interpreted as our medium. So the way of "doing" church utilising our preferred style, becomes the medium by which things are expressed. So, for example, when we invest large amounts of money into an ornate building which we say is for the worship of God, what we are really saying is that the building is more important than people. It does not matter how much we say that of course, people are always more important. However, the medium tells the story and makes a point.

Likewise the style/medium of our meeting will often give messages and tell stories that sometimes – and maybe often - is different to our words. We could, for example, talk about relationships being very important when the medium/style of our coming together conveys totally the opposite message. Especially if we have everyone sitting in rows looking at the back of the neck of the person in front. Very unrelational! So persuading and influencing is very important, and we are all doing it all the time. Sometimes the medium we use will be saying the opposite to what we say we believe. We are all aware of the way things are said to us as well as what is said. The medium is the message!

The Good News of Jesus is to be conveyed in the best possible way. The medium is the message. God does it by incarnation, or, using Bible words from John 1:1 and then verse 14 in the New Testament, "Verse 1. In the beginning was the Word, and the Word was with God, and the Word was God. And then verse 14 The Word became flesh and made his dwelling among us. We have seen his glory, the glory of the One and only, who came from the Father, full of grace and truth." This is from the NIV version.

What is actually happening here is that God is using words, the words of Jesus, but he is incarnate in those words. So the words become not only words, but the medium/style, the very message themselves.

That is why Jesus Himself is the Word - not just saying the word. And, of course, that principle is still very much the way the Good news of Jesus should be told, i.e. by incarnation, medium, style, words and message are all in agreement and not contradictory. That way we can effectively change what needs changing and make a difference for good.

We can do it. We can be incarnated. We can become both message and medium and with a none contradictory style. That means that we will do things with integrity.

In a recent article, I noted that I am often invited to speak on a subject that I don't like speaking much about, as I think it is somewhat of a non-starter. However, I end up talking about it anyway. Evolution that is with people like Richard Dawkins on the Teachers Channel, More 4 News and the like. Then again, I took a phone call the other week from a very nice young lady who said she wanted to interview me. I said "Oh yes! What about? Let me guess. It's for TV and it's on the subject of Evolution." She replied, "It is sort of on that subject. But it is more than just that subject that we have reason to want to interview you." I asked the obvious, "What channel is it?" "Oh! It is not a channel," she replied. "This is a special market research."

(To be specific, the research was part of a programme commissioned by **Theos,** The 'Public Theology' think tank and funded by the Templeton Foundation. **ESRO** has been commissioned as independent researchers to carry out the work. As with all research that ESRO conducts, they adhere strictly to the ethical guidelines laid down by the Association of Social Anthropologists (ASA): http://www.theasa.org/ethics.htm. (Dr. Robin Pharoah & Tamara Hale)). "Market research on evolution?" I responded incredulously. "Yes! Sort of." she replied. "So why me?" I asked." "Because," she said "Our Company concentrates on the sort of research that eventually produces reports for public use.

These reports could be used by anyone. This one is funded by a public "Theology think tank," and we specialise in finding people that we know are thought – leaders, or opinion leaders." What? My response was, "It is nice to be thought of as "an opinion leader," or a "thought leader," particularly as I know that thinking is the beginning of all action, and if we want to change action then we need to change our thinking. So; do I want to do that? You bet I do!"

[107]

What do I want to change? What do I want to influence? I would like to change how we look at Refugees for a start. Also: How Social Services works. How people treat asylum seekers in the UK. I would like to change those young people who think that they cannot effect change in the world in which they live.

Influence is a very powerful thing. Often time's, people on committees and boards and things say to me, "I am not sure what I do hear. I am not active *per se*. I just attend." The thing is; How much do you persuade? Are your plans good? At what level is your integrity? Do you make things possible for others? Are you a door opener? In other words: How much are you affecting change by just being there? You bring change by just creating new thoughts, new ways of doing and being, by being a pioneer, being a thought leader and opinion maker instead of just a follower. Supply good thinking right thinking.

Out of the box thinking.

You could even be an incarnation style message with the right medium that really makes a difference. Why not?

Upstream Issues

I heard someone telling a story recently about how they were working in fish conservation and checking on clean water in rivers and streams in the UK. Apparently they found an area of a stream where the fish were struggling for oxygen and dying. How was it resolved? Workers take out any dead fish and it is apparently then possible to push oxygen into the water. Often the water agencies do this by, as the Environment Agency tell us, pouring Hydrogen Peroxide into the water upstream. This practice releases extra oxygen into the water. Such action appears to somewhat reduced the potential fish kill.

Obviously one can keep doing this sort of thing, but of course, what is really happening is that one is dealing with an event, like an illness, or a tragedy that sometime keeps occurring, where one can put it temporarily right. However it appears again at a later date.

Often in the case of the fish dying, checking up stream one may discover that there is a factory that periodically discharges its waste into the stream. This waste is toxic and depletes the oxygen in the water, thus killing the fish. Conclusion: It is better to deal with the cause of the upstream issue, rather than create the results downstream of fish dying.

It seems to me that this is often the case in our society at large. We deal with the results - and never think about the cause. I know it's not the whole answer, but in this country we constantly hear how we are short of houses. When one asks people what is the upstream issue, they will tell you it's immigration. I am sure that is true to some extent. However, is there another factory upstream creating the need? What, I would like to ask, happens when people get divorced? Oh yes! There is often the trauma for the couple - definitely for any children involved. But then, what about housing? Do they still live in the same house? Or are now, two houses needed?

I think there are lots of upstream issues in our world where we need to look upstream to really help, rather than just sticking a plaster on the hurt at the point where the upstream issue has impacted.

Let's think about some of the things we are reacting too.

What about the current government tax receipts shortages? Are the upstream factories putting poison into the system? At the moment we have more children coming into the care system than ever before. 2014 hit the highest need for Foster Carers for children than ever before. We are doing our best with help and plasters. However, is there an upstream issue we should be looking at? In 2013, there were 68,110 children in the care system costing the taxpayer £2.5 Billion. The predicted increase in 2014 was said to be around 7%. Will it go up again in 2015, 16 and 17? Are we dealing only with symptoms? Or is someone looking upstream? If so, what is the cause?

Number of children looked after at 31st march each year up to 2014:

- 2010   64,470
- 2011   65,500
- 2012   67,070
- 2013   68,060
- 2014   68,840
- 2016   69,540

What is it now?

I have picked up here on just a couple of areas of our society and I am asking the question. It is great and very necessary to care, and to deal with society's symptoms of sickness, just like we would care in any situation such as a road accident for example. But, would it not be better to put things in place to stop the accident from happening if we could. Surely we should try and examine the upstream issues – don't you think?

I is for "In the Beginning"

In the Beginning there was nothing – which exploded.

My Blog: "Where does my tax pound go?" generated a lot of comments. Thank you to those who joined in the big bang conversation. I note also that some of the 'followers of the way' are getting a little excited by my response about the need to have the right and freedom to talk in school about creation, and actually to teach creation.

I am not, at this stage, concerned with the thought of evolution or not, but want to make you aware that there are many people who want to silence those who are followers of the way, that is, those who believe that Jesus Christ rose from the dead and who believe that there is a "God who is there," who is the source of all things, who created the universe and the earth, as well as time and space outside of himself.

Those who oppose the teaching of creation are not just advocating "You must teach evolution." What they are advocating is that, "You must not say that there is a God who created the world, however he did it. God must be kept in the private place of religion so called, or special dedicated buildings, or maybe we will let you talk about that "myth" in the confines of religious instruction, though we rather you did not!"

I listened to humanists discussing the subject on TV last Sunday morning. They were vehemently opposed to bishops in the House of Lords. I might even agree with them there. However, when pushed, they slipped back into their usual rhetoric of, "Why should we allow schools to talk about God or faith? These myths belong outside of those areas and should be stopped, as well as bishops in the House of Lords." It is not evolution that they want taught. It is God and the fact of the Lordship of Christ and the resurrection that they do not want taught, or talked about in the public arena. This agenda of humanists has always been so. There has always been the pressure to keep one's beliefs private. But that is not the way of it for the person of the Way. We are commanded, as followers of the way, to share the good news that God is a personal God. He is there, He is not far away and a way of reconciliation has been made to Him via Christ.

And that all goes back to the beginning, that likeness that we have to the God who is there, that ultimate responsibility/answerability we have to Him and that we actually, as humankind, rebelled against Him. That is a "public place announcement"- and must remain so!

Let's go back to the beginning. Which beginning? The humanist theory of beginnings is that there was nothing, then there was a big bang, and after billions of years we have you and me, and a few billion others. However because the bang, "just happened," we need to understand that there is no meaning to it, as many of the people I am talking about, when pushed, will, of course, be honest enough to tell you. There is no meaning in love, justice, or morality. When one is dead, one is dead. There is nothing else to it. No purpose in life. It's all just a really bad joke.

Of course you can enjoy life while it's there, but don't think that any of it means anything. Love is just the firing of neurons in the brain. It's a chemical reaction with, perhaps, a physical outcome. It is about pointless survival. There is nothing there and no reason for it. Everything is simply a great big accident of nature, whatever nature is. God is dead. In fact, God never existed. Man is also dead. If we think about it for a moment, we will move into total despair at such a pointless, meaningless existence.

Rather I would want our students and everyone else to know, the fact that we do have meaning because we were created in the image of a personal and loving God. That gives us meaning, and intrinsic worth. That actually is true truth. That is why we need to respect each other. That is why we can have meaningful love, both towards other humans and to God. That is why love can be reciprocal. That is why life, the universe, me, and you have real meaning and value.

My old friend George Canty used to say to me, "Why do people think that they can have faith in faith? That is so irrational? If you are in despair, without faith you might have faith in faith, or drugs or alcohol or sex without love, or take a leap into any nonsense." "Rather," George would say, "Put your faith in God.
That is something rational, true, checkable, reasonable, and verifiable."
Being a follower of the way is not illogical or irrational. It is truthful, sensible and rational.

[112]

There are those who would say science has replaced the need for God. Interestingly, Julius Robert Oppenheimer, a scientist, theoretical physicist and professor of physics, who was not a Christian, actually acknowledged Christianity was needed. He believed it Christianity was required in order for modern science to exist. He believed this for the simple reason that Christians, he said, created a climate of thought which puts people in a position to investigate the form of the universe in which they exist.

Many early scientists had the view that a reasonable God had made a reasonable universe, and having created reasonable man we could scientifically examine this reasonable universe and discover how it works. The problem for the modern humanistic mind is that all the time they try to examine the irrationality of the universe and the accident that we are her, they are discovering that they are examining a rational world.

Going back to that TV programme the other Sunday morning, I noted what they said about bishops in the House of Lords. The humanists said, "We don't want them there." And, as I said earlier, maybe I agree. Then they said, "We don't mind people being Christians. But they must not impose their ideas on others, particularly children in schools," even though they feel it is perfectly OK for them to impose their ideas wherever they like. I know their answer to that criticism, as I have discussed it with them many times. They say, "Ah! But what we are teaching is true!" As if they had the monopoly on truth!

Well I don't want what I have discovered to be pushed into some private corner, limited to a religious education class, or a special building. And what I have also discovered is truth. It's all about a Person.

Adrian on Darwin

Running a Christian School within the Independent Sector often means that we are contacted by TV to do this or that.

The often asked question is about Evolution and Creationism, as if somehow we did nothing else. Even people like **Richard Dawkins** has spent time grilling us on our views for his documentary **The Root of all Evil**. Funnily enough, we don't usually think much about Darwin or Evolution, between those TV times.

From what I know of Darwin he was a good family man, doing interesting research. However, what is very important to me is what people really think. I think that Darwin himself was still in the realm of theory as to how and why. Today, we tend to be more dogmatic and sure as per Richard Dawkins, when maybe we ought not to be so proud of our certainties.

Our thinking is that, if the Bible is correct, (and I believe it to be so) then our thoughts are the things that mould us and makes us (*"as we think in our hearts so we are"* - *Proverbs 23: 7),* for our thinking is that which generates the way we act. So, if we think that the universe is some mechanical process, then we tend to treat people like a machine. If we think that we are just an animal then, we tend to treat each other like animals.

It seems to me that Hitler believed that Darwin's view of how life worked was correct and much more than theory. From this belief he decided, *(thought)* "Then let me speed up the process and create an evolutionary jump and make the master race."We know the results of Hitler's thinking processes.

If, on the other hand, we believe *(think)* that there is a mind behind our universe, and that we are created in the image of God, then surely that thinking should encourage us to treat one another with dignity and respect! Richard Dawkin's argument with me on TV, was that he was more honourable than me as he did not need a God to stop him from pillaging and raping. His implication being that I did! My problem with that argument is that one person cannot negate what is going on in the world with great swathes of destruction and man's inhumanity to man. Our thinking that we can play God, and our devaluation of each other, is a daily fact whatever Richard thinks

So what do I think of Darwin? Interesting theories. But believing them to be so totally correct without criticism leads to dangerous thought.

[114]

MORE 4 NEWS
Richard Dawkins on Teachers Channel
All on the Same Subject – Adrian Hawkes Comments

While recently doing a two minute spot for channel "More 4 News," I thought to myself, "Actually, this piece is only two minutes long. *Half an hour of interview edited down to two minutes?*" In fact, I thought, the subject was – and is - quite important, important to our freedom of speech and freedom of thought! Let me explain.

As I am part of a Christian community that runs 4 Independent Sector Schools I often get asked to do programmes like this, and it is always about the same subject; Evolution. It's as though, as a Christian, and one that believes in the schools that I am involved with, the only thing we ever talk about is Evolution. Not Maths, English, Computer Science, Social Studies or Citizenship, to name but a few, but rather Evolution. Actually, this latest programme was because we were at the 150th year anniversary of Charles Darwin's lecture that started all the talk. But it does seem to go on and on, disproportionately to the priorities of the substance of schooling.

An interesting thing about this programme for More 4 News, was the gentleman who came on and said, *"What we need to understand is that Evolution and its teachings are not an attack on Faith."* The thing is, that each time I go on one of these programmes I usually get emails, post and even the occasional phone call. The Evolutionists write and tell me what an idiot I am. The Christians write and nicely tell me I was not strong enough in my presentation and then guide me with literature to better my opinion. I think that in the middle of it there must be a public that is bemused.

Why am I saying that I think this subject is important? Talking with Richard Dawkins for his programme and listening and reading some his work, I conclude that actually it is not just about Evolution, the big issue is with him is that, "There is no God," and any thought that there is, is dangerous to society. Furthermore the attitude seems to be one of, "If I can stop people like you Mr Hawkes, from doing or saying anything to suggest that there is a God, I am going to stop you."

[115]

Listening recently to a Radio 4 programme from the Cheltenham Science Festival in Gloucestershire, Professor Peter Atkins stated that as a, 'believer,' in evolution, he had the truth. The program host asked what he thought about people whose view is that there is a designer/creator God? He simply replied that they had some sort of mental problem and could not possibly be scientific much less a proper scientist.

What we really have is a kind of Religion from these proponents. It is a religion without God. It is a religion that propounds with evangelical fever, *"There is no God!"* I said that on Mr Dawkins' programme, which I think somewhat annoyed him, but that comment, of course, lies on the cutting room floor.

After one of these TV occasions, I am not sure which one, maybe it was from my time on the teacher's channel on which I was quizzed on the same subject. I had an email from one of these people that write to me after such occasions. He basically accused me of being a child abuser for believing that there is a God and teaching children such.

And this is what is so worrying about this particular lobby. For although the nice man on More 4 news said, *"This is not an attack on Faith,"* nevertheless, the people who I found, the vocal lobby for Evolution, are the same people who are aligned to the, *"there is no God"* lobby. So does it matter, in the name of free speech, that they express that opinion? Perhaps not, providing they allow me the same courtesy of speech and thought, but not if they want to go down some Orwellian state line that prevents me from speaking, or even thinking for that matter.

I am not surprised that the TV channels talk to me. I at least will talk. It seems that the Muslim schools were not willing to express their views on TV. Neither were most of the Christian Schools.

I have to add that when I have agreed to go on these programmes, many of my friends phone me and say, *"Do you think this is wise? They will make you look very stupid!"* Maybe I do. However, even if I do, it still worries me when I hear statements like those coming from Professor Peter Atkins, who I think would silence any opposition to his point of view if he could.

[116]

Then there is Richard Dawkins, who believes that Religion is the root of all evil and should be outlawed. And don't forget my emailing corrector, who said, and I quote: "*I honestly believe that what you are doing is mental child abuse, and we are working very hard on trying to once and for all outlaw your type of brain-washing propaganda. There is no god. Move on.*"

He pointed out to me that he was a BA (hons) MA,

What I notice from all of these people is there is an almost Taliban fervor to marginalise my opinion, keep me silent and make sure I am outlawed!

God help us if they are allowed any kind of legislative power!

25 YEARS IN SWITZERLAND

The weekend of the 9th May 2008 saw Partying, celebrating, thanksgiving and just great fun as the Tamil churches we have founded during that time, in Switzerland, celebrated their 25 years existence.

From very small beginning 20 years previously, refugees began to enter Switzerland away from the continuing war in Sri Lanka. By this time there was already a Tamil church operating in France, so they needed to celebrate too.

Pauline and I reminisce about those small beginnings. Refugees with nothing. Often living in cramped rooms, shared with more people than should have been allowed to live in such a small space. That said, we remember some of the prophetic words about blessing, both material and spiritual, that would be coming their way. Now we can see that God is faithful and His word is true. Prophecy is more than words. They are happenings - though probably not yet finished in their fulfillment. These Tamil people now have homes that are spacious, good cars and jobs that pay well.

Nada, one of the leaders now, remembers that sometime there were only two or three at the meetings they held. Now we are not sure how many people are part of NLM Churches in Switzerland. Perhaps 1,000, with around 10 meeting groups/congregations.

I thanked the gathered crowd for their generosity in their financial support back in Sri Lanka, which has enabled the work to grow there with Schools, Clinics, Vocational training centres, churches, orphanages and the like.

The huge gathering of Tamil people honoured people like Jenny Sinnadurai and Karen Dey, for their continued faithfulness, Pauline and I, for being there from the beginning - and still being there. They also expressed thanks for the Pioneer Network, for facilitating people to teach, lead and input folks folks such as Stuart Lindsell. They honoured the leaders in Switzerland for their humble approach to leadership and also for their faithfulness. People like Nada and Kala, Albert and Joy, Ravi and Sugandi, not forgetting also leaders in Bergdorf, Lausanne and all those who are still there doing a great job.

The Saturday finished with a great explosion of joy and celebration with everyone leaving the building with bunches of gas balloons allowing all who would see them, that Jesus is good, all the time.

The London Training Consortium (College) Story

In 2005, Phoenix Community Care formed a new company called "London Training Consortium." The reason for forming the company was actually precipitated by misinformation from an accountant. We were told that we needed to take this action in order to register for VAT purposes. In the end, that intelligence turned out to be incorrect. However, by the time we had discovered the truth, the company was already up and running.

PCC was already addressing some of the needs of the young people. For example, looking after unaccompanied minors, foster children, vulnerable adults and young people who had been through the care system and were moving on to independence.

We quickly understood that many of those we were seeking to help needed to be able to speak English to progress in the UK. For that reason English Speaking for Other Languages (ESOL) classes were born. During the seven years since the inception of the London Training Consortium (LTC) we have seen many young people helped by the tuition given. We have run the classes and somehow found the money to pay the staff. Although, most of the time I have no idea how (God alone knows). At other times we were fortunate enough to receive grants from the European Social Fund via the London Development agencies. Each year we wonder how we will find money to train the next batch of students.

In spite of the challenge of ongoing funding, the college has expanded its services and now helps those young people, who the government euphemistically refer to as NEET (Not in Education Employment or Training). We have helped many to access further education, enter into employment, and often most importantly, change their attitude to life, success and progress.
I remember the whole office applauding one young man on achieving his Oxford Cambridge Royal Society of Arts (OCR) certification in

[119]

Literacy and Numeracy; which is equivalent to a General Certificate of Secondary Education (GCSE). He was full of delight by the fruits of his hard work.

LTC is registered as an examining body for various courses leading to qualifications such as OCR, (Oxford Cambridge Royal Society of Arts), City and Guilds and ICCE. There is an enduring thrill observing young people, who thought they could never achieve such qualifications, smile confidently as they receive their certificates. We are still talking to the people who offer grants, and help folks to fill in their application forms. Each year, in excess of fifty students undertake the various courses offered by LTC. The courses are tailored to get the best for the individual concerned. I am fascinated by statistics and thought perhaps my readers would like to see some.

First of all, here are the various nationalities that have gone through our college. It reads a bit like United Nations doesn't it? The interesting thing is; you can often tell where the wars in the world are, by looking at these statistics in numerical order:

Afghanistan 84, Britain 71, Eritrea 25, Albania 22, China 21, Congo 12, Kurdistan 11, Somalia 10, Kurdistani Iran 8, Kurdistani Iraq 8, Turkey 7, Bangladesh and Iran 6, Iraq 5, Sudan 4, Kosovo, Poland, Afro-Caribbean, Uganda and Guinea 3, Ivory Coast, Romania and Sierra Leone 2, Algeria, Ethiopia, Gambia, Korea, Burundi, Switzerland, Vietnam, Kuwait and Pakistan 1.

Finally we seem to be more than just a training college helping many of the students to fill in forms, find housing, offering help and support with the many challenges that life brings. Many of the students are without family or relatives to help them with these issues. As one staff member commented recently, "I often feel less like their tutor and more like their Mother." She went on to say, "what most of these young people are looking for and what they really need to progress, is someone to sit and listen to them." And that is exactly what we do. It's called, "Going the extra mile." The reward for us is their success. One of the most special elements of being involved in LTC is that some young people who commenced as students end up as long term friends.

J is for Justice

Justice

Cuts Care and Development (Children in the Looked After System)

In what direction is the care area in the UK heading? The current government promised that it would not cut front line services, particularly for those most in need. I am sure you will agree that those who are on the "At Risk Register," or those actually in the Looked After system of the UK are very vulnerable and in need. One London borough actually said it was going to cut foster care rates by half. That seems to me to be moving in the opposite direction of what has been previously announced. When I contacted central government on this issue I was told, "Very sorry! This is a local decision, nothing to do with us!"

There is a vast burden of regulations imposed on those who care enough to foster or to adopt. Many of the regulations are very good. However, like all things human, they work at the whim of the human beings applying the regulations. There are excellent Social Workers out there who, I would say, have the ability to apply the CS factor (that is, common sense, a commodity which often seems to be very uncommon). However, in my experience, there seems to be many social workers for whom the "power" of being a social worker has gone to their head. These people treat all others as lesser mortals.

I overheard a conversation recently between a key worker for vulnerable adults and a social worker. The key worker has good university degrees and is a good worker, with experience and expertise. I noted that the key worker was being very polite and patient. When the social worker had finished and left, I asked, "Are you alright?" "Yes, I am, I suppose," was the response. "But why is it that social workers think that I am stupid, when I am not? And why do they think that it is OK to treat me in that way and talk to me like dirt beneath their feet?"

It isn't acceptable, but many social workers seem to display that same attitude. Why is it? Is it the training? Or is it the pressure of the job? Is it, perhaps, that they are emotionally insecure? I don't know why it is, but I wish it would stop.

I do not believe the code of practice is the problem. Below are some extracts:
The General Social Care Council (GSCC) codes of practice states that Social Care workers must:

• Protect the rights and promote the interests of service users and carers.
  • Strive to establish and maintain the trust and confidence of service users and carers.
  • Promote the independence of service users while protecting them as far as possible from danger or harm.
  • Respect the rights of service users whilst seeking to ensure that their behaviour does not harm themselves or other people;
  • Uphold public trust and confidence in Social Care Services; and (i.e. in their dealings with other professionals and working collaboratively)
  • Be accountable for the quality of their work and take responsibility for maintaining and improving their knowledge and skills.

However, talk is cheap, or rather, the words on the page are not worth a jot if they are not observed.

Then there is the element of need. The number of looked after children is around 64,400 on 31st March 2010 according to government statistics. That does not include those on the At Risk Register, which is probably about the same number. This brings us to an approximate total of 128,000 children in need of care. Can we afford to cut our service delivery in such areas? Or should we be improving the delivery and the training of those who are willing to foster or want to adopt. Alongside the compelling argument to avoid funding cuts, perhaps we should also be looking at the reasons why we have so many children in such need. I wonder also if smaller agencies might actually deliver a better service for less cost, particularly if the checking procedures were strengthened that are currently delivered by OFSTED.

Since the '60s, the whole adoption scene has changed dramatically. At that time, single parenting was much less common. Abortion and birth control were only just commencing. There were 27,000 adoptions in 1968. Large numbers of children were released to adopters, many almost straight from birth. That whole scene has now changed. Now the children who require adoption are more likely to come from parents that have been neglectful or abusive, either physically, sexually, or by the use of substances that damage the children as well as themselves. Adoptive parents can often face the choice of waiting for years for a young single child, or months for older sibling groups. The reality being, that as those children get older their experiences of neglect and abuse are likely to be significantly higher due to the length of time they have remained with neglecting parents. The knock-on effect is that adoptive parents are often left to clean up the emotional fallout of their adopted children, plus the support given is minimal and *not* a statutory requirement. Often the training for adopters remains negligible. It has not changed much since the 60's. I would reiterate that the kind of children coming into the adoption system has changed dramatically. Should not this be more of a priority in designing the way we help these vulnerable children and how we guide today's adopters? The number of children available for adoption has, of course, dropped as single parent families have become more culturally acceptable. There are now around 3,500 children each year who go from care to adoption. To make matters worse, those in the know tell me that of current adopters, something like 1 in 4 situations break down. In other words, the child goes back into foster care, or back into a children's home. The high emotional and public cost of this surely needs investigating.

And where are we going with the large and unwieldy Social Services department. Sometimes, just because of the size of Social Services staff and the number of potential foster children, they seem to treat the foster carers and adopters more like a commodity than like people. I wonder if smaller agencies might actually deliver better service for less cost. Particularly if the checking procedures that are currently delivered by OFSTED were strengthened.

These big departments are being hit by cuts. Whatever central government is saying to the contrary, departments have been slimmed down. In some instances this may be the right decision, but in light of the cuts, can they still deal effectively with those 64,000 children in a manner that does not increase the damage, that all agree, should be avoided? The fact remains that those in the looked-after system are less likely to leave school with good qualifications. They are also more likely to end up in the prison system, with all the ensuing expense, or, as Big Issue founder John Bird likes to say, "They could become a great "Big Issue" seller!"

It is also still true that if you are part of the black and ethnic minority, your chances of being in care are greater and your chance of finding an adoptive parent less likely.

26% of children within the English Child Care system were from a black or ethnic minority origin in 2010, as compared to 11% within the general population (Department for Education, 2010; Office of National Statistics, 2010). Frazer and Selwyn (2005) noted that in 2003 only 10% of approved adoptive families were of Black, Asian or mixed parentage. In the same time period, only 13% of all the children adopted were from a black or ethnic minority origin.

It may be that smaller units of foster care, and a better training programme for adopters would be a step in the right direction. I know that a lot of work has been done in this area in the past, and, of course, tragic events like baby P make us all want to see change. However, after the press fever has died down, we go back to doing what we did, and sort of forget. These young people can be a great resource to the nation. We should not short change them. The current round of cuts should force us to take a fresh look at how we can improve their life situations. (25,000 children leave care each year)

Further reference:

Frazer, L. and Selwyn, J. (2005) "Why are We Waiting? The Demography of Adoption for Children of Black, Asian and Black Mixed Parentage in England," Child and Family Social Work, Vol 10, pp135 – 147.

Great Britain. Department of Health (2010) DfE:

Children Looked After by Local Authorities in England (including adoption and care leavers) - year ending 31 March 2010 [Online]. Available at:
ttp://www.education.gov.uk/rsgateway/DB/SFR/s000960/index.shtml (Accessed: 23rd April 2011).

Office of National Statistics (2010) Adoptions. Available at:
http://www.statistics.gov.uk/CCI/nugget.asp?ID=592 (Accessed: 12th April 2011).
Figures quoted are usually for England and Wales, Scotland and Northern Ireland have separate statistics.

K is for Kicking

Kicking against …The Thought Police

Today I want to rant. I want to rant about those people who want to stop me thinking, or restrict my freedom of speech. I want to rant about those who want me to think just like they do. I want opinion, I had better keep my values and beliefs to myself.

Netlog lit the fuse to my rant. I have a blog on Netlog. They have removed two of my blogs. Their reason? They do not allow people to talk about religion on the blog. As it happens, I hate religion also and I don't want to talk about it. What I do want to talk about is values, beliefs and relationships. Two of the Blogs they took down were about relationships. So much other junk is allowed - but I am not allowed to complain about that, am I?

I am greatly disturbed that in many countries people are prevented from speaking about their beliefs and values. And when they do speak out in disagreement, they must be killed, as happened recently in Pakistan where government ministers who spoke out in opposition were executed.

Do those who want to kill people for their beliefs have such weak beliefs themselves? I don't get it. I have friends in various countries who have been imprisoned for no other reason other than their beliefs. One friend used my home as a safe house after fleeing his own country. He and his family narrowly escaped death. They were shot at because of their beliefs.
Are people so insecure about their belief systems that the only way to hold on to them is to block out any other viewpoint, to imprison or kill those who differ? I make no apology for my rant.
This "Thought Police" attitude is pandemic and going global.

Why do gods need defending? I get upset if you insult the God I worship, love, and serve. Of course I do! However, it would never cross my mind to kill you if you disagree with me, or lock you up because you have a different point of view. Do I even think that I have to defend God? That would be ridiculous! Any god that needs defending by a mere human is no god at all.

[126]

Yet this is the attitude that is rife in some religion - and I include the religion of atheism. I have emails from very learned atheists (who take the trouble to put their university qualifications at the bottom) in which they tell me that if they had the power they would silence me from spreading my views about a God who doesn't exist, and in their opinion had no part in my existence or any creative involvement with the world. They know these things, of course, because they have explored every corner of the cosmos. There is no God.

Even pressure from the UK government makes me want to rant. They are currently stating to schools, "There is no God, and if there is a God, he certainly had no involvement with any kind of creation." This is implied by their stance.

Are we are sure God does not exist? Are we sure that he played no part in creation? The opposing arguments are so strong that anyone with these beliefs are ridiculed and gradually, will be silenced. The default position is rapidly becoming, "We will not allow you to speak such things! Our arguments are so good and so strong and so right that you must not be allowed to have a voice!"

... RIOTS

Now that the riots have calmed, and the papers and newscasters have left the subject behind, I have some questions about it all.

I have listened to the Prime Minister and various Politicians talking about the fact that this was just "gang culture." It is "robbery," and that is it. I did hear a couple of people asking what the causes are of what was going on, but not a lot of comments were coming back on that score.
Some have cited cuts and closures, but I would like to ask some other questions, and I think my questions just might touch on causes.

The last government spent a large amount of money on trying to cut down underage and very young age pregnancies. They failed, the figures went up. So:
Question one: How many of our rioters come from very young mothers, who really, are possibly only children themselves?

[127]

We have terrible figures for marriage breakdowns. I note that the Prime Minister said, "Lots of the rioters have come from dysfunctional families." Maybe! And if so…

Question two: What make those families dysfunctional? I noted that the ,

Question Three: If one is taught that one is just a machine, or a collection of genes that all arrived by accident, is there really any need to take responsibility for my actions? Just asking.

Question Four: Jim Wallis in his book *Why the American Right Gets it Wrong and the Left Doesn't Get it* - states that "A budget is a moral document." Is he right?

Question Five: Talking of Morals, where do they come from? Are they truly there? And, if so can we talk about them? Is there a law giver and ultimate judge? Can I make my own mind up as to what is right and wrong? And if I should decide that looting is right, who is to say I am wrong?

One young lady with a tee shirt covering her face was asked by a reporter, "How do you feel about robbery? Do you feel good about what you have just done?" She replied, "I'm only getting some of my taxes back!"

Question Six: Many have said, these rioters have nothing to lose. Maybe they haven't if they are just machines in an accidental universe, which is what they have been "educated" to believe. Are they, then, right?

Just in case you think I live in an ivory tower, I actually live in Wood Green, London. Many of my family live in Tottenham. I am white, but personal friends of mine who are black had to take their small child and run from their flat which was just above the first carpet shop that went up in flames, in Tottenham!

Also I am involved in trying to help NEET young people (Not in Education Employment or Training). It is true that many of them have given up on themselves, do not know where they fit in, or feel they do have not stake in society and therefore feel that they have nothing to contribute. Many of them are not knowing that God loves them, regards them as highly valuable, and has purpose for their lives.

[128]

Question Seven: Politicians and police have talked about the "fact" that this is gang related. I meet some of the gang youngsters who are afraid to go out of their own post code in case they get attacked because they are in the wrong place. Our training centre is in "the wrong place" for some of them and we have had to give them rides to and fro so they can improve their education. But here is my question: Why are they in those gangs? Is it because their family is dysfunctional and family life is not there and so they need to belong? They need a family even if that family is a gang?

Question Eight: Is it my imagination, or am I right in thinking that if you talk about right and wrong, or dare I say Evil and Good, or worse still Sin, then the PC crowd and government is on it like a ton of bricks, telling you, "No its just behavioural; and you should not talk in those terms?"

Question Nine: Dr Donald Howard, an American Educationalist, said "Discipline is not something you do TO someone. It is actually something you do FOR someone." Am I right in thinking that this is now out of fashion - discipline that is - and very un PC?

Question Ten: Do we need to find a purpose in life? Do we need to look for a lawgiver? Is it possible that even though our families are dysfunctional there is a family that wants to include us, and bring us into responsible relationship?

Sitting down inside

Funny to see recently on Face Book the fact that Richard Dawkins is wondering if we need Christianity as it is not blowing people up, or saying that those that do not believe should be killed. Maybe he needs to take an even deeper look.
What really puzzles me Is why people think that a forced acceptance of something, means that I or anyone else has really accepted that premise, belief, thought. What a silly idea.
It also puzzles me that people think that if you are not allowed to speak something different to their point of view, their perspective then that is fine, they must be right, again what nonsense.

[129]

Yet this is our world, people have views that I don't agree with, lifestyles that I think are wrong, attitudes that I think that if followed by lots of people will lead to their destruction and sometime the destruction of lots of others too, however I am not allowed to say opposite to what is the P.C. position, my view must not be heard? Now does that mean that the argument, position, life style of the others is so wrong that they cannot bear to hear anything opposite to what they have chosen right or wrong?

I joined a political party once, just to go along to the meetings and understand how they thought and how it worked. I tried to sit at the back and keep quite. One day they announced that they had made a terrible mistake, they had invited someone to speak to the meeting, and discovered he was a member of another party.

They said *obviously* they could not listen to him. I being very naïve asked a question, this was my question, "Why are you afraid to listen to another point of view or perspective, is our own position, argument, perspective, so weak that we cannot possible listen to someone we might disagree with and disagreeing with him come to understand our position thoughts are after all correct"?

The answer puzzled me, the answer was "but he is not a member of our party"! I tried again, "yes but does that mean we cannot hear what he has to say"? The answer again, "you don't understand, he is not a member of our party and so he will say what we don't agree with so we can't hear that"? I gave up!

So we live in a world where people are being killed because they disagree, don't believe what you believe cannot possible hear even a view that is different from the party line. So this year in Brunei, Somalia, Tajikistan all banned Christmas celebrations as it might damage the thinking of the rest of the population apparently it was because of fear that people would be led astray. I wonder how weak the thinking of those people is.

I remember one of those stories, apparently a little boy was would not sit down at the meal table, he was only small and insisted on standing to eat, I think his opinion was that the food went down better that way.

[130]

His Father got really upset and kept trying to make him sit down remonstrating with him with many words. The little boy refused, in the end the Father got fed up with discussion and arguments, and putting his hand on the little boys head pushed the little boy down until he was sitting.

The little boy looked at his Father and recognised that he definately was stronger than him, but then he said,

"Dad, I know that you have got me sitting down at this table, but I want you to know I am actually standing up inside!

There is a lot of us around that are actually standing up inside!

L is for Leadership

Leadership for all

I've written a book on this subject and it's called 'Leadership and...' I wrote this book for anybody and everybody, so far it's sold very well and it's on its third re-print. The problem is, a number of people have said to me, "I have seen the book, but I didn't buy it because I'm not a leader." I think, perhaps, I should have given it a different title.

The thing is, from God's perspective, he has called us all to be leaders. Yes, that means you, even though you may never have thought about being a leader until I just said it. I watched a programme today on TV, there was a discussion on whether or not it's okay for women to be in leadership. Obviously it was one of those theological type discussions. I was puzzled; I thought that in the body of Christ that there was neither Jew nor Greek, in other words our earthly citizenship type does not matter, our ethnicity has no bearing in the new kingdom. Neither does our gender, as there is neither male nor female, we are all sons. This is what Galatians 2 verse 26 to 29 says:

[26]You are all sons of God through faith in Christ Jesus, [27]for all of you who were baptized into Christ have clothed yourselves with Christ. [28]There is neither Jew nor Greek, slave nor free, male nor female, for you are all one in Christ Jesus. [29]If you belong to Christ, then you are Abraham's seed, and heirs according to the promise.

So we are all sons of God. That might sound funny if you are a female. But don't worry, the men have issues to, we are also called the bride of Christ.

Some of our words just don't quite explain it accurately when we are talking about the kingdom because we are trying to use concepts that perhaps don't apply in the new kingdom of God dimension.

What about the leadership angle that I just mentioned and the fact that perhaps you didn't even know you were a leader?

1 Corinthians 6, 1-3 says:

¹If any of you has a dispute with another, dare he take it before the ungodly for judgment instead of before the saints? ²Do you not know that the saints will judge the world? And if you are to judge the world, are you not competent to judge trivial cases? ³Do you not know that we will judge angels? How much more the things of this life!

What this is saying, in simple terms, is that the saints are called to "rule," "judge," or to use my word, "lead," because that is what leadership is; judging, discerning, ruling. And everyone is called to do that in the world to come, so perhaps we had better get into practice.

God has called us to be many things, prophets, priests and kings in His kingdom. All of these positions are leadership based and that leadership preparation does not start when you die. Here's the thing. We need to learn and understand how to be good leaders. We need to start learning now, and that includes you. All of us are sons and all of us are called.

I have a friend who leads a church community and who often receives requests for his leadership team to visit conferences and the like. I asked her, "How do you decide who you will send?" Her answer was funny, yet appropriate. "I send anyone from the community who is willing to go. The whole church is full of leaders." Her answer says it in a nutshell. We are all leaders - and you are one of them. God the Father makes us sons, prophets, priests and kings no less.

Leadership – Servant style

I was in one of those meetings where the preacher goes on and on. The more he went on the more irritated I got. It was not because he was going on, but because he was getting it so badly wrong. He was preaching from Luke 7:8 where the centurion seeks healing for his sick servant.

The preacher had obviously not read the passage, or at least had not paid attention when he read it, because he kept saying that the Centurion said to Jesus that, "He could see that Jesus had authority like he had authority." How embarrassing, what the centurion actually said was that he was *under* authority and perceived that Jesus was also *under* authority.

Jesus saying he was under authority is a very interesting and enlightening fact. He was telling us that the things he was doing were at the command of the will of his Father and not His own will. In Matthew 20, it's interesting to see that there were those amongst the twelve disciples who wanted to be in the top tier of leadership, and they asked Jesus if they could be at his right hand and left hand, (actually they got their Mum to ask, but anyway, I digress).

Jesus demonstrated a completely different style of leadership, one I am afraid that the church, as a whole, still does not seem to grasp. The style is called "Servant Leadership."

Jesus outlines this style very clearly, both in words and actions, in Marks gospel, chapter 9 verse 35, when he says, "If you want to lead or be the first, you need to be the last, or rather the servant of all." Then he demonstrates this very process as he takes a towel and a bowl and washes the disciple's feet. In the account in John 13:5, Peter is very upset. He does not think that master Jesus should be washing people's feet. Nevertheless, Jesus carries out this act to clearly underline and promote the servant style of leadership.

It's helpful for us to understand who, in the culture of the time when Jesus was here, would be doing the foot washing. I've walked around in Africa quite a bit and I can understand the need to wash feet. Even when I am wearing socks and shoes, my feet still need washing, my socks need changing and my shoes need shining, because the roads are so dusty. So, who exactly would have had the responsibility of washing feet in that culture? It would have been the job of the very youngest, most junior servant. If the home did not have servants, then the youngest child would do the job. Now we can see how mind-blowing it would have been to the disciples to see Jesus taking up a towel and washing their feet.

The King of Kings, the Lord of Lords, the creator of all things, in fact the very reason why all things were created, is now washing feet! It's mad isn't it? But that is the kind of leadership that those who lead in the church need to practice.

Being a follower of Jesus is unusual. If it's real, it is counter-culture and so at odds with what people would think normally. That's what makes it so fantastic. It is so very different and totally opposite of what is the expected norm in any culture in the world. The trouble is, we are so influenced by our culture and the way the world runs that we don't realise how different we are called to be. The early church had the same struggle, as we can see in 1 Peter 5:v2, *"Be shepherds of God's flock that is under your care, serving as overseers—not because you must, but because you are willing, as God wants you to be; not greedy for money, but eager to serve; not lording it over those entrusted to you, but being examples to the flock."*

Have a look at it and you'll see the words, "serve" and, "not lording it" (that is being the big heavy handed boss) all in one sentence.

So, you feel God has called you to lead. It is servant leadership that he's called you to. That is so different to what we see in the world around us. However, it is God's way. This is the way he wants us to lead in his world. Are you ready to lead?

Leadership of Self

The most important person we need to learn to lead is our self. In other words, we need to be in charge of ourselves. The thing is, if we cannot govern, control and lead our self, how would it be possible or even thinkable to lead others?

It is obvious from scripture that Jesus thought of himself as under authority. That is, under the authority of his Heavenly Father, He was doing, saying and being all that his father wanted him to be and do.

In servant leadership, which is the style of leadership that is required by God, the phrase, "Do as I say, not as I do," just does not hold water! Self-discipline is a must. But what does that mean?

Well it includes things like controlling our tempers, or should I say temperament. The excuse that I often hear from people who lose their temper is, "That's just how I am!" That excuse will just not do. It might be how you were before, but now that you are a new person in Christ, as it says in 2 Corinthians 5:17, "Therefore, if anyone is in Christ, he is a new creation; the old has gone, the new has come."
;
Many times I hear people say, "Accept me for who I am, God does!" Of course, in some senses, that is true. God does not wait for us to change before we come to him, so in that sense he certainly does accept us for who we are and just how we are. It is like the old hymn says, "Just as I am, I come".

But hang on! It doesn't stop there. The scripture is very plain about this. God's plan for us is to change us. There are many references similar to the one I quoted from 2 Corinthians. Here is another example; Colossians 3:10, "and have put on the new self, which is being renewed in knowledge in the image of its Creator." So it is obvious that God does not plan to leave us as he found us in that "Just as I am," state. The plan is to change us and to make us like his son Jesus.

So how does he do that? Or, how do you or I do that? That is: How do we change to be more like Christ? It's not as complicated as you might imagine, though it does take some action on our part. God is alongside us, helping us, encouraging us, strengthening us, being with us every step of the way. I often ask people what is it that we or God uses to change us. I get a variety of answers, including praying, going to church, reading the Bible, as well as "by the Holy Spirit." These are all good answers, but not the right one methinks.

The right answer is "to think." The battle ground, from God's perspective and from a biblical perspective, is our thinking and our minds It is the changing of our thinking and our minds that makes us into good leaders, in control of ourselves, able to lead ourselves and therefore able to lead others.

The Bible has lots to say on this subject, about "putting on the mind of Christ."

There are so many references in the New Testament about having the mind of Christ, that I decided to encourage you to get hold of a concordance and have a look for yourself. You could start with Philippians 4:8, "Whatever is true, whatever is noble, whatever is right, whatever is pure, whatever is lovely, whatever is admirable, if anything is excellent or praiseworthy **think** about such things."

You could also take a look at Romans 12:2 which tells us we need to renew our minds. "Do not conform any longer to the pattern of this world, but be **transformed** by the renewing of your **mind**. Then you will be able to test and approve what God's will is, his good, pleasing and perfect will."

If you do that, it changes everything. Computer geeks say that if you put rubbish into your computer, then you will get rubbish out. They call it GIGO, "Garbage In, Garbage Out." It's the same with our minds. What we need is right thinking that will change us so that we can lead ourselves and then lead others.

Honest Leadership – i.e. in the family

For many years I led large youth camps both in the north and south of England. I often feel I have spent almost as much time camping as Abraham did!

What has camping to do with leadership? Which, of course, is the subject we are discussing. On those camp sites, with almost 400 teenagers thrown together in close proximity, there were many human problems. One of the camps regularly had young people who were referred from various departments within Social Services. One can imagine how there were lots of pastoral issues and much time spent just talking, answering questions and dealing with teenage matters.

It may surprise you to know that the group of young people I probably spent the most time with, due to their unruly behaviour, usually after midnight sitting on a hill around a fire (well it was a summer camp), was the church leader's kids.

My conversations with many leader's kids over the years became very repetitive. It went something like this:

"I know your father and mother. They lead that large church in Anyshire. Why is it, that amongst all these young people, you are giving me the biggest problems?'
Their response invariably began with, 'Huh!' Then with a teenage shrug, "You might think you know my Mum and Dad, but you only see them when they are at a church meeting. You don't live with them. You don't see you how my Dad treats my Mum. You don't see how my Mum speaks to my Dad. You have no idea what they are really like!' And, of course, they were right.

Out of the hundreds of disciples who followed Jesus, he chose twelve of them. Then he lived with them. This was the basis of his teaching. He didn't give them a lecture now and then for a couple of hours, he was with them 24/7. It's a well-known saying that you don't really know someone until you have lived with them. When I was at college sharing a room with 5 other students, one of the guys had a very appropriate rhyme which was, "To live with the saints in heaven above, I'm sure that will be glory. But, but to live with the saints on earth below, boy, that's another story."

When we're at a church meeting and someone asks, "How are you doing?" It is so easy for us to put a smile on our face, be very spiritual and say, "I'm fine." But when one gets home, the façade drops and their real character appears. That's a rather hypocritical lifestyle. At home it's much harder to be a Christian, a true follower of the way, a leader who maintains consistency in words and actions.

Does that mean it can't be done? I don't think that's true. We do need, however, to change our thinking. We need to put on the mind of Christ. We need to have a servant attitude in our heart, and we certainly need to lose the, "I am lording it over you," approach that so many of us pick up so easily. It is strange how quickly we learn to boss people around and take the high ground. And I'm not just referring to leaders.

Next time you are at a Christian function, take a look around at the people who have been given some responsibility.

[138]

They may be sporting a badge, or a walkie-talkie. Notice how quickly they begin bossing people around, putting others down and making small rules seem like mountains to climb or an instrument with which to whack others. This bossiness is in us all and we need to be on our guard when it rears its ugly head.

If we desire to be a Jesus-style of leader, we need to be honest with ourselves, we need a heart "make-over," and we need to say to Jesus, "Help me to be a servant-style leader that effects real change in the world." We need to consistently seek to maintain that attitude in the most important place, our home.

Investment into People

One day, a little boy was being driven by his Mother along a motorway. In front of them was a large lorry filled with rubbish, it was obviously not going very far as lying spread-eagled across the tarpaulin sheet used to cover the rubbish, was a man. At a guess, he was doing this to save the time and trouble it would have taken to rope the tarpaulin to the sides of the lorry. The man lay on top of it to stop it from flying away as they drove along.

The little boy studied the lorry and the man spread out on top of the rubbish, he was puzzled by the almost lifeless form of the driver's mate. Suddenly, a gust of wind lifted one corner of the tarpaulin causing the man to react quickly to bring the large sail under control by throwing his arm over the offending, flapping corner. The little boy turned to his Mum and said in a horrified voice, "Look mummy, somebody has thrown away a perfectly good man!"

Leaders must never throw away perfectly good people. Scripture reports that Jesus said, "I will not quench a smoking flax nor break a bruised reed." What exactly does that mean? I reckon it means that Jesus will not put on one side even the weakest or most damaged person, but rather He will use them. They too are leadership material.

Sadly, many are tempted to throw people away because they're not clever enough, or too clever by half, the wrong colour, the wrong culture, funny, silly, awkward or just plain weird.

Leaders work with people and need to get them motivated, activated, committed and following us, because we are following Jesus and of course helping them to develope into leaders themselves.

If we, even in our thoughts, dismiss people or mentally throw them away, then that is completely opposite to the Jesus style of leadership. Scripture is full of success stories about people whom others had thrown away. If you want to lead "Jesus style" then you will want to discover people whom others have thrown away. I am talking about people who if taken and carefully nurtured and polished, will turn into diamonds whose bright light will dazzle you. These people, you will find, by careful handling, will not only become useful kingdom seekers but also powerful leaders, kings, prophets and priests.

We must learn to love others, be good at directing people and never deriding them. You are there to help them in whatever way possible. We need to remember that Jesus came to lift people up not to push them down.

We actually need to make people, other people, our offering of worship to God. God has great things in store for all of us. We are called to be his leaders, his prophets, his priests, and His kings. *All* of us! God has put great value on us. He seems to know the value of every person and he is never willing to discard anybody. He will never throw them away. The only manner in which they can be thrown away is if they throw themselves away. Jesus never throws people away, He died for people, all people. We should never forget that.

Leadership and the cost - in time and space

It seems to me that there is a great gulf Between most people's understanding of leadership and Biblical style leadership. In many ways those of us who think of ourselves as follower of Jesus are more often than not influenced by Greek thinking and philosophy than we are by Judeo-Christian thinking and influence.

What is worse is that we think that the Greek way of thinking and its philosophy is actually Judeo-Christian - and it isn't!

We are talking at this time about leadership. The whole Judeo-Christian/Greek thing is another issue, but I have mentioned it now because of the way that Jesus led and I contrast that with what is often perceived when we lead in today's' world. What we tend to do is preach, or perhaps we would use the words teach or even lecture. Usually that takes place from the front of some building and what is really happening is information being passed from someone's brain though their vocal cords out of their mouth and into, they hope, their listener's ears. This then is regarded as leading, and of course it is, but actually it's a Greek style of leadership.

In contrast the Judeo-Christian style of leadership is much more involved, and we see it very clearly in the servant leadership style of Jesus. From out of his many disciples he choose twelve of them, then said "Follow me." For three years they followed him, or if you like, followed His leadership. That "following" is very involved, for Jesus and for the disciples. They are living together, walking together, eating together, watching what Jesus does, sometimes helping him do what He does, like distributing baskets of bread and fish. Sometimes Jesus will say, "Off you go and do it by yourself." Then, when they hit problems, they go back to Jesus and say, "We can't seem to do this. Please help!" Jesus also regularly spends time in what perhaps we would now call a tutorial group. In these times He is talking to them and answering some of their questions. Often to our modern frustration, his answers are asking new questions. Yes, Jesus occasionally preaches, but actually that is quite rare, most of the time he is walking, talking, doing and showing.

Here is a couple of my stories to illustrate what I'm talking about.

Some years ago one of our leaders said to me, "Why does so and so do what you ask them to do, but they often don't do it when I ask them? I am a leader just like you." I didn't go into detail about the principles of leadership, but I responded with, "Actually they lived in my house for two years. I saw them every day. They had breakfast with me almost every morning.

They came home at night and I was there. In fact, I was probably with them more than they were with anyone else. Perhaps my life input to them has influenced them strongly and they are therefore willing to help me, or to do what I ask." The leader replied, "Oh! But I don't want other people living in my house, or to be involved with them to that extent." To which I replied, "That is why you don't get the response from them that I do. This is how life works!"

The second story happened some years ago. A young lady came to me and said, "This is my brother." I said, "Hi," and then she said, "I want to give him to you." I looked a little surprised and said as politely as possible, "That's fine. Thank you! But I don't want him." "No!" she said. "You don't understand. He has been to a Christian camp and has become a Christian." I answered with an appropriate and sincere, "I think that is great! Fantastic!" "No! No!" she said again. "You still don't understand! That happened to him last year - and the year before - and the year before that. But two weeks after he gets home, he is a bad as ever. I know that because I am his sister." By now I was very curious. "So what do you want me to do?" She told me, "I want you to look after him and take him with you, wherever you go."

And so I did, much to the disgust of my girlfriend at the time. Why? Because every time we went out, the guy was in tow. It was a pain. I did try to share with him what little bit I knew, and so wherever I went he went too. And just in case you're wondering and wanting to ask; No! He isn't following me around anymore. He is, however, still a strong follower of Jesus, and leading others.

What I am trying to say, and hoping my readers get it, is that this kind of Judeo-Christian leadership has at its heart the servant lifestyle to start with. It is quite costly. Costly personally I mean. It will take a lot of our time, our total commitment, and to have people with us a lot – it can sometimes be a real pressure. What you are really giving to the people that you are leading is, in fact, your life. When you think about it the person we so often claim to be following did just tha. He gave us his life, that we might live, and lead others. Do you want to be a leader? Can you give your life?

DIFFICULT PEOPLE

Let's be honest. There are difficult people around, aren't there? There are also people, who claim to be followers of Jesus, who think we need to be nice to everyone.

The problem with being nice is that sometimes "nice" means, in modern parlance, "untruthful." When we are untruthful, we need to ask the question: Are we really helping the other person?

Let me illustrate where I am going with this. Have you noticed how people who tell you they are Christians sometimes say, and usually very loudly and firmly, "You need to accept me as I am, because God says He accepts me just as I am. He tells us to come to him just as we are, so you should do the same." And that is the problem with sound bite truth. Of course, what they are saying is true. However, it's neither the whole truth nor the whole story. We so love those sound bites don't we?

The truth is that God loves us and calls us to come to Him as we are. However, he also calls us to change. This is made clear in scriptures like, "Be transformed by the renewing, or the changing of your mind." He also plans to conform us to the image of His son Jesus as in Romans 8:29. These scriptures give us the clear understanding that although God accepts us as we are, it isn't part of His plan to leave us as He finds us.

May I be honest? Thank you! Sometimes, when people say, "Love me as I am," I am thinking, (but of course I don't say it), "You really are horrible! You need to change!"

Then there are people who say, "Do you know, I never have these problems at work, or at my book club. I only have them when I am here in the church community." And the first thing that goes through my head is, "Uh oh! They are not telling the truth!" Perhaps they think they are, but actually, they are not.

For many years I have run Christian schools. Sometimes, I have a parent sitting in front of me saying, "Do you know, I never had this problem with my child in their last school?"

What they fail to realise is that I have a file on the child from their last school describing the behaviour issues and have read the problems that the staff at my school are experiencing - and I know my staff! Sometimes, of course, people don't realise what they are doing. At other times, let's be totally clear, they are not being honest. They are trying to circumvent their own problems.

That leads me to my next issue with people, namely, that of their own problems. There are those who want to dump their problems on others, especially if those on who they are dumping have assumed any form of leadership role. What happens is this; someone will share their problem with you, and, because you care, you really put your mind into it. After they have poured out their problems to you, they go home and sleep soundly, while you toss and turn and worry about their problem. It is not good to allow people to dump their lives on you. We need to try and help people to find ways through difficult passages in their lives, and be as helpful as possible, but ultimately it is for them, to work out their own resolutions.

Scripture tells us that we are to work out our own salvation. That, again, could be a sound bite, but of course God is there working with those who have problems, and, no doubt, if you are caring leader, you also will be alongside them. Do not allow people to make their lives your responsibility. God wants us to grow up, to be mature and to work-with Him as we work through difficult periods in our life. He promises to turn them round and help us learn from them, maturing us and changing our own thinking.

Finally, to help any of you reading this who do lead, and are going through one of those terrible times when some person you have been trying to help turns around and blames you for the problem that they have, even though the problem was there before you even met them, or they list the terrible problems that they are having with you that sends you home feeling a complete and utter failure and a really useless leader - in fact a useless person - here is my little formula which I hope might help you.

Ask yourself, "Do other people have this problem with me?"

If the answer is "Yes!" then perhaps the critic is right and you do have a problem. If the answer is "No!", and I have to say it usually is "No!" then you need to say to yourself, "Because other people do not have this problem with me, then it is probably not my problem but theirs."

Then ask yourself, "In my observation of this person, do they have a similar problem with other people that I know?" If the answer is "Yes!" again it confirms what I have just said. It is not your problem it is theirs. Often we end up beating ourselves up when we should not do so, simply because we haven't thought through the situation. We have simply reacted negatively to criticism, and blamed ourselves for something that is not our fault or our responsibility.

I hope today that I haven't caused you to no longer want to lead, or help those difficult or problematic people. God does love them; I just don't want you to live in condemnation. Happy helping, and be blessed.

Leadership – In the big wide world

I have been looking at leadership in these short articles in the context of those who are followers of Jesus. However, I hope that I haven't given the impression that these skills of servant leadership are only relevant and appropriate to the church community. If I have given that impression let my try and correct that here and now.

I have spent a large chunk of my life establishing some Independent Schools. We have two in North London, one in Sri Lanka and one in Nakuru, Kenya. When people ask me, "What is their purpose?" I answer that I am interested in affecting the thinking of young students. Also I want to produce tomorrow's national and international leaders.

I hope you don't think what I say next is too strange, but even if you do, I believe it to be so. If you really are a follower of Jesus, and you are walking with him, then certain things will apply to you and your life.

First of all, you are in touch with wisdom. I do not believe that wisdom comes from any other source but from God. He is the source of wisdom. Knowledge on the other hand can come from a variety of sources. If you are a follower of Jesus then you should have a world-view that gives great credibility to any leadership role into which you enter. Followers of Jesus also have a clear perspective about the future, ie: where it's all going. Why we are here? And, what is our human purpose? You are also in touch with the ultimate lawgiver and ruler. Therefore you understand what it means to have a moral base or a moral compass. Scripture talks about our thinking producing who and what we are, and that can, should and does reflect into the wider culture locally, nationally and internationally.

I learned a lot of my leadership skills from following Jesus rather than from management training, or other training schemes. I have discovered that it is very easy to transfer those skills into what we sometimes call, the secular world, (although I don't like the word secular, as I know that the Kingdom of God can be found in every area of life and do not like the false dichotomy of secular and spiritual). I have been able to use the leadership skills obtained as a follower of Jesus in Social Services, education and business to name but a few.

Just the other day I was listening to a discussion about an emerging economy on the Radio. They were talking about how the country could be improved by business, by politics, and by new laws. Yet, there was an element that was missing from the debate. There was no mention of how people think, or, if you will, the philosophy of a nation.

In the UK, whilst I would never want to call us or think of us as a Christian nation, we do have a strong Christian heritage which can be seen in our laws and the way the country works. This heritage is, I believe, currently being rapidly squandered and eroded, but some of it is this is still there. This tends to make us generous and caring. It affects levels of honesty and corruption.

If you look at national cultures in other parts of the world, you will see clear differences to the UK culture, due to the underlying philosophy.

[146]

For some, there is a lack of concern for others outside of their own country. Some place a low value on human life and some have very corrupt systems. I am sure business, law, politics and education can all help those things if a nation's culture is wrong. However, ultimately one doesn't really change things unless one changes the thinking and the underlying philosophy of life in a person, a family, an ethnic group or a nation.

As one American president once said, "If you educate an evil man who was stealing from the railway, it doesn't change his actions, it just makes him clever. Instead of stealing from the railway, he steals the whole system." What we often see as requiring a structural change actually needs a change of heart, or from my point of view, Jesus style leadership in all areas of life. So how about you, where and how do you lead?

Leadership – Getting it wrong

I hope you have remembered what I said at the beginning of this chapter of "L is for Leadership," which was that all of us are called to be leaders; or to put it in Bible language, we are prophet's priest and kings.

Alongside this universal calling there are always several people in each church community who take special responsibility for others, and that brings with it all sorts of pressures. One of those pressures is the problem of being right. I guess you have all seen that joke that sometimes sits on a manager's desk which says, "Rule number one: The boss is always right. Rule number two: If the boss is wrong, refer to rule number one." The reality is, of course, that being in leadership does not always mean that you are right.

That in itself presents another pressure; one of our culture and our age. Generally, people do not like or expect anyone in leadership to be wrong. Just watch what happens when a politician tries to admit to being wrong and having missed the mark. The response is rarely, "That's great! They have admitted they are wrong. Let's forgive them and move on." Usually it is quite the reverse. Immediately, there is a flurry of frantic digging in order to reveal further failings and the public demand they resign – no! that's not enough – they should die.

Even that is not enough with some. There are those who want to dance on a their grave.

Coupled with the possibility of being wrong, there is also the cultural pressure whereby we want our leaders to know the answer to everything. I am a leader, and sometimes I am wrong. Sometimes, I do not know the answer. What is worse, sometimes I can see a problem, which I am sure everyone else can see. I know this because they come and tell me, often in conspiratorial tones, "There is a problem." I know there is problem. I didn't need anyone to tell me what I already know. What I need is for someone to give me an answer to the problem, as I don't have one.

So what can we do? Firstly I think that it is very helpful to admit we are wrong as quickly as possible and learn to put up with people's reactions and disappointment. We should also look for help both from God and our fellow travellers. Perhaps when they see us admit that we are wrong, it might encourage them in their own struggle to get things right.

Secondly all of us need to treat those who lead us with respect when they say that they do not have an answer to some particular conundrum. Possibly, accepting and believing that they simply do not know.

Thirdly, and this is a hard one, I am convinced we need to learn to say "I am sorry." That can be a great help to all. But isn't it a hard word to use?

Let me finish by telling you a positive story to illustrate what I mean.

For more than thirty years-I have been involved in running Independent Christian Schools. In two of them, I hold the role of principal. A while ago a young lady of around twelve years old was brought to my office for some misdemeanour. It was my job to tell her off. I did so, very sternly. The young lady ended up with tears running down her cheeks. She left my office very, very subdued and quiet, so I thought I had done the job well. The next day, to my horror, I discovered that I had reprimanded a totally innocent person, who was in no way guilty of any wrongdoing.

What should I do? I asked a member of staff to find the young lady and bring her to my office as quickly as possible. She walked in with fear in her face. I asked her to sit down. She did so, very carefully, her hands folded meekly in her lap.

I explained to her that on the previous day I had made a terrible mistake when I told her off and I said I wanted to apologise. I looked into her fearful eyes and said, "I'm sorry. Please forgive me." The transformation was instantaneous. The fear disappeared and the young lady burst into the largest smile I have ever seen. I was afraid that her face would come apart if she smiled any more.

Suffice it to say, she went away very happy. I must admit, I also felt good. Being wrong and saying sorry really made my day. I think it made her day too. I am pretty certain that the story got repeated many times to her schoolmate's.

Did being wrong in that case make me a lesser person? I don't think so. I think dealing with being wrong after the event *in the right way* made a positive difference. Don't you agree? Unlike how some of us react to our fallible politicians, she didn't want to kill me. It was just the reverse. I think she thought she had a received a fantastic present. Don't kill people for being wrong, be like our God, full of grace and forgiveness.

Leadership – the book, Vision

Scripture says that where there is no vision, people perish. Maybe it's just the people I mix with, but there has been a bit of a backlash against the subject of "Vision." Maybe you are not aware of that. If not don't let it worry you. The thing is that people react (and I understand why they do) against the fact that leaders want everyone to buy into *their* vision. Sometimes they even exhaust people in trying to see things achieved and the vision reached.

Why their vision anyway? Why not mine?

Well here are some answers;

[149]

Do you have a vision? People regularly come and chat with me, seeking advice about the direction their life is taking, or not, as the case may be. They may say things like, "I don't have a vision. I really would like one. What should I do?" I'm sorry but I have a stock answer which is, "Get on board someone else's vision!" Don't forget that scripture says, without one, people perish.

As leaders, aren't we all called to lead? Yes we are, but we are also called to follow. Scripture states that we should be under authority, and if we are all practicing servant leadership then things will work really well. I would also hope that as a leader you are following a vision God has given you, one that reflects what Jesus said, "*I must be about my Father's business.*" Or let's put it another way: The Father's vision is what I plan to accomplish.

So let's think again about those who have no vision, if it is the Father's vision that your leader is following, why not get on board? A key point to bear in mind is that the Father's vision is broad enough to encompass other visions. For the church community to function smoothly and effectively, we should all be following a God given vision. That does not eliminate the possibility that God can also give you a vision, at which point you should be able to say to the leadership, "Hey! I really want to do this and accomplish what I believe God has shown me." If we are all under authority, in close relationship with the Father and his purposes, it should be equally possible for the leaders to say, "That's great! That extends the vision in this area and makes things work better in that area. How fantastic that we are going in the same direction." Often when we cannot respond in that way, then perhaps what is wrong is that the vision is too small.

In many ways God has given us the broader visions, outlining them several times in scripture. He wants us to catch His vision, the top priority he give us is to *"seek FIRST the Kingdom of God."* We are also told, *"Tell the good news."* I know you know it, but let me say it again: The good news is about a person and that person is Jesus. He is the good news. We are told to, "*Tell it in Jerusalem, in Samaria and the uttermost parts of the world.*" That's a big job, and a huge vision isn't it?

Finally we are told to, "*Make disciples of the nations.*' I think that gives most of us enough to do for the rest of our lives. Don't you?

A vision keeps you fresh; it actually keeps you alive and moving forward. I have a little saying that some puzzle over. "The worst enemy of better is very good." The thing is, when things are bad, you can usually see that there is a need for some vision to make them better. However, it is when things are going well that can put you in the danger zone. Unless you are alert, you could end up settling down and dying off. Don't do it! We have not arrived; the kingdom has not yet come, there are still dreams to dream and a vision to have.

Get a vision of leading, forging ahead, keeping going and kingdom seeking! If you haven't got one then get on board with someone who has. There is a promised land to be possessed, there is a Kingdom to be sought after and we have the power to bring it to earth if we know our God. That's why he told us to pray and work. "*Your kingdom come your will be done on earth as it is in heaven.*" Happy seeking!

M is for Morality

Morals and Conscience – Do we have them? Where do they come from?

I have written about this subject a lot. From that you will gather that I think it's important. Especially in the light of some the recent events in the UK, such as the riots. However I believe they are only a symptom of something deeper.

Politicians, of all shades, including the prime minister are discussing this subject. It is playing central stage on many TV and Radio Programmes. Perhaps, then, it really is important. There is also deep concern about our schools and our young people. How, the politicians and TV pundits ask, can we install morals into young people so that they do not smash up our streets and destroy our society?

Many responses to my books and blogs can be summed up as follows, "Morals don't need to come from the Bible, The Koran, or from a god. They surely can come from within ourselves." To which I respond, "Yes! Of course they can. But what sort of moral guide would that be?"

We need to go one step back and ask, why we need to have morals at all, and what is it that propels us to even ask these questions. My answer encompasses the whole issue of conscience.

What is conscience? What is our conscience? My argument would be that conscience is a part of us that we are all born with. Some people disagree with this concept and say that we don't have a conscience, but I strongly believe that we do. We each have our own individual conscience, unique to us personally. That means that it only works for us, it doesn't work for anyone else. What it instils in us is the general sense of right and wrong. In a nutshell, right and wrong for you might be different to the right and wrong for me, but there will, most definitely, be a personal right and wrong. This concept is far beyond the idea that we do things because they are convenient or inconvenient or because we know we can, "get away with it."

How does conscience work? For the individual, and I do stress the individual, in any given situation it will say to the person, "Yes that is right. Do it!"or, 'No! That is wrong! You should not do it." Your conscience does not impel you, it does not force you in any direction, it will only hint at the decision you should make. The final decision that decides the action is the result of your own decision making process, which I would call "the will." When you have carried out an act, you know if it is wrong without anyone telling you. You will feel uncomfortable and disturbed. The pendulum of your conscience has swung into the negative zone. For many people when they obey their consciences and do what they feel is right, they often say they feel good. When they disobey their conscience they feel bad, or despondent. However the despondent feeling does not prevent them from disobeying.

Interestingly the Bible has some comments on this. John 1:9 is obviously talking about Jesus the Christ. The implication is that there is a "light", or the word I use, "conscience" that is there in every person. Romans 2:14 says "for when Gentiles, who do not have the law, by nature do the things in the law, these, although not having the law, are a law to themselves." In other words we all have it, and we use it, that is our conscience, personally.

This means that we all have different views of right or wrong according, first of all, to us, and then, as we grow and develop, according to what we learn from our family and surrounding culture and education. The problem is that we all break our own rules, and go against our own conscience.

Conscience can, of course, be educated. That is where the moral discussion enters the stage. Who will define that moral code? Will it be just me? Will it be my culture? Or will it be God? It is possible for our conscience to be developed and refined by all sorts of external things, including education. But who should define the moral code? Which one will we adopt?

We need to understand that the moral code that Jesus defines is quite amazing, in that it is contrary to all other moral codes that I know anything about. However, please tell me if you know something different.

[153]

Think about some of those moral imperatives and how counter-culture they are. "Love your enemies. Do good to those who do bad to you," for starters. What sort of Moral code do you want young people to follow? What moral code is required for our culture to follow and for you personally?

Morals, where do they come from?
Looking up something recently on Wikipedia, I discovered lots of comments about myself in discussion with Richard Dawkins. Many of the comments following on from the discussion are statements like, "How ridiculous to think that morals come from any kind of God."

Usually, in this kind of debate, there is a tendency to ridicule things that I have said. That is fine. I guess it goes with the territory of getting involved and not being afraid of what I believe and understand, and being sure that it holds water and can robustly stand up to cross-examination.

I suppose I do get somewhat irritated in debates when people tell me what I believe, and then tell me how ridiculous it is to believe it, while attempting to prove how stupid I am. However, all the time I am thinking, "I never believed that in the first place. You have not given me space to say what I really do believe, or think." It's what I call, destroying straw men. One puts up an argument and then knocks it down. But if I did not believe what they thought I believed initially, it was no argument in the first place. What is that? It is destroying the straw man that does not exist.

In TV debates, especially those that are not live, there is the possibility that what was said is on the cutting room floor. I remember in one debate with Richard Dawkins, he said to me that he was more moral than me because he did not rape or pillage, and he did not need a God to stop him doing those things, whereas I did. My reply, which must be on the cutting room floor, was, "Bully for you, Richard. You ought to watch the news more often. If you watch the news you can see that there is an awful lot of inhumanity and suffering in the world. I live in one of those areas where young people can be stabbed, or shot just because they happened to have strayed into the wrong post code area.

[154]

My questions are: Why are we so awful to each other? What has happened to a moral basis? I would argue that as we move away from an understanding of a God, who ultimately will judge and question our life responses, we become more selfish and less inclined to care for each other or have any basis for moral decisions. Our moral compass deteriorates.

The humanist argues that our morals come from the fact that we are simply human, and they develop out of our selfishness and survival needs. Or, as Richard Dawkins would argue, the selfish gene is simply protecting itself by being moral towards others.

I often ask the question, Why do we have right and wrong? From where do we get such concepts? The arguments on Wikipedia, in answer to what I said about morals, seem to conclude that it's just because we are human. I'm sorry, but that just will not do. If doing wrong gives me an advantage, and I can avoid getting caught, why not go ahead and do it? Morals like that don't seem to me to be moral at all.

In a discussion on morality, Richard Dawkins was asked: *"If we do not acknowledge some sort of external [standard], what is to prevent us from saying that the Muslim [extremists] aren't right?" Dawkins replied, "What's to prevent us from saying Hitler wasn't right? I mean, that is a genuinely difficult question, but whatever [defines morality], it's not the Bible. If it was, we'd be stoning people for breaking the Sabbath." The interviewer wrote in response, "I was stupefied. He had readily conceded that his own philosophical position did not offer a rational basis for moral judgments. His intellectual honesty was refreshing, if somewhat disturbing on this point."*

It brings us back to the question: Who is the law giver? If there is no ultimate lawgiver, or God, then morals become irrelevant. We are left with anarchy. If we can get away with it, then why not? Whatever it is, right and wrong are just words without meaning. What is right for you might be wrong for me. But so what!

Dr. Bahnsen says that, *"If the God of the bible does not exist, all principled or moral complaint about what Hitler did to the Jews is irrelevant. In a godless universe, what one "animal" does to other "animals" is ethically irrelevant. There is no basis for indignation or outrage. What happens, happens: period. We are left with the feelings and desires of others versus the feelings and desires of Hitler – with neither having any more "right" than the other."*

If we support liberal freedom, then in a true atheist worldview we should defend Hitler's freedom to do as he desired!

Dr. Bahnsen sets forth a rational, objective case for the existence of the Christian God, a case which fully takes into account the crucial function of one's worldview in his reasoning. He is quoted in the tabloid for the Tabash debate as saying: *"Pursued to their consistent end, the pre-suppositions of unbelief render man's reasoning vacuous and his experience unintelligible; in short, they lead to the destruction of knowledge, the dead end of epistemological futility, and to utter foolishness."* (http://www.tabash.com/)

I question here the argument that atheists and humanists do as much good in the world as the likes of Robert Raikes, Wilberforce, Shaftsbury, Cadburys, Fry's, Rowntree . The reality is that the Christian ethic, the moral bias of serving a living God, gives us great reason to care for His world and the people created in His image.

Interestingly Dinesh D'Souza took Richard Dawkins to task for engaging in historical revisionism when it comes to the atrocities of atheist regimes and declared Dawkins, "reveals a complete ignorance of history". In a recent interview D'Souza declared:
"Richard Dawkins argues that at least the atheist regimes didn't kill people in the name of atheism. Isn't it time for this biologist to get out of the lab and read a little history? Marxism and Communism were atheist ideologies. Stalin and Mao weren't dictators who happened to be atheist. Atheism was part of their official doctrine. It was no accident, as the Marxists liked to say, that they shut down the churches and persecuted the clergy...

Dinesh D'Souza stated in another interview:

"As one writer put it, "Leaders such as Stalin and Mao persecuted religious groups, not in a bid to expand atheism, but as a way of focusing people's hatred on those groups to consolidate their own power." Of course I agree that murderous regimes, whether Christian or atheist, are generally seeking to strengthen their position.

But if Christian regimes are held responsible for their crimes committed in the name of Christianity, then atheist regimes should be held accountable for their crimes committed in the name of atheism.

And who can deny that Stalin and Mao, not to mention Pol Pot and a host of others, all committed atrocities in the name of a Communist ideology that was explicitly atheistic? Who can dispute that they did their bloody deeds by claiming to be establishing a "new man" and a religion-free utopia?

These were mass murders performed with atheism as a central part of their ideological inspiration, they were not mass murders done by people who simply happened to be atheist." Joseph Stalin's atheistic regime killed tens of millions of people.

The thing that I noted most as I looked through Wikipedia and other web sites and the arguments against my moral perspective was that no one seemed to talk about 'conscience,' that strange inner-voice with which we are all born.

No one asked, "Where does that come from?" The Bible says in John chapter 1 that there is, "…a light that lights every man." John is talking about Jesus in his Gospel, however there is also that 'conscience' light that every person has, and why would that be a surprise?

If, as I believe, we are made in the image of God, why would it be strange that there is that a part of us that is God-like, telling us about good and bad, right and wrong?

[157]

Conscience is a strange thing, it tells us these things but does not make us do the right thing or stop us from doing wrong. Dinesh D' Souza says it much better than me:

The Surprising Fact of Morality

Evolutionists have some ingenious explanations for morality. But do they work? Morality is both a universal and a surprising fact about human nature. When I say that morality is universal I am not referring to this or that moral code. In fact, I am not referring to an external moral code at all. Rather, I am referring to morality as the voice within, the interior source that Adam Smith called the "impartial spectator."

Morality in this sense is an uncoercive but authoritative judge. It has no power to compel us, but it speaks with unquestioned authority. Of course we can and frequently do reject what morality commands, but when we do so we cannot avoid guilt or regret. It is because of our capacity for self-impeachment and remorse that Aristotle famously called man "the beast with the red cheeks." Aristotle's description holds up very well more than 2,000 years later.

Even people who most flagrantly repudiate morality — say, a chronic liar or a rapacious thief — nearly always respond to detection with excuses and rationalizations. They say, "Yes, I lied, but I had no alternative under the circumstances," or "Yes, I stole, but I did so to support my family." Hardly anyone says, "Of course I am a liar and a thief, and I don't see anything wrong with that." What this means is that morality supplies a universal criterion or standard even though this standard is almost universally violated.

Morality is a surprising feature of humanity because it seems to defy the laws of evolution. Evolution is descriptive: It says how we do behave. Morality is prescriptive: It says how we should behave. And beyond this, evolutionary behaviour appears to run in the opposite direction from moral behaviour.

Evolution implies that we are selfish creatures who seek to survive and reproduce in the world.

Indeed we are, but we are also unselfish creatures who seek the welfare of others, sometimes in preference to our own. We are participants in the fame of life, understandably partial to our own welfare, while morality stands aloof, taking the impartial, or "God's eye," view, directing us to act in a manner conducive to the good of others. In sum, while evolution provides a descriptive account of human self-interest, morality provides a standard of human behaviour that frequently operates against self-interest.

So if we are mere evolutionary primates, how to account for morality as a central and universal feature of our nature? Why would morality develope among creatures obsessively bent on survival and reproduction? Darwin himself recognized the problem. In The Descent of Man, Darwin argued that "although a high standard of morality gives but a slight or no advantage to each individual man and his children over the other men of the same tribe, yet . . . advancement in the standard of morality will certainly give an immense advantage to one tribe over another."

Darwin's point is that a tribe of virtuous patriots, with each of its members willing to make sacrifices for the group, would prove more successful and thus be favoured by natural selection over a tribe of self-serving individuals. This is the group-selection argument, and for many decades it was considered an acceptable way to reconcile evolution with morality.

But as biologists now recognize, the argument has a fatal flaw. The question we have to ask is how a tribe of individuals would become self-sacrificing in the first place. Imagine a tribe where, for instance, many people shared their food with others or volunteered to defend the tribe from external attack. Now what would be the fate of individual cheaters who benefited from this arrangement but hoarded their own food and themselves refused to volunteer to fight? Clearly these scoundrels would have the best deal of all. In other words, cheaters could easily become free riders, benefiting from the sacrifices of others but making no sacrifices themselves, and they would be more likely to survive than their more altruistic fellow tribesmen.

So do I still think morality or conscience is something that comes from the 'God who is there,' after reading all that is said about my opinions in the various discussions, Wikipedia and otherwise? Even more so!

Morality

The subject I observe presents such problems.

I was part of a government think tank looking at OFSTED inspections of schools. One of the things they look at is the moral part of the school's ethos. My problem is how does one obtain morals? In my small discussion group there where Muslims, Catholics, Jews, Evangelicals, and humanists. All of us, apart from the humanist, agreed that morals have to come from some kind of Law giver, and actually, in all of our thinking it was agreed that it must be God, apart, that is, from the humanist, who said there isn't a God, so morals must come from somewhere else.

I went on to argue that in terms of generosity, in such things as tsunamis, famines and the like, the UK is actually quite generous in its giving, I put this down to the Judeo-Christian influence in the background of the nation. The humanist said, "Now don't be silly. It is due to the fact that we were once great colonists." To which I responded, "I thought that was about greed, trade, and getting lots of things for ourselves!"

I was one of those interviewed by Richard Dawkins for his 'Religion is the Root of all Evil' programmes. After which I found stuff all over the internet, usually from many of the so called, "learned" atheists, poking fun at my opinions. Funnily enough I have read Richard's book, "The God Delusion," and one of the things that struck me is how often the base of who we are and where we are comes down to "luck," at least according to that book. God seems a better thesis to me.

And of course both in the programme, on the net, and definitely in Wikipedia comes the discussion of mortality.

I am amused that in at least one article, the fact that we live in a moral universe and one "without God," according to the atheists, is argued from the fact that some fish have a symbiotic relationship with "cleaner" fish. The action of the one fish on the other actually protects them. From this the atheist argument claimed that therefore, this is why we don't go around on our streets killing each other because it's wiser not to.

Richard Dawkins often says that being an atheist is not to be one with a depressing philosophy, actually he say it makes one appreciate life more and love life. Again I say, 'Bully for you.' The problem is that you don't have to travel very far to find people who are starving, people who have been enslaved, people who have every reason not to love life. If you now want them to believe that this atheism is the truth, and not be depressed by such a philosophy all I can say is HELP! It's the most depressing view of life that I can imagine. Thank God it isn't the truth!

So where does morality come from? I note that even some of the comments on what I think that are listed in Wikipedia. Note that I am saying that we live in a moral universe, and there is a base line for morality, and that sense of morality comes from somewhere. And I would say it comes from God. Yes that is what I am saying. Morality without a Lawgiver is craziness. It is not morality. As Charles Finny would have put it:

"Opposed to this is willing self-gratification; a practical treating of self as if the gratification of our own desires, appetites, etc., were of supreme importance. Now in this ultimate choice of the good of universal being, or of self-gratification as an ultimate end, moral character must reside. Primarily, surely, it can reside nowhere else. It is this ultimate choice that gives direction and character to all the subordinate actions of the will; that gives direction to the volitions, the actions, and the omissions of all our voluntary lives. This ultimate choice is the root or fountain from which all volition and all moral action spring."

I guess even Richard would agree with some of that. Finney's basic premise is that morality only comes from our own selfishness to survive or not be killed.

[161]

That is why we don't have mayhem on the streets. Although I wonder if we perhaps do. I live in an area where we have postcode crime, knife and gun crime, so the morality is, one does not live in my postcode area. If one does live in my post code you must need killing. That seems a great morality!

Going back to that statement I made earlier, "Bully for you," seems to take no note of the Hitler's, Pol Pots, and Stalin's of this world, which again makes me think if morality is only up to our moving to a value system that selfishly benefits us only, and we can get around it, then why not? If it is to my benefit to circumvent the law? If there is no ultimate sanction or moral law giver?

It has always interested me that the Bible talks about giving 'light' to every person who comes into the world. What is that light? Personally I have always seen that light as being the conscience that dwells in each and every person. We can obey it or disobey it, it is, if you like, a little bit of God in us, if we obey it we feel good, if we disobey it we feel bad, but it does not force us either way, we have the freewill, we have choice. Again to quote Finny on conscience, he talks about moral insanity:

*"Moral insanity, on the other hand, is will-madness. The man retains his intellectual powers unimpaired, but he sets his heart fully to evil. He refuses to yield to the demands of his **conscience.** He practically discards the obligations of moral responsibility. He has the powers of free moral agency, but persistently abuses them. He has a reason which affirms obligation, but he refuses obedience to its affirmations".*

So where do I think morality comes from? I think it comes from the lawgiver – God. He has created, and designed a moral universe. It is a universe that ultimately works towards the best good for all, the created order that means us, as well as God Himself. We can pretend it is not there, we can work against it, we can refuse to listen to our conscience, we can ignore it, but none of those things make it "not there."

[162]

The problem of Morals

For many years I was Chair of Governors for a large North London school. We would regularly receive directives from Government departments asking us to work hard to create "good citizens." Well educated ones, of course. I sympathised with their desires.

In Ofsted "speak" and enshrined in Government legislation runs the "SMSC" theme. This requires schools to work on these four areas in the lives of the children; Spiritual, Moral, Social and Cultural. I am pleased that the Government, and in turn, school inspectors acknowledge that human beings are made up of more than just the physical.

The Bible has a strange little phrase: "As a man thinks in his heart, so is he" (Proverbs 23:7). Have you ever considered how strong your perceptions of yourself are? They are so strong they make you become what you think you are. This is why and how you project yourself, which is why self confidence is so vital.

Let's take this a little further and argue that if we think we are just mechanical beings, then why should we not act mechanically? If we are mechanical beings, what we do to each other, or how we do it is not really that important, we are, after all, just machines. Conversely, if we are just animals, then we can act like animals to each other. Some animals are nice to each other, some are not and will attack their own species, even eat them. For many species, mating is something to be fought over and has no connection with faithfulness, or reliability, and there is no moral basis to sexuality. If I am an animal, then that is how it is.

I recently worked with a committee comprising of Muslims, Jews, Christians and a variety of other religions, and in my sub-group, a humanist. We were debating morals in the light of the legislation mentioned above. My question is always, where do morals come from? The humanist argued that it is just part of being human. But is that true? In the sixties, I had a friend who told me he always had at least £700 in his pocket. I was, at the time, earning £15 a week, which was not a bad wage at the time. I asked him how he managed to obtain so much money at the ripe old age of 9.

[163]

He shrugged his shoulders and said, "I steal it." I asked him how he could justify this, and what his family thought. He explained that the only crime his family would beat him for, was "being caught." As far back as he could remember with his parents, grand-parents and great grand-parents, their life was simple. "No one steals from us. And if we steal from them it is only what they deserve. They should have been as careful as we are." Needless to say, I pondered if that would be a good moral base for school children.

The question remains: Where does a moral base come from? My wealthy young friend and his thieving family worked it out from a "human" point of view. The humanist would say, "That's how we get our conclusions." But is it?

On the other side of the debate, my Muslim, Jewish and Christian friends would all agree that a moral imperative must come from some kind of lawgiver, rather like the law of the land, produced by the legislature. That seems logical to me. Is the ultimate lawgiver God? A higher standard, from which to set a moral base?

I also pose the question: Does our Christian heritage affect how we respond as individuals and as a nation? When crisis strikes in Africa, or some other far flung place, appeals are made and the UK public responds and is well known for its generosity. I would argue that this response is due to our Christian roots that echo down the centuries, reminding us how we need to help those in need.

I discussed this with my humanist friend, pointing out that there are countries equally as prosperous as the UK, yet without the Christian heritage, who respond by saying, "This is not our problem." Why the different response? The humanist explanation is that Britain's colonial history solicits this generous response, whereas other countries did not have the power of the Empire in their history.

I have problems with that explanation. From my reading of history, it seems to me that the Empire mentality was "Get what you can for us." Perhaps I am wrong. Can you help me out? Can you shed some light? Laws suggest a lawgiver. Morals suggest to me that somewhere there is a moral ideal, invented by a moral lawgiver.

[164]

Or should we just come to our own conclusion, like my 9 year old friend with a big, fat, stolen wedge in his pocket? "If I don't get caught, what's the problem?"

Here is one of the questions I received while airing my views in the public forum.

Does it muddy the waters to pay attention to some other-than-charitable national behaviors characteristic of nations that supposedly have a "Christian" heritage? If we were to ask which nations in the past invaded, pillaged and manipulated other nations during the era of imperial expansionism, where would the "Christian" nations rate on the damage-done scale? Or any complicity in the slave trade? Any involvement of "the Christian church" in those enterprises? In what civil war were there more casualties for that country than the combined casualties during the two "great wars" and the Korean war?

History indicates that it was an "in-God-we-trust" nation. The same nation, so U.N. financial records apparently indicate, that announces great aid packages but defaults on their pledges as a matter of course? How are nations with a Christian heritage doing on the moral-social issues of illicit drug trade, consumption of pornography, prostitution, getto-isation, instutionalised corporate greed and political corruption?

Doesn't it seem that the broader our studies and the more careful our analysis, then the more difficult it is to make a case for significant positive moral impact on the basis of historical or resident religious heritage? Or does it just depend on what we take into the study?

My response was:
I don't think it muddies the waters, it does mean that the conversation has to go further than a sound bite. I know that the country involved in more war's than any other over the last 200 years is the UK. However, I am bringing this down to the personal level, and whilst nations and governments do wrong things nevertheless there are underlying moral principles that come from heritage that affect the individual in countries. So why are individuals in one country more generous than in another? Why are woman freer in one area of the world than another?

We, I think, must not rule out the underlying thinking that molds a culture and persuades it in certain directions. One guy said, "I love Hinduism but I don't like India." I think he was referring to some of its injustice such as the caste system. The difficulty is, which comes first, the chicken or the egg? Does the philosophy mold the thinking thus creating the injustice. Or does the injustice mold the philosophy?

At the end though, the question is: Is there a moral lawgiver? I still think if we look at the big picture where nations enact legislation and we teach a philosophy that reflects the lawmakers' moral prerogatives, we get better results.

So generosity has its own blessing. Respect for the individual has its own blessings. We don't have to be followers of Jesus to benefit from the blessing of moral base do we?

Another question at the same forum from the same man was:

I think I understand your basic thesis. And to a degree, I think you're right. However, I'm carrying some qualifiers in my brain that make me reluctant to very quickly embrace the notion that folks, at "the personal level", are found to be more beneficent when they live within a national Christian heritage. To be fair in developing that thesis, there are a few things that would seem to require refinement.

What are we talking about when we say "generosity"? Is a dollar/pound given by an average individual in the UK equal to a dollar/pound given by an average person in, say, Ghana? In other words, are we going to take relative resources into account when we define generosity? Is dollar/ pound giving per capita the way we discern the generosity per capita? It seems to me that the pennies given by a destitute widow turned out to be extravagantly generosity, while the larger "gift" was rather meager! Should we perhaps be measuring sacrifice, rather than only amount? I've been treated with extreme and crushingly humbling generosity as a guest in very destitute villages, villages that know nothing of Christ.

Another thing. Can we, in talking about this, really ignore the national expressions/impulses?

[166]

If we say, we're going to build our thesis based on just "personal" example, won't we be forced to acknowledge that the "Christian heritage" has failed somewhat if the nation's practice is rather different than we're seeing at the personal level? I'm asking this question on the assumption that it's the people who comprise a nation and shape the national morality.

So if we're talking about kindness toward women; Is political freedom the criterion? Or should we look more broadly? Who consumes pornography if not individuals? Who fuels prostitution? Individuals, at a "personal level" or some institution?

If I sound cynical, I am somewhat. Anything that can modify that cynicism for me?

I replied:

OK maybe I share the cynicism. However, my thesis is that where there had been a Christian influence, even when that influence is corrupt, which it often has been then, there is a better chance. Not that anywhere has arrived but things are always "in the process of" – where the influence is appropriated. This, I think, is a process. You mentioned slavery. I would argue that the Gospel lit a fuse that eventually had an effect on slavery. The more of us that take up the cudgels for current slavery, based on our moral understanding together with Kingdom perspectives and thinking, then big changes can and still need to be made.

I suppose what I am talking about is trying to compare like with like, if that could ever be possible. I take your point about real sacrifice and accept that without qualification. But if you take somewhere like Japan which probably has just as good a per capita income compared with the UK, then we note that the willingness to be generous would not be the same. The approach would be, "That is another country which has nothing to do with us." That wouldn't be the UK approach, although, the more we erode what we started with then I am sure we would certainly get there eventually. I agree, often those with less are more generous than those with more.

I also have been on the receiving end of great generosity from those who have very little in Ghana, in Kenya, in Sri Lanka and in communist times in Poland, where one church pooled their meat rations for the month to feed us for one meal! When looking at the different philosophies that pervade, I am thinking about the "national broad brush scenario."

I mentioned Hinduism. That is a way of thinking. We need to ask, "What does it produce?" Or Communism; "What does it produce?" Or Shintoism; "Does it produce?" Or even Islam; "What does it produce?" Even Christianity, in its broad brush scenario; "What does it produce?" I think if you put a map of the world down and asked the question, "Where has Christianity been? Has it had a national effect for good or evil? Even bad Christianity? Then we need to ask: "where would I rather live?' As a Nigerian said to me recently, "I know there is a lot wrong with the UK, and other countries where Christianity has had an influence. However, I would rather live where they have had that influence than where it has not been."

So I don't think you should give up the cynicism just yet, but rather press for an increase in "real" followers of Jesus, "real" Kingdom seekers who are pulling down handfuls of Kingdom, bringing justice, righteousness, freedom and care. This is what James calls "true religion."

Blasphemy

I note from the Guardian that the Irish Doyle is suggesting that there should be, in Ireland, an extension of the blasphemy laws to include all offences to all religion whatever flavour that may be.
Atheist Ireland, an organisation that claims to represent the rights of all atheists, responded to the new law by publishing 25 anti-religious quotations on its website, from celebrity figures including Richard Dawkins, Björk, Frank Zappa and the former Observer editor and Irish ex-minister Conor Cruise O'Brien, who are all opposing the law by trying to be as blasphemous as possible. I guess they hope publicity from their publication, after being taken to court, will generate more interest in their cause.

If you look at Pakistan, or India or places where blasphemy laws exists, it seems to me that they are often used by people not against blasphemy per se, but rather to settle other scores, such as property disputes, or just to attack people that one does not like. Or, as is often the case, it is used to attack people with another belief system that one does not agree with.

It is also rather strange that we want to stop people saying things against that which we believe. As if what we believe is not strong enough in its essence to defeat such nonsense. It seems to me that if my arguments for what I believe in, or where I get my value system from, are so strong that another's argument cannot stand against it, the other must silence me, or worse -kill me. This seems an extremely strange way to defend one's opinion. Is your opinion so weak that you cannot argue back, and therefore you can only deal with me by silencing me or by my death?

Let me also say that my mail tells me it is not the so called "religious" people who are guilty of such nonsense. I have emails from a very learned atheist telling me that he would like to silence me, and that if he had the power, they would most certainly use it to see to it that my views had no air time! "Soon," he said, "The mental child abuse you inflict upon innocent children will be outlawed." (sent to me by a BA (hons) MA person). This is a direct quote from one of those emails that I received when talking on TV about God. Even when there is televised debate, the view being portrayed is not necessarily dealing with the real argument, those real arguments are often on the cutting-room floor.

I note from the Guardian article that Richard Dawkins is trying to be as rude as possible about God (http://www.guardian.co.uk/world/2010/jan/01/irish-atheists-challenge-blasphemy-law?utm_source=twitterfeed&utm_medium=twitter). As a Christian does his view offend me or upset me? I don't like what he says, and just because he says it, does that make it right? I obviously do not think so. Do I think that I need to defend The God who is there? I don't think so.

I think he is quite able to move to his own defense if He thought it worthwhile, which I doubt.

In terms of the word "Blasphemy," what is the dictionary definition:

Blasphemies A contemptuous or profane act, utterance, or writing concerning God or a sacred entity.

So it seems to me that you can't get a more contemptuous act than that of the crucifixion of God, which is what happened. I think *'The God who is there's answer to that act is splendid. The Resurrection! (*"The God who is there" phrase was first used by Francis Schaefer of the L'Abri community in Switzerland.)

Metanarrative's

Many who read this page probably do not know what a metanarrative is. That does not matter. You will have a metanarrative of your own. The word really means "the big picture." However, we often use it in terms of a paradigm, or "world- view." "What's that?" you might ask. Be assured that even though we don't think about it often, we all have one. And the thing about "worldviews," because it's the way we think, it ultimately will affect the way we live, our actions and all that we seek to do or not to do as the case might be.

There are lots of worldviews out there. Christianity has its world view - its big picture if you will. One's worldview is how you perceive the start and the end of life and all things. Communism has a world view. Atheism has a world view. Hinduism has a world view as does Buddhism.

Very often we do not think about our 'worldview,' yet we are, nevertheless, living by them. When a lot of people adopt a particular worldview it has an effect on our nation, our culture, our laws in fact - it has an impact on everything in life.

There is a great move in the UK and, in fact, in many western countries, to push us into a materialistic worldview.

That world view will ultimately change lots of things if more of us agree with that, even subconsciously accept it, even though we may never have sat down and analysed our "worldview," even though we have, perhaps, never thought about "worldviews" until you read what I am saying now.

I had a small discussion on TV with Richard Dawkins. He got somewhat upset with me when I said that he was a good evangelist for his religion, i.e. Atheism. He, of course, does not see it as a religion. I do, and certainly his religious view will, in its stinging tail, give us a worldview that, if we accept it, will lead us in certain directions.

I don't know if you ever saw the TV series of Faulty Towers, where Basil's car breaks down. First, Basil shouts at the car. Then he beats it with a stick because it won't start. Richard Dawkins uses this skit to explain his "moral" position, and show us how we should act if we hold his worldview/metanarrative. Here is what he says:

"Let's all stop beating Basil's car

Retribution as a moral principle is incompatible with a scientific view of human behaviour. As scientists, we believe that human brains, though they may not work in the same way as man-made computers, are as surely governed by the laws of physics. When a computer malfunctions, we do not punish it. We track down the problem and fix it, usually by replacing a damaged component, either in hardware or software.

Basil Fawlty, British television's hotelier from hell created by the immortal John Cleese, was at the end of his tether when his car broke down and wouldn't start. He gave it fair warning, counted to three, gave it one more chance, and then acted. "Right! I warned you. You've had this coming to you!" He got out of the car, seized a tree branch and set about thrashing the car within an inch of its life. Of course we laugh at his irrationality. Instead of beating the car, we would investigate the problem. Is the carburettor flooded? Are the sparking plugs or distributor points damp? Has it simply run out of gas? Why do we not react in the same way to a defective man: a murderer, say, or a rapist? Why don't we laugh at a judge who punishes a criminal, just as heartily as we laugh at Basil Fawlty? Or at King Xerxes who, in 480 BC, sentenced the rough sea to 300 lashes for wrecking his bridge of ships?

Isn't the murderer or the rapist just a machine with a defective component? Or a defective upbringing? Defective education? Defective genes?

Concepts like blame and responsibility are bandied about freely where human wrongdoers are concerned. When a child robs an old lady, should we blame the child himself or his parents? Or his school? Negligent social workers? In a court of law, feeble-mindedness is an accepted defence, as is insanity. Diminished responsibility is argued by the defence lawyer, who may also try to absolve his client of blame by pointing to his unhappy childhood, abuse by his father, or even unpropitious genes (not, so far as I am aware, unpropitious planetary conjunctions, though it wouldn't surprise me).

But doesn't a truly scientific, mechanistic view of the nervous system make nonsense of the very idea of responsibility, whether diminished or not? Any crime, however heinous, is in principle to be blamed on antecedent conditions acting through the accused's physiology, heredity and environment. Don't judicial hearings to decide questions of blame or diminished responsibility make as little sense for a faulty man as for a Fawlty car?

Why is it that we humans find it almost impossible to accept such conclusions? Why do we vent such visceral hatred on child murderers, or on thuggish vandals, when we should simply regard them as faulty units that need fixing or replacing? Presumably because mental constructs like blame and responsibility, indeed evil and good, are built into our brains by millennia of Darwinian evolution. Assigning blame and responsibility is an aspect of the useful fiction of intentional agents that we construct in our brains as a means of short-cutting a truer analysis of what is going on in the world in which we have to live. My dangerous idea is that we shall eventually grow out of all this and even learn to laugh at it, just as we laugh at Basil Fawlty when he beats his car. But I fear it is unlikely that I shall ever reach that level of enlightenment."

So now I see the moral perspective that the atheist would have us come from, that is the world view.

No responsibility, no blame, a mechanistic world view no less. Let's just fix them or replace them (does that mean we just kill them?) I do think that 'following Jesus' gives us a much more enlightened metanarrative world view. What do you think?

N is for Never

To structure or not to structure, that is the question

The people I mix with have got somewhat bored with, and no longer wish to think about or discuss church structure. That's rather a shame as I believe it is important and perhaps seminal to the current time and the cultural collapse in the West.

If pressed into a debate, they say that it doesn't matter what form of ecclesiology the 'local' church takes, as long as we love God. The problem I have with this train of thought, the sentiment of which I understand, is that tradition and form often has a huge molding effect on our thinking, and thus our actions. And as we know, wrong thinking leads to wrong actions, and wrong principals lead to wrong values.

There are also those who constantly plead for a return to New Testament church practice - as if anybody knows precisely how it was organised. Even if we did, are we going to avoid development and live in the past? A problem with this debate is that the antagonists generally don't distinguish donkeys from Daimlers, or a slave based structure from a democratic society. They also seem to overlook the problems experienced by the early church and its practices. Much of the New Testament was written to correct such practices and problems.

As I often say to theology students, beavering away on their degrees, with ambitions to take up positions overseeing a local community following their graduation: "Hmmm… not quite sure your ideas would work out too smoothly in a church in ancient Corinth. I don't think I would want to be a leader sorting out those crazy values." But idealistic students do tend to have this rosy view of what church life is like, and have very black and white answers on how to deal, "theologically correctly," with problems of church structure.

So we have this rejection of structure, and as I have stated above, I do have sympathy for this point of view when I see what some, "structured churches" are like, or, what I would call "organised religion."

[174]

However, I don't believe it's the structure that is at fault. As human beings, we need structure and regularity in our lives, even if it is only to remember a basic requirement like cleaning our teeth each day.

If you look at history in general, and church history in particular, one can see how it ebbs and flows. There will come a time of refreshment, increased knowledge of God, a renewing of horizontal and vertical relationships. It is followed by a period when man takes over. The whole organism of the church then solidifies, stultifies, settles and secularises. This says more about our sinful nature that seeks money, power and sex, than about the virtue or lack of it in the structure. Ultimately we can even end up allowing God's power to corrupt us so that we rule and lord it over people, bringing them under our control rather than into God's love and freedom. Eventually the organisation or denomination takes on a life of its own, often far removed from Godly values. Power rules and people ask the legitimate question, "Is this how a simple follower of Jesus would act?"

We need to remember the foundational building block which is, Jesus said, "I will build my church." Perhaps we think that as he has gone away and that we should now take up the baton on His behalf. When we do that, what a mess we make! This is because we confuse the "Church" with the "Kingdom." God told *us* to *seek* the kingdom. He said *he* would *build* the church. The church is not the kingdom, and the kingdom is not the church. The church should be seeking the kingdom, which is so much bigger than the church. We get sidetracked *building* the church, when actually we should be *seeking* the kingdom.

The challenge therefore is to be kingdom-minded. Here are a couple of quotations which you may find helpful as you take up this challenge;

"The church gets into trouble whenever it thinks it is in the church business rather than the Kingdom business.
In the church business, people are concerned with church activities, religious behavior and spiritual things. In the Kingdom business, people are concerned with Kingdom activities, all human behavior and everything God has made, visible and invisible.

[175]

Church people think about how to get people into the church, kingdom people think about how to get the kingdom into the world. Church people worry that the world might change the church, Kingdom people work to see the church change the world!" Howard Snyder.

"The Kingdom is a dynamic greater than the church. If you pursue the church you won't find the Kingdom, but if you pursue the Kingdom you will find the church." Simon Markham.

O is for Oh

OH!

A strange story

Some years ago I was invited to speak at a church meeting. My theme was "Getting Involved." Pauline, my wife, was with me and she also spoke along similar lines, emphasising the need for people who call themselves Christian to "get their hands dirty" and care for God's world. James 1:27 (NIV) tells us, *"religion that God our Father accepts as pure and faultless is this: to look after orphans and widows in their distress and keep oneself from being polluted by the world."* I spoke about the shortage of foster carers in England and Wales. Another 10,000 are needed. The people in this community responded in a positive way, and quite a few became foster carers and adoptive parents. 10 years on it's encouraging to see the fine results that those people have achieved.

I got to know one couple very well, and when I went to visit them I was struck by how small their house was compared to how large was their willingness to get involved. I said, "You need more room!" We sat down and looked through their finances, as they had said they couldn't afford a bigger house. I am an eternal optimist when it comes to such things, and so I said, "I think you can - but that's just my optimism. Let me send you a financial advisor to see if he agrees with me." They agreed and my financial advisor went to see them and came to the same conclusion as me, he even arranged a mortgage for them. All that was needed now was to find the right house and sell their small house. Eventually they found a house and when we saw it we were staggered by the size and the extensive land that surrounded it. The price was a stretch for their finances, but after we had prayed together it seemed that this was the right place and would help this couple to achieve all that was in their heart.

Offers were made and accepted. Their small home sold quickly. We were just getting ready for celebrations when there was a twist in the tail. I received a tearful phone call from the couple, telling me that their house was sold, the contract signed, moving in date arranged, but the large house they wanted to buy was no longer available. The seller had called them to say he was removing it from the market. Instead of celebrations, commiserations. Instead of a large house, homelessness. No wonder there were tears and prayer requests.

The next few months were very tough, the couple and their permanent lodger, moved in with a relative who had a house almost as small as the one they had sold. They were living in a nightmare and didn't know what to do next. Then one day, the wife did something very weird. Even to this day she has no idea why she did it.

Her husband cycled to work every day. She strapped a large sack of salt to the back of the bike. Her husband assumed that it was to help him to keep fit, as he was having to push those peddles very hard to propel himself *and* the huge sack of salt. (It was impressed on me how enormous the sack was). At the time she said she had read in the bible somewhere that people who are followers of Jesus should be salt in his world. A rather mumbo-jumbo interpretation of that concept, but because things were so difficult and stressful at the time, the husband decided to humour his wife and kept on cycling every day, with the sack of salt in tow.

The months went by and then I received another phone call, the wife told me she thought she had heard God speak to her. She thought He had told her to take the sack of salt that her husband had been towing around on his bike, go to the house that they had wanted to buy and pour the salt all around the house (outside the property boundaries of course!). To avoid people thinking she was a "nutter," she and her husband drove to the house at around 1:00 am and quickly poured the salt out, as they thought God had said they should. The next morning they received a phone call from the owner of the house saying he had decided to put the house back on the market, and were they still interested. If they were, they could have it at the price they originally agreed. With joy in her voice she told me, "He wanted it to happen quickly. We signed the same day and we are now moving in."

I told you it was a strange story, how can anyone explain that! I went to the house warming celebrations, and over the years joyfully watched their many adopted children growing up in a warm, loving and nurturing environment.

This story remains a mystery to me. I don't begin to understand the ramifications. I only know that sometimes when we are a "follower of the way," God asks us to do strange things, and we do well to obey his instructions. I don't think that gives us an excuse to be weird and off-the-wall. I think perhaps there are enough people around who are like that without you and me joining them. But the moral of the story is how good and pleasant it is when a follower of God is obedient to His request.

Is it just me that thinks this is all Mad or what?

I have listened to stuff recently on the place of woman in certain places. Things like In Saudi Arabia if you are a woman you cannot drive. Very un-womanly apparently. Recently I noted on our local news that in Stamford Hill, a Jewish school was saying that they would not accept new students for the school if a woman drove them to the school.

Again, apparently, women who drive, "lack decorum." What? The London Evening standard reported in what is thought to be the first formal directive of its kind in the UK, that rabbis from the Hasidic sect, Belz, have told women in Stamford Hill who drive that they go against "the traditional rules of modesty in our camp."

Then I hear that Malala was saying that in Pakistan even 13 year olds are in prison because they confessed to someone that they had been raped. Some reports say that up to 80% of women in Pakistan prisons are there because they reported a rape and now have been arrested and placed there because of fornication. By Pakistani law, it seems that, in order to prove their rape they would need to bring to court 4 Muslim men who saw it happen. Each of these four men would be required to be, "of a pious and trustworthy nature."(source The Guardian) Of course, non-Muslim men would not be trusted in their report and neither would a woman! However four "godly" Muslims who stood and watched a rape would be acceptable. Please!

The obvious conclusion is, "Don't admit to Rape or you will end up being imprisoned and receiving lashes." And, of course, that allows men who rape to get away with it and rape again and again with impunity.

Again: Is it just me? But when one try's to argue the case, use logic, or even accept that there might be a different point of view, or even worse that they might just possibly be wrong in their thinking, none of that works even as a discussion point. The answer to my point of view, my logic, and my pleas, is that I seriously ought to be executed and killed, because I do not subscribe to the "right" view of life and the universe. If I can be killed *before* I express my views - all the better. I guess that just demonstrates that my view, and logic is correct and the argument of those who would silence all that do not agree with them are so weak that they cannot tolerate any discussion whatsoever. "Believe what I say or face the sword!" Am I missing something here?

Speaking from one who would be a follower of Jesus, it seems to me that he is putting a nuclear bomb of thought in some cultures with regard to woman. I know that at that time, 2000 odd years ago, a woman in the country of His birth would also not have been allowed to speak in court, she also would have been kept out of sight wherever possible, covered in clothing. She certainly should not have been out of the house if she was ceremonially unclean like the woman who touched the hem of Jesus' garment and was healed.

Jesus obviously did not understand the culture having risen from the dead and asking a woman to be the first one to testify if the event. I know that "Christianity" has tried to perpetuate the whole myth of woman as second class persons, and in my view twisted various people's words taking them out of context to maintain an order that I do not see God supporting. As I say, "Jesus just got it wrong didn't he?"

I also have recently heard a lady on Radio 4 talking about these issues in the Middle East. She went on to say that she was a Muslim, but really felt, culturally, badly treated, put down and misplaced.

She said that she lived in an intense Bible Belt area of the USA, and found that their the same attitudes underlined male cultural values towards woman. Oh! Help! I am sure she is right.

Of course we are trying in some countries to redress this nonsensical balance. But really - I don't see anywhere where we have yet got it right.

P is for Prayer

Prayer Questions

Thinking about Prayer. There are lots of things that puzzle me. Let me ask you some questions.

Why is it that Prayer through the night, all night, is better than prayer through the day, all day?

Why is it that some people have to shout loud when they pray? Perhaps God is a little deaf. That happens when you get older, though it would surprise me if that has happened to God. Though I have to say that I doubt that he is frightened either so shouting probably doesn't bother Him.

Why is it that when some people pray they pray so quietly in a whisper? Maybe it is because someone told them that if you whisper people believe you, even if it is not true, and they hope to catch God out.

Why is it that we close our eyes and bow our heads when we pray? Again as you get older that's a recipe for dropping off.

Why is it that when some people pray they have to scrunch up their face, which they don't do when they are talking to other people? Is there something spiritual about scrunched up faces?

Why is it that when people talk about prayer, and of course fasting, they make a big announcement about it? What is that about anyway, are we trying to twist Gods arm and persuade Him to agree with us? Strange that when Jesus talked about fasting, in that odd instant, He said, "When you fast, do not look sombre as the hypocrites do, for they disfigure their faces to show men they are fasting. I tell you the truth, they have received their reward in full."

I have thought a lot about prayer. When I was a youngster, around my late teens, I got it into my head that praying was very good. It is! However, I went along to our regular weekly church prayer meeting, every Tuesday evening. It was a bit strange really. I was the only one under about 50 years old there.

Most times it was very boring. Let me be honest. The strange thing was, there was one man who always prayed at 8.40pm every Tuesday evening. It was a long, long prayer. Actually I don't really know or remember what he prayed about. I just remember that there were lots of "Father"s, "Jesus," "God," "Lord," "Our Lord," "Our God, "in it. It did seem as though the sentences where joined up by those words rather than, "and," or, "but" or "anyway," and things like that. The thing I noticed was that when he stopped, the leader of the meeting would say, "Amen!" and the meeting would be over.

Now I am older I often wonder why I went there every Tuesday. I guess I thought it was the right thing to do. Perhaps it was. It taught me other things, even if it was not about prayer. Things like patience, stickability and consistence, to name a few.

So! Anyway! These are some of my questions about prayer for you to think about. Maybe you could email me your questions or tell me of your personal puzzling issues about prayer.

Oh! One more thing! Why does God need us to pray? He knows what we will say anyway. Let me tell you a story. I think this is a strange story that happened to one of my prayers.

I was asleep in a guest house in Wales, when I was woken up. I cannot explain quite what I mean by that, but it was a bit like "God shook me" and said to me, "Get up and pray for your friend and He even said his name" I was only in touch with this friend spasmodically. I met him some years previously in Italy. He was Finnish. So I got out of bed and prayed for him, praying I know not what because I didn't really know why I was praying.

I suppose I could have stayed in bed and prayed, but it seemed it was serious, so I didn't. I even kneeled down. That was a bit unusual for me I must confess. I kept talking to God about my friend and finally felt, O.K. God I reckon you have heard my prayer and answered it, whatever the answer is!

By the way this is before emails, mobile phones and text messages, but I did write a letter to my friend and ask him where was he at 3.00am on such and such a date, and what was he doing?

[183]

A few weeks later he wrote back and told me. He said "I was out late at night talking with people about Jesus. Finally I was by myself and a man came up to me with a knife and pushed me down a dark alley. I thought it was the end. He was obviously trying to rob me. I was up against a wall with the knife to my throat, when suddenly he dropped the knife and ran away. I don't know why. There was no one there and no one came to my rescue. Why do you ask."

What I really want to ask is this. God obviously knew what the situation was, and he obviously did something about it - but why should I be involved? I guess I was encouraged by the timing and the answered prayer, even though I didn't know what I was praying for or about, but it's still strange isn't it. Maybe it's because God just loves to involve us in what he is doing.

MONOLOGUE

Another thing: Why is it that, for lots of people, it seems to involve lots and lots of talking? I guess they think it's a one way conversation, a monologue rather than a dialogue.

I have travelled quite a lot and seen many things concerning prayer. Prayers that are written on paper and then pinned to trees tend to flutter in the wind. Lots of religious people seem to have things like beads to pray with. Perhaps these things are helpful. I don't know, but it still all seems like one way traffic. Monologues with God. Once, when I was abroad, travelling in the back of a taxi, the driver suddenly stopped the car, scribbled something on a piece of paper, jumped out of the car and put the paper and some money into a box on the wall. When he got back into the car I was curious and asked him what that was all about. He smiled and told me, "It was a prayer."

In another country, there was a crowd of people around a big glass box with a statue in it. I sidled up to one of the people on the edge of the crowd and asked, "Do you speak English?" I find that's always a good way for me to start a conversation. "Yes," they said with a smile. So I asked him what the crowd of people were doing. He told me"We are praying to our god." I asked him, "Why is your god in a big glass box?" He smiled benignly and explained. "You see, if the god was not in a box, everyone would touch the god, and the god would get dirty!"

[184]

It seems to me that the gospel, the good news of Jesus Christ, his birth, death and resurrection is all about repairing the broken relationship between us humans and Father God. For a relationship to be a real one, it does seem to me that there ought to be two-way communication, rather than just one way.

I know that some people do talk a lot and expect others to just listen to them, but I really don't think God is like that. Jesus said to his followers, "I don't want to call you servants, because a servant does not know what the master is going to do. Instead, I call you friends because you do understand. I have told you what the Father has told me." That's in John's gospel, chapter 15, verse 15.

I don't think that two way communication ended with the first followers. I am a follower and a disciple of Jesus and maybe you are too. I want to know what the Father's business is. Don't you? Yes! I know we have the Bible, but this is a new age and whilst the values don't change some things do. For example, I don't worry too much about falling off a donkey like Paul, but I do worry about crashing my car! So yes, I do want a two way conversation. I think He does too.

So it seems to me that I need not only to talk to God, to pray, but I also need to listen to God to see what He is saying to me.

Let me tell you a little story, I was working with a guy called George Canty. He would sit on the platform in church meetings and often tell me things that were going on in the lives of people sitting in the audience - people he had never met before, and neither had I. I said to him one day, "Why does God tell you these things and not me?"He said, "Maybe you're not listening. Maybe you talk too much." I remember going home, lying in bed and saying to God (praying that is) "God, I do want to talk to you, but I also want to hear you. Can you talk to me?' What next? I would say God spoke to me.
However, it wasn't a voice I heard with my ear. It was more of a perception in my mind. It seemed as though God said to me, "Yes! I will talk to you. I have always been here and wanted to, but you have been busy talking to me and not listening." So, I said to God, "Okay, if this is you talking to me, and not something I am making up in my head, and it's not me having a conversation with myself, help me to know that it really is you."

God said to me, "Well now, what does this verse say?"" and he gave me a chapter and verse in a certain book in the bible. I lay there quite a while, thinking and thinking. Finally, I said to the voice in my head, "Actually, I don't even know how many chapters are in that book. And I certainly don't know what that verse says, even though I have thought and thought."

The voice in my head said, "There is that many chapters in that book, and this is what the verse says …" and the words of a verse ticked through my head. Then the voice said, "You have a Bible right by your bed, on the cabinet. Look it up now and see if that really is what the verse says." I switched on the light, picked up the Bible and thought, "Oh dear! This is not the version I usually read, so what it says in here will not be in the right language, it won't be in the words that I originally learned. I've got this completely wrong. This is just my imagination." And then I heard the voice say, "Did you think that I didn't know what version of the Bible was by your bed!" How embarrassing! I turned to the verse and it said, word for word, what I had heard in my head.

I know God wants to talk with us. Learning to listen is the hard thing. Hearing correctly is sometimes even harder.

Men in White Coats

Let's talk about the problem of hearing right when we are praying. By praying, I mean not just saying things to the ceiling, but an actual two way conversation with God. Of course, I don't overlook the problem these days, that in the west, if you tell people you are talking to God and listening to Him, they might rush you off to a place where they put people who are "hearing things."

That almost happened to me once. One day I was visiting a person in hospital. Actually, they had been sectioned because they were, "Hearing things." I'm not sure where from. I had brought a friend with me to visit the patient. My friend was a doctor of medicine, not psychiatry. We were chatting to the psychiatrist, discussing the prognosis of the patient. My friend happened to mention that he himself had heard from God. I was instantly very nervous. I thought the psychiatrist was going to have my friend sectioned as well.

[186]

Therein lies the problem: Some people are hearing "Things" rather than hearing from God.

Let me tell you a story. This is one of the stories in a book I wrote called, "Hello. Is that you God" which is all about hearing from God. Some years ago I took a crowd of young people to a friend's church. The group were mainly English young people. Most of them were Londoners, born and bred. The church we were visiting was a Ghanaian community. In the past when I had spoken there, they had run their meetings in their own language, providing me with an interpreter. Although the church was based in London and the majority of the members spoke English to a greater or lesser degree, they felt it was easier to run meetings in their first language. On this occasion, as I was visiting with a group of English speaking youngsters, they decided to run the whole service in English. It was a long meeting with lots of singing, dancing and preaching. It was all in English to accommodate the group I had brought along for the experience, and they all seemed to be enjoying themselves.

Towards the end of the meeting I turned to the group I had brought and said, "Isn't it kind of them to run the whole thing in English because we are here." Without exception, they all looked at me with a bemused expression. Then one of them said, "But no-one has said a word of English the whole way through!" It was now my turn to look bemused. I didn't know what they were on about. I said, "What do you mean? they're singing in English now!" "No, they're not. We can't understand a word," they said to me.

As the song went on, I pointed out the words to them. Admittedly, the words carried a heavy West African accent, but gradually the light of understanding dawned on the faces of my young friends. "Wow! You're right," they said, "They *are* singing in English!" My conclusion was that because I had been there many times, and listened to the people sing and speak, I was now easily able to understand the accent and hardly noticed it was there. However, for my friends, this was their first time, something entirely new and their understanding was clouded because of the accent.

It is interesting that the same kind of phenomena occurs in the Bible.

For example, when Jesus was baptised and God spoke to him it is obvious that Jesus heard and understood the words he heard, but for the crowd of onlookers, they just heard a noise, a little like my friends at the Ghanaian meeting.

Then again, in the account of Paul on the Damascus road, he sees a light, falls off a donkey and then hears Jesus saying, "Why are you persecuting me?" Paul clearly hears the words, and his life is turned around, yet those with him didn't hear the words. They said that it thundered. So it does seem to me that sometimes, perhaps many, many times, God is speaking to us, but we don't hear him. What we hear is thunder, or what we think is our own mind, or worse, the effects of the drink or cheese from the night before.

So where do we go from here? Like a young child learning to talk, understanding comes gradually, and takes practice. The same applies to an older child learning a new language, and all its various sounds. It takes practice. Watch a young child experimenting with language. They are practicing. They don't always get it right, but they don't always get it wrong - and the practicing doesn't seem like hard work, it's fun. To hear from God will take practice too. And I don't think talking to God is hard work, it's often just fun. There will be some serious talks, which may not be so much fun, but perhaps that's another subject for a discussion. It would be great to hear your stories and opinions.

Prayer – Serious and Funny

I said above that prayer, i.e. conversation with God, can be seen as fun, not just as what many people see it as? A chore? A pressure? A duty? What a shame, why isn't it fun? Why isn't it just normal life?

Before I tell you about that serious conversation, let me first tell you a story. A good friend of mine, in a sort of half-serious conversation, asked me if I thought that God could or would tell jokes or make fun. I think he was a little unsure of my reaction. I thought about it for a moment and said, "It seems to me that if God is our designer, and we can enjoy jokes, we must have been given a sense of humour. Therefore my guess is that God must also have a sense of humour as he invented us that way."

[188]

I sensed he was relieved by my answer, because his next remark was, "Would you like to hear a joke that God told me?' I wasn't sure what was coming next, but I definitely wanted to know.

My friend told me that he was in a church meeting. He was there because he was taking part in the meeting. However, he was not enjoying it. He was sitting by himself at the back of the hall and feeling really bored. He didn't like it and he didn't want to be there. Nothing that was being said seemed relevant to life. He thought to himself, "This is so boring, I bet God isn't even here." Then he started to pray in a light-hearted way and said, "Father, I don't like this meeting, it's boring. It's irrelevant and I don't think you are even here." My friend said that it seemed God spoke to him and said, "Oh no son. You are wrong. I am here. Omnipresence has its problems." Sitting at the back row of the meeting, my friend had put his hand over his mouth to stifle a chuckle. He said he gave better attention to the people that were there in the meeting after that joke.

So, onto that serious stuff I was referring to. I work in a very busy office with lots of busy people. My wife also works with me, or rather, we work together. Sometimes people give me messages for my wife when she is not in the office, then they say to me the next day, "Did you give your wife the message?" And I answer, "Sorry, I haven't had a chance to talk with her." They often frown at this comment and ask if I actually live with my wife, and if I do, do I actually talk to her. Well I do live with my wife and I do talk to her. However, there is talking and then there is talking. My home, as well as my office is a very busy place, usually we share it with at least four or five other people, so exclusive conversation is not always easy. Both my wife and I understand this.

Sometimes, I will say to my Pauline, my wife, "We need to talk." Of course, I am talking to her in that very sentence.

However, Pauline understands what I mean when I say "We need to talk," and she will respond by saying, "OK! Let's go out for a coffee," meaning, "Let's make personal space," for a sharing of ideas, perhaps making plans, sometimes trying to solve some knotty problem or difficulties that we or others are facing. We use this exclusive time to air our thoughts and ideas in a more in-depth manner.

[189]

This talking time goes beyond our surface conversations which would not work at times like these.

My point when talking about prayer is this: I often take that same approach with God. I find it is possible to talk to God in very general terms and to pray for all sorts of things. I like to think of it as the sort of conversation that goes on between friends all the time. Of course, good friends don't need to be talking all the time. That can be frustrating, can't it? Friends can just be together and not talk. There is even genuine communication in silence.

So, my communication approach to Father God is often the same as with my wife,. Of course we talk all the time at a certain level, but as you can see, there are times when I say to her, "We need to talk." I do that with Father God. I say "God, we need to talk. I know you know where I am at. I know we have had conversations. However, I need to talk to you seriously, and more importantly, I need to listen to you seriously, I need to understand what you want, think and expect from me right now. I need you to help me understand where this situation is going.' That's what I call the serious conversation. That's what we could call "Serious Prayer." However, it's still talking to God, it's still two-way, and actually, sometimes, what God does say to us can be very surprising indeed - and that might throw us - particularly if we have a view on how God works with his friends. But that's another subject.

The great thing about talking to God is that He can share in the fun stuff as well as the serious stuff. We can talk to him on every level, and if we listen, He'll respond to us in the same way.

Who Answers your Prayers?

I have something to say about the strange things that we get in terms of answers from God. I do wonder if we only think they are strange answers because sometimes we have a peculiar view about what God is like. I remember one guy at my theology college praying for hours asking God not to make him marry so and so because he didn't like her. I don't quite know where he got the idea that God wanted him to marry her anyway.

However, I do think he thought that God would only chose things for him that were hard or difficult, or things that he wouldn't normally like. A very strange view of God indeed. And by the way, he never did marry her.

It is very strange how some of us view God. How we view him must colour the way that we expect him to answer prayer. Sometimes, the colour of our perception is so strong that we can't see clearly what He is doing and it blurs how we hear what God is saying to us. I am often surprised when people say what they think they have heard, even if it is something I have said. I know what I said, and I know what they are saying - and I know they have heard wrong. Has this happened to you when you are doing pastoral work. Someone comes to thank you for something you said to them, saying that it really helped them, and you are sure you never said it, but "Hey!" It helped anyway!

The colouring of our views is a very strong thing, or if you want to use a big word, it colours our presuppositions. Those are the things that we have already in us that make us come to the conclusions we come to, whether we realise it or not. Presuppositions make us expect things to occur in a certain way. It is a bit like when you have spoken to someone on the phone and have built up a picture in your mind of what they look like. Then when you meet them, they look nothing like the presupposition. And what a shock that can be. The thing is that we do that with God. And we do it when we pray. We have often presumed the right answer in our head, and often not only the right answer, but even the method of delivery.

I have always loved the story of Naaman in the Old Testament in 2 Kings 5. There are lots of things that can be seen in that story, and maybe one day we could go through it together. However, for now, let us just think about the part of the story where he finally gets to his right destination, the prophets front door.
He knocks on the door and never actually gets to meet the prophet, only the servant, who tells him how to get well from his sickness. If you know the story, then you will be aware that at this point Naaman gets mad because he doesn't like the method that is offered for him to get better. Actually what is happening is that his presuppositions are kicking in and it shows by his reaction.

Naaman says, "This is not what I expected. I thought that the prophet would come out of his house, strike the place of my sickness and I would be healed!' Where did he get that idea from? I wonder if he had been watching too much Christian television! Only joking!

So when we pray what are our expectations of the method of answer, as well as what the answer will be? What are our expectations of what God is like? The thing I think we need to have in mind is that this is the God who said he wants to call us friends. Not only friends, but he wants to be our Father. Not only to be our Father, but He wants to share with us the inheritance of his only begotten son, Jesus. So, what kind of answer would that kind of God give to us?

I think one of the most humbling things that God does to his children, his friends, is to say things like, "What do you think?" or, "What would you like to do?" I often want to reply to God when he says something like that to me, "God, it's little me that you are talking to. Perhaps you think I am making up this idea. Remember, Lord, I'm not like Abraham. You said in Genesis, "This is what I plan to do, but before I do it, let me go and ask my friend Abraham what he thinks." That is amazing, the king of kings, the creator God, asking a mere human for his opinion! But then, if we don't have a presupposition of that kind of God, then we will not, of course, expect that kind of reaction from Him. When God speaks to us in that way, we will be so surprised, so amazed that we will be totally sure that we have not heard from God, but that we have made it up. That's why I say, sometimes God's answers are very strange.

When you think about it, particularly in the area of doing things that God wants, if you love God wouldn't you want to do what He wants. And if you love Him, why should it be a surprise that when we ask Him, "What do you want me to do?' He who loves us, and knows that we love him, should reply, "What would you like to do?" If your desires and actions are coming out of your love for Him, I should think you will probably want to do what He wants anyway. And the more you know him, the more you will get it right, and the end result will be that you will be pleased to do it. God will be pleased you did it. Isn't that great!

Why are some prayers answered and some not?

I have a friend that I worked with, who, when I was with him saw many answered prayers, particularly for sick people. But not everyone was healed. I asked him one day, "Why is it some are not healed and some are?" I have never forgotten his answer. He said, "Lots of people ask me why some are not healed, and do you know what my problem is? My problem is the question: "Why is it that some *are* healed? Why does God answer prayer?" In other words, he was saying he was as puzzled by the answers, as much by the non-answers.

Sometimes prayer can be dangerous. Particularly answered prayer, because that puts us on the spot. If one thinks about it, there are lots of times when God answered prayer in scripture that God didn't want to answer. There isn't time in such a brief article to go into them in detail, but if you know a bit about scripture, you can see them there. For example, God did not want Israel to have a King, but they kept asking and in the end He answered their prayer and gave them Saul. Then the problems started! Then there was another King (Hezekiah) who God told, "Put your house in order, you are going to die." The king begged God, in prayer, for more time. God answered his prayer, but oh! What problems his lengthened life gave to everybody else! So be careful of nagging God for an answer. Especially if God has said it's not a good idea.

I have a little phrase that fits well with prayer. It goes like this; "God will not do what you can do. If you want God to do what He can do, then do what you can do and you will find that He will then do what only He can do." Please don't make that into some kind of doctrine, as God might just do something that you haven't even thought of. However, I do often find people are praying for things that they could very well do themselves.

For example, one might pray, "Dear God, please send my friend that small amount of money that he needs," when actually one has that amount of money in one's pocket, and maybe one should just give it to their friend anyway and say, "Thank you God, that you have given me money that I can now pass on to my friend."

One of the stories from scripture that I think illustrates this well is the story of Nehemiah.

He prays "Oh God! The walls of Jerusalem are broken down. It is such a shame. Do something." He then mentions it to the King, as he was the King's cup-bearer and food taster. The king provides him with God's answer. "Why are you so miserable?" he says to Nehemiah.

It was a very bad thing for a cup-bearer to be miserable. It may have been that the King's wine was poisoned and he was not saying. But obviously the King trusted Nehemiah. It's good when people of the living God can be trusted. Nehemiah told the king what he had been praying about and the King says, "OK, off you go, build the walls up, and I will supply the money and the materials." I am sure that was not the answer that Nehemiah expected when he made the prayer. I do find though, that often God will say, 'OK! Heard your prayer! Now get on with the answer and I am with you!' Scary stuff praying isn't it?

The thing is that God is with us, and I believe that he knows us better than we know ourselves. So, when he tells us to be the answer, or part of the answer, then also we should know that he is not leaving us alone. I remember when I left college to take charge of a church community, I said, "God, I don't mind where you would like me to go. However, please, if you don't mind … I don't want to go to Ireland or London."

After five years in the North of England, the opportunity came for me to move to London. I wondered if God had forgotten my prayer. I decided to go and have a look anyway, and then decided to give it a try, and so we moved to London. I've been in London now for nearly 40 years and I can't really imagine being anywhere else. I just have this feeling that God knows me better than I know myself. I am sure he was not forcing anything on me, but was actually saying, "I know Adrian. If he just tries to do this with me, he is going to enjoy it. I know he thinks he won't, but let's just see, shall we?' And of course God is always right. Sure, praying can have that dangerous edge to it. When God says, "OK, you have prayed. Now I want you to be the answer to that prayer - but I am with you, and because I am with you nothing will be impossible to you. You are going to really feel actual enjoyment doing it for me and with me."

Good job that some Prayer is not answered!

When you start talking about prayer, someone is always bound to ask, "What about prayer that doesn't seem to get answered?" Are they saying, "It's not answered because it's not what I wanted or expected?" And, of course, we mustn't forget that the answer could be, "No," "Yes" or "Wait." It might even be, "That isn't going to be answered because it's the wrong prayer."

I remember praying for a lady who said she was feeling very sick. I was young at the time. At least that's my excuse. I prayed, "Lord, deliver this lady right now." Deliver is not a word I use very often. I'm not sure why I used it at that moment. A few weeks later, the lady came back to me and said, "I'm still being sick. But by the way, the doctor says it's because I'm pregnant." I sent a very quick prayer of thanks to God that he hadn't answered my prayer for deliverance The baby would have been delivered very, very early!

In certain conversations I tend to switch off. I think, "If I start to answer this question I'm going to be here for a month. And this person will be bored after 10 minutes. What's more, it won't be the answer they want. They only want a quick sound-bite." Part of the problem is our culture, but God does not fit into our expectations there.

Sometimes we just don't understand. We might ask a good question, but we won't get an answer, even if the words make sense to us. When my youngest daughter was five, someone asked her a daft question, "Who are you going to marry?" I was impressed with her answer, she said, "I'm going to marry my dad." What a great choice, I thought. But obviously a five year old could not comprehend the concept, and would not have understood if someone had said to her, "No! That's not how it works. As good looking as your Dad is, that is not the person you will marry."

In the Old Testament there was a prophet named Habakkuk, who went into his tower and said, "I am going to pray to God for an answer, and I am not coming down from this tower until I have the answer." God speaks to him about all sorts of things, and he eventually comes down from his tower.

But guess what! The question he asked in the first place, the reason he locked himself away in the tower, that question never got answered. It's almost as though God is too polite to say, "Sorry! Daft question! Answer not relevant. I wish you hadn't asked."" I'm glad that there are some questions He leaves unanswered, and there are also some questions I wish I had never asked.

In the New Testament it strikes me as funny that Jesus rarely gives a straight answer to a straight question. Often he answers a question with another question, or He doesn't answer at all, or answers in a strange way. For example; "Show me a coin. Whose head is that?" In our culture we think we have a, "right" to an answer, to everything, all the time. "And make it short please. We don't want to wait around and be bored. A sound-bite will be fine." Jesus does not fit into this mould.

I notice that, in the Bible, people struggle with the answers that Jesus gives, because their understanding doesn't stretch to His concepts. Just like my five year old not understanding the concept that she couldn't marry her dad.

So, as you talk to God, do be prepared for a non-answer to some of the questions you ask. Maybe, one day, it will be clear - just not today. Rather like my 5 year old daughter. When told she couldn't marry her dad, she replied with irritation, "Why not? I will if I want to!" She now has a husband and three children of her own, so I'm sure she now understands. And one day you will too.

Getting to Know You

My editor tells me that she likes these articles on prayer because I am not giving a 10 point formula for you to follow to get your prayers answered. As I've said before, prayer is a conversation that we have with God, of both light and serious issues. The ability to have that conversation developes as our relationship with God developes. The fact is that the gospel of good news is about a broken relationship being repaired. It's not about following a religion, it's about getting to know a person, Jesus. It's about a restored relationship with God, Father, Son and Holy Spirit because of what Jesus has done.

As with any relationship, you can't treat your relationship with God like a slot machine. You put in a coin and out pops a chocolate bar. You put in a prayer in the right way and, hey presto, the answer appears. It isn't like that. There isn't a set of rules or a formula. Can you imagine a married couple working out their relationship like that: The formula is; I have to tell you I love you three times a day because that's what the manual says. That would be a terrible relationship on the way to a rapid breakdown. Relationships don't work like that, and deep down, you already know that. Relationships are fluid. They develope and they grow, especially where love is involved. The God we want to have a relationship with is a God of love, and loves us passionately. That's a great foundation for building a good relationship, and as we get to know God, our love for him will grow.

I have been married for forty years, and yet my wife, Pauline, still says she is getting to know me and that I still have the ability to surprise her both by my actions and my words. That is what is so special about relationships, they can go on developing and developing.

In a strong loving relationship, sharing with each other is ongoing and on many levels. Gradually, you understand each other. It takes time, but it doesn't feel like a chore because you are developing a relationship with someone you love. Over time you even know how each other thinks. It's just like that with God. As you talk to Him, learn about Him and get to know Him better, you find that you want to share even more with Him, to talk to Him more, to hear from Him more. A formula is the last thing on your mind. You just want to talk to your Friend.

And have you noticed, that in loving relationships people have lover's names for each other, names that only they understand. From my reading of Revelation 2:17, it seems that one day God will give you a name that is only known to you and Him. I like to think this name is his deeply intimate lovers name for you, one of those names that only work between two people who are very close.

Yes, I know these talks are about prayer, but my goal is to switch on the light of understanding to help you realise that prayer is simply on ongoing conversation with God. It's all about developing your relationship with Him. Sharing every detail of your life with Him.

Asking Him "What shall I do?" "What do you want me to do?" Gradually as you get to know Him better, you will find that you are thinking like Him. You are doing the things that please Him willingly because you want to please Him. Eventually, what you want to do will be what He wants you to do because you have spent so much time with Him. He will have affected your thinking and your actions and your desires. You will find that the communication flows, you are in unity, you want the same things, you think the same things, and He really does know your name and you know Him and it's personal and intimate.

Getting to know a friend is not a chore, and having conversations with God will not feel like that either. Here's something to think about: What is your name? And what does God call you?

God Loves to Surprise us!

As we think about prayer and hearing from God, there are some things that we should do. Firstly: Remember. Remember what God has said to us and done for us. We see this, "remembering," frequently in scripture. The Israelis continually remembered the good things that God had done for them, as they celebrated God's actions. If you have Jewish friends you will know that the many things that God did for them are still remembered and celebrated today. It's good to remember.

Secondly: Be thankful. God is with us, speaks to us and loves us. And maybe, we should say "Thank you!" If you have done something for someone, and they don't say thank you, it feels as if they are ungrateful. I notice that people are ready and willing to ask God for lots of things, and I sometimes hear them complaining about what God is doing, or not doing. But thankfulness is in short supply. It's good to remember what God has done for us. It is equally important that we say, "Thank you." We have a friend, the king of kings, the God who is there, the God who is willing to be in a friendship relationship with you and me. That is a very good reason to say thank you.

Thirdly: We need to rehearse what God has done. I like stories. Don't you?

My grandchildren pull my leg and tell me that they know all my stories and all my jokes. The younger ones are not so sophisticated, they like to hear the stories again and again. These stories rehearse and remind us of what God has done and that does us good.

May I tell you a story about a prayer that was answered? My children are now married with children of their own. However, when they were about 7 and 9, they brought home a form for me to fill in, asking for permission for them to go on a school trip which would cost £5 each. It was not a lot of money, but at the time we didn't have much money. We signed the form and they duly took it back to school. A week later, they came home from school and said they needed to take the payment to school the next day. I looked at my wife and she looked back at me with a shrug. We didn't have the money. In the morning, as the girls were getting ready for school, they kept reminding me that they needed to take the money in for the trip. I have to confess it was hard for me to tell them, "Sorry kids. I don't have the money. But I do have an idea. Why don't I come up to the school and ask if we can pay in instalments?" That was just not good enough. They were very unhappy with my suggestion. The eldest looked at me with a stern face, "Dad we need to pay today!" It was 8:40 in the morning, with the kids due to leave for school in five minutes. I only had one answer; PRAY!

I said to them, "I'm sorry kids, I don't have the money, so we need to pray and ask God to sort this out, because your Dad doesn't know what to do and you won't let him come and use his negotiating skills." Their faces were defiant. They definitely did not want me speaking to their teacher about lack of money.

We stood in the kitchen, they in their uniforms, my wife looking on in desperation, recognising that this was something so very important to the children, and me trying hard to put a brave face on it as I prayed. "Dear God, my girls want to go on this trip. I've signed the form and now we can't pay. We are embarrassed - and it's only £5 each. Sorry God, we don't have the money. Please can you help us?" We all said a loud "Amen," and stood looking at each other wondering "What now?" "Let's get you to school," I said, "and I'll come back later and…" I didn't know what to say next.

[199]

It was a very windy autumn day. I opened the front door to leave the house and a gust of wind blew into our hallway, bringing with it a swirling heap of leaves. It was blowing them through the door like a mini whirlwind. I shut the door again, thinking I would wait a moment for the gust to die down. My wife got busy with the dustpan to sweep up the load of leaves and I stood by the door, surrounded by leaves. Then … I looked down and there in the middle of the mess, was a £10 note.

You can talk all you like about coincidences, and question why, just as we finished praying, that the wind had blown it into our hallway. I don't know the answers, but let me tell you my kids were very impressed with God's quick answer. I still remember that it happened. I am still thankful, and I still rehearse the story with those of my grandchildren who are willing to listen to me.

Cheese, Wine, Coincidence, Hallucination, or God?

OK! Last article on P for Prayer. I want to tell you about my book on prayer. It's called "Hello. Is that you God?" If you buy it through UCB I'll throw in "Jacob" free. That's another of my books. But this is not an advert. I want to tell you about the book if you don't mind.

I wrote it because I believe, as I have been saying throughout these articles, that God wants to both listen to us and talk to us, but many people seem to get stuck at the first stage. I also think that many people don't understand when God is talking to them.

I also realise that some people don't even believe that there is a God to talk to or listen to. I feel very sad about that. I wanted the book to reflect the idea that some people do not think that God would really talk to them. So, at the end of each chapter, I pose questions. For example; what do you think is going on? Was that God talking? If not what was it? In many of the situations that I describe, I am hard pressed to think of anything other than it was God speaking to me. I really cannot put it down to cheese, wine, coincidence or hallucination, I believe God spoke.

There is a lady I know in my church community, let's call her Mary, who had purchased a copy of my "Hello" book and she was reading it on the way home. This is what she told me:

"I was sitting on the bus enjoying reading your book and I thought to myself, "It's alright for Adrian to hear from God, but He never speaks to me." Then, do you know what? I heard a voice in my head that said, "That is because you never listen." Mary was more than a little shocked. She prayed a quick prayer. "If that was you, God, I'm listening now. Is there anything you want to say to me?" "Yes," said the voice. "There is a lady two seats in front of you. Go and give her the book, she needs to read it." Mary told me that she just sat there, somewhat embarrassed and a little unnerved. When the bus stopped, the lady got off. "It was not my stop," Mary continued, "but I jumped up and got off as well, and very timidly, I went up to the lady who was walking in front of me, and said, "Excuse me, but God just told me to give you this book." I felt very self-conscious, but she didn't seem at all phased by a stranger appearing at her side and offering her a book. She simply asked me what the book was about, I said it's about hearing from God, and to my surprise, she said she had been thinking about that for ages, and wondering if it was possible. She said she would very much like to read it, thanked me and went on her way."

Another lady I know, I'll call her Sue, received the book from a friend as a gift. Sue said much the same as Mary, "It's alright for the author, but God doesn't listen to me." Sue also heard a voice in her head which said, "Well, talk to me." Sue is a widow, and to make extra income she lets out rooms in her house. She had been trying for many, many months to get a new tenant but to no avail. The agency who had the room listed had not found her a suitable tenant. She lay in bed one Friday evening thinking about the book and then she spoke to God. "Dear God, if you can hear me like the book says, please, please, I urgently need a new tenant for my room. Can you please help me? This room has not been let for months." Sue then snuggled down in bed and went to sleep. Saturday morning at 9am her phone rang, it was the agency and they said, "We think we have the perfect tenant for you." He was and still is.

Was it coincidence or was it God hearing and answering prayer? I know what I think, what about you?

Q is for Questions

QUESTIONS

Progressive Humans

A few of my friends have commented on this subject of late, which has set me thinking. Every so often we have this "**flash**" of how progressive we are today, how clever we have become and how sorry we feel for those older or past that did not have our knowledge and progress. Oh! How civilised we have become!

I think that was the sort of zeitgeist around 1913, particularly in Europe. And then, of course came World War One 1914 – 1918, with all the "civilised" countries of Europe and then the world trying their best to annihilate each other.

Then of course, the talk was that this was the war to end all wars. We would then become civilised. The progress of humanity could continue. We know so much better than those throughout history, our forefathers and the like. The dream was, of course, shattered by World War 2 1939 to 1945, with its mayhem and destruction and inhumanity to mankind by very "civilised progressive humans."

It doesn't take long for things to settle down. I would guess that there was positivity in the 1950's, and certainly, there was "Peace and love, man" in the 1960's, and we are back where we started. The "accident" of the universe allows us to get better and better. After all, we know so much more than those who went before. Yes, we have access to information at the touch of a button, we can get it on the internet. Not that we always remember what we learnt, or even had the wisdom to use what we know, but surely we are getting so much better, so much more civilised. Aren't we? Perhaps we should not mention the Stalin regime, or Pol Pot or maybe Iraq, Syria, Rwanda, Kosovo, Bosnia Herzegovina. Do I need to say more?

I think about our modern propensity to think that we are so much cleverer, wiser and knowledgeable than those who have gone before us. They didn't know much did they?

[203]

Very superstitious and often using God to explain those things that they did not understand. At least, that is exactly what some would have us think.

I am reminded, as I think about this, concerning the "Clever us now," argument - or was it a discussion? –between C. S Lewis and a hypothetical protaganist. He relates it in one of his essays. The question is put: "How silly it would be to imagine that if there is a God, He would be interested in this tiny place Earth. Of course, the argument goes, "in history they looked up and saw the sky and they did not know how large it was, therefore it could seem that the Earth was the centre of the universe. Now, of course, we know better." I imagine Lewis pulling a book off the shelf and reading as follows, and perhaps saying "Is this the sort of thing you mean?" and reading from the book he has pulled. "In relation to the distance of the fixed stars, Earth must be treated as a mathematical point without magnitude." Is that what you mean?"

 I am sure the protagonist would reply "Yes. That's just what I meant. It shows what we now know." Then Lewis, checking, as if he needed to, saying "Oh! This is from Almagest, Book on, Chapter five. It was written by Ptolemy 2,000 years ago, so they obviously knew that then!"

I can hear the protagonist saying, "What about the nonsense of the virgin birth then? We certainly know how children are produced, and maybe Joseph didn't understand." That would be strange," Lewis may have replied, "for then I wonder why, if Joseph did not know the normal course of pregnancy, he would record that on discovering his wife's condition he was "minded to put her away." Matthew 1:19.

We really must stop thinking that those ancient people did not have knowledge, were stupidly ignorant of normal processes of life, and therefore were duped by what the Bible would list as miracles.

Are we really progressive humans, infinitely more knowledgeable, wiser and definitely more civilised?

Where are we now?

VALUES

Many people do not understand that spending a heritage is like draining capital. In this case it is cultural capital.

Many do not understand that our UK cultural capital has been laid down over many centuries via a strong Judeo-Christian emphasis. That does not mean that I believe we have ever been a "Christian country," whatever that means. But we have inculcated values that help us live, keep us safe, make us generous and help us to treat each other with respect and dignity.

Each time a bit of the law of the land reverses that cultural capital, or erodes it by practice, it makes many things harder for all of us. "In what way?" you might ask. Well, in very practical ways. For example:

- The pressure to keep married if you are married. As someone said on Radio 4 question time recently, we have dismantled the family and replaced it with the welfare state and it really isn't working.

- The pressure to stay sexually healthy.

- The pressure to benefit your children with a stable home and good role models both male and female.

- The pressure to stay financially solvent.

- The pressure to care for the stranger who comes into our country.

- The pressure to work and care for others.

We need to understand that these values are in the culture, and actually they did not appear from nowhere.
Recently I was in a government think tank environment and we were asked to come up with ways that OFSTED inspectors could judge if a school is working well "morally."

[205]

OFSTED are required to inspect a school on that issue by UK law. We were told we couldn't change the law, but we could advise best way forward. My problem straight away, was how do you get a moral base unless you have a moral giver, or to put it another way, a lawgiver.

In my group were Muslims, Sikhs, Jews, Hindus, Roman Catholics and some from ACE Christian schools. Oh yes, and one humanist. All agreed, moral imperatives don't come from nowhere, all except that is the humanist. I asked him why is it that Britain is often so generous to other countries who are far away but who are going through natural disasters like earthquakes, or famine or floods. Why is it the British are actually very good givers, yet there are other nations who are as rich as we are if not richer yet they see no need to help? His response was, "That's their problem we have ours."

The humanist argued with all those who expressed any kind of faith, saying to me, "We are generous because we used to be a colonial power!" Hang on a minute. I thought colonialism was, to a great extent, about getting what we could from others, or did I miss something?

Yes, I know it was about trade, and Christians went along as well to share the message of good news, but there was a lot of exploitation too. In the end, I said to the humanist, "I am so glad you disagree with me," (he did on every subject). He looked puzzled and asked why. I said, "If you agreed with me I would think I must be wrong!"

People of a faith may disagree on a lot of things, but they know one thing, and that is moral prerogatives do not come from inside mankind, rather it comes from another source. Each time the culture takes its own, supposedly "amoral" direction, which is more often than not, an immoral direction, we have squandered a little more of our "culture value capital." In the end, we are morally broke, and that's worse than having an economic downturn or financial cut backs or being financially broke.

STRATEGY

I worry about those who think there is no strategy with people of the way, or that we do not need one. I am sure we do, but not one that hems us in, or turns us into 'religious' people, or that becomes humanist, corporate, institutionalised and fixed. We need that Celtic wild goose experience that is God led, and let me tell you He has a strategy.

Why do you think in the early first century, people like Paul set their face toward Rome? It was a lot more than the tourist in him. He knew that Rome, at that time, was influential and he wanted to influence the world. Why did Jesus set His face toward Jerusalem? He was determined to go there. Scripture says it was *THE* plan. It was the Fathers strategy for rescue.

So what is our strategy? It ought to be to influence, to be salt, to be light, and not to attack. Notice, Paul starts at the point where people are. He circumcises Timothy, because he believes that he should be so, not because he was willing to go in that direction, but to enable others to hear him. On Mars Hill, he starts where the people are. He says "I see you have an altar to the unknown God. I have come to show you Him!" Does he start by quoting scripture at them? No! Rather, he says, "Your poets have said..."

Our strategy must not be condemnation, but friendship and cooperation, without letting go of who we are and what we hold dear. How many Muslim, Hindu or Sikh friends do you have? You need them. If you haven't got any then go and find some. Understand them, understand their culture, understand their ways. Not for false compromise, but because scripture says that he that who wins people is wise, very wise.

One of the frightening things that we do is to dehumanise people. We do this by giving humans strange names that make them less than human, which then enables us to treat them as other than wonderful beings made in the Image of God. I noted in the Northern Island troubles that Catholics would refer to Protestants as "Prods," and the Protestants would refer to the Catholics as "Papists," both, in a sense, dehumanising each other.

So, it's almost as if, when you kill them, you are not killing a human being. Phrases also used in war like: "body count," or "Civilian Collateral Damage." For those phrases, read, "Dead people," or worse still, "Mothers, sons, fathers and daughters. The words change our perception. Do not dehumanise people. They are people whom God loves.

VISION

What will it look like?

Do we know what we are looking for? Personally, I want to be obedient to the command to "Seek first the Kingdom of God." If we are seeking it, we should have some idea of what it will look like when we find it. "Our Father who art in Heaven … Your Kingdom come. Your will be done **on earth,** as it is in Heaven." Peace, righteousness, justice, wholeness, let's find it, Let us be the salt/influence that brings it to earth. Let us be a light that shows the way. You cannot do that without being involved in the culture, changing it, seeking the Kingdom in it, in the areas that make and mould the culture, i.e. Education, the Arts and Media, Politics, Business. We can't do any of that, without getting our hands dirty and being involved. That means touching all the people, not just the ones that you perceive are nice enough to become Christians. Whatever that means.

Where The Tax Pounds Go
    http://www.guardian.co.uk/education/2012/jan/15/free-schools-creationism-intelligent-design

It was disappointing to watch the glee with which Richard Dawkins greeted the announcement made by Michal Gove who stated he will not fund any school with tax money that teaches anything about creation in a science lesson (The Guardian Jan 2012).

Disappointing too, was the level of comment by most guardian readers to the article. The content was somewhat juvenile and ill informed, for example, "I don't want my tax pounds to go towards teaching that rubbish!"

I, too, am a tax payer, and 53% of UK citizens think creation should be taught in school. Setting aside the rights and wrongs of the subject, there did seem to be the sound of the jackboot, which in fairness, some guardian readers did say that they could also hear.

I think I could also hear the Taliban style fervour coming from the atheistic religious lobby. Having been in discussion with some of these people not too long ago, on a news programme talking about evolution and creation, one kind man emailed me and said, "I should not worry, we are not anti-God, just anti creationism in Science." You, sir, were very kind, but in general that has not been my experience. In fact, quite the opposite. Not only would this lobby like to remove creation from being taught anywhere in any shape or form, but please, (although they almost never say please) you shall not mention God at all anywhere. We have seen this kind of thing before, in Albania, in Romania, in Russia and for decades in North Korea, and see what accepting and balanced societies that attitude produces.

At least Richard Dawkins was honest. When questioned about the morals of Hitler, he replied "What's to prevent us from saying Hitler wasn't right? I mean, that is a genuinely difficult question. But whatever [defines morality], it's not the Bible. If it was, we'd be stoning people for breaking the Sabbath."

It's the arrogance that I find so difficult to swallow. Either you agree with me, or you should be silent. And yes, I have been at the receiving end of such statements. I have been told by certain people that if they had the power they would do all they could to silence me. What are they so afraid of? Richard Dawkins seems to spend more time attacking a God in whom he does not believe than anything else.

A world view is bound to colour our expectations and the way we look at things, mine has been coloured and I freely confess to that. The problem is that the atheistic lobby admits no such colour. They are speaking truth, as they see it. They have been everywhere, understand all things and clearly there is no God. Should those who have met the God who is there, say anything that opposes this view, they are ridiculed mercilessly, and told how stupid they are.

I recently listened to a radio four science programme in which two eminent scientists discussed a recent science exhibition. Towards the end of the programme the interviewer said in a friendly manner, "It's quite interesting isn't it that one of you is a Christian and one of you is an Atheist yet you are both equally qualified and in the same discipline." He asked the Christian what he thought about that, the Christian replied, (and I paraphrase) "Well I am a follower of Jesus and that of course affects my world view." He asked the same question to the Atheists who responded, "No person who says there is a God, or calls themselves a Christian can be a genuine scientist."

I wonder about these people. They are so sure there is no God and yet are afraid when we so-called idiots believe that God is there, and very involved in His world. Why do they get so hot under the collar when we believe God is behind the whole idea of Earth and human history? If it is all so terribly stupid why are there draconian attempts to regulate and silence us? Are we that fearsome?

I am finally reminded of the song writer in Psalms 14:1 and 53:1 Amp Ver. "The empty-headed fool has said in his heart, there is no God."

Power

It's an old adage and probably correct, that power corrupts and absolute power corrupts absolutely!

Thinking about the subject, I am somewhat puzzled by a.) The unwillingness and fight against federalism in the UK. "We don't want it at any price,'" seems to be the politicians' mantra. What is the difference, Scotland, London or Wales? b.) Isn't that localising government some form of Federalism?

The plus side say that you bring government and decision making down to the local people and that must be better. The negative side, from my opinion, is that what actually happens is that it is easier to be a big fish in a small pool than a big fish in a big pool, and so we get small, narrow minded, power hungry, "I must protect my insecurities by projecting power," kind of people which actually is not beneficial to anyone. Is that not what happens?

Working in Social Services and connected areas, I constantly come up against (and it may be because where I work is small and local) the power hungry, insecure people who are splashing their power around, often wrongly, often with damaging results. They love to tell me their qualifications, and who they are pointing at. That is why their decision will stand, whatever Minnows like me think – and it will not be considered if, maybe, I just might be correct. That does not matter - they have the power.

One senior management person recently said, on being confronted about caring for the staff that worked under him, "I don't care about my staff." Great! I hope they don't have the investors in people mark. And how stupid not to know that caring for staff is the best way of getting a good job done.

I have to say that the other people I find I constantly clash with are social workers. They always love to tell me that they are qualified (not that all their qualifications attained are very good ones). Is that coming from their insecurities? One of them reminded me why we started an agency for foster care recently. Having fostered for a local boroughs, and observed several boroughs, and talked with many foster carers, the thing that I noted was partly, that social workers were very busy, carrying too big a case load. So, by default, the foster carers did not get looked after well. Foster carers are very aware of that. My thinking is, one has to look after the careers as well as possible, that way they will look after the children as well as possible. It is not a case of look after the children and forget the carers or look after the carers and forget the children. It is neither. It should be both. So as I was saying, one of them recently reminded me of those things, on a dispute on what should happen. They said "I really don't care about foster carers, they are just paid to do a job." My opinion? Completely crazy! It is the power factor badly at work again.

So these little fish, have a degree. They are now so qualified, they are the fount of all knowledge. And so, it does not matter about anyone else's opinion, be they good staff or great foster carers or just the Minnows who happen to be on the receiving end of this power projection. They have the power.

[211]

So my question is: Is it better to have the large pool where it's harder for these insecure fish to get to positions of power, and badly use it?

Or: Is it better to have a big pool where maybe the insecure don't quite swim to the top so easily and therefore power is exercised with more thought and care.

R is for Relationships

RELATIONSHIPS

Days out in the country

Claverdon Nr Henley in Arden

In the early 1960's I was part of a team of young people who wanted to see change. The team, by the way, was call Ribbons of Faith (RoF). Please don't giggle. Cut me some slack! It seemed like a cool name at the time. We planned to change the world! I don't know about everyone else, but I still do.

Changing the world can be laborious, and sometimes just persuading people to come and meet "The best Friend you could ever have," is harder that you expect.

One of the team members, John Moore, became very concerned with the fact that the villages of the UK did not seem to know much about our "Best Friend." He wanted us to do something about it. We couldn't think of anything imaginative, so we decided to go to a picturesque little village called Claverdon, about 30 miles from Birmingham. The village didn't have much in the way of a centre apart from a community hall and a big Anglican building. We got to know the local Rector, Canon Ross, who welcomed us with open arms when he heard what we wanted to do. He gave us the community hall for free, to use once a month for whatever we liked. And so we began to see if we could get Claverdon folk interested in meeting Jesus.

All we did was walk around the village and knock on everyone's door to say "Hello." We had a newspaper, funnily enough called Challenge, which we gave people to read and also offered them books by Billy Graham. The community hall became our lunch centre as we trundled into town from the big city. Our convoy usually consisted of three vanloads of people.

[213]

Why was it funny to be using a newspaper called Challenge? Three young men, who we did not know very well, offered to come and help us distribute Challenge newspapers. We thought this was kind of them and gratefully accepted their offer. After three months, we discovered they were distributing the communist newspaper of the same name. This did not make us popular in middle class Claverdon as their demographic was definitely not pro-communist.

Today I believe that the UK has changed considerably. There is a new openness towards spirituality, not only Christianity, but spirituality in general. In the early sixties there was a much greater resistance to anything connected with God or spirituality. I am glad of the change taking place.

As a result of the sixties resistance, our door knocking in the middle class village often resulted in a very polite English response which included a smile, but the subtext was an unmistakable brush off. "Oh! How nice for you. Now, please go away. We are very happy in our lostness. Please leave us alone." Nevertheless, month after month we went back although we appeared to have little response.

Billy Graham came to the UK in those days and this seemed like a golden opportunity for our team. We continued to knock on doors and we booked some large coaches. When people opened their doors we offered them an invitation and a free ticket to come with us to hear the American evangelist who was coming to London.

The outcome was that we filled three coaches, we went to London for the day with our villagers, and many of them made a real commitment to Christ at the Billy Graham meeting. This was not the end of the story. We continued to go back to the village, but now the villagers themselves were reaching out to their own neighbours and introducing them to their new found Friend.
 The Anglican Church was blessed and we felt that contact was worthwhile. This one village had received some impact from the good news that is Jesus.

First Principles

When I was in college, one of my assignments was to write a thesis. I forget how many words it was, but I do remember it was a lot! It is probably still gathering dust somewhere in my loft. My subject was "Man qua is a Religious Being." I won't bore you with the intricate details of my thesis, which was a very fat tome indeed. I will just give you the fundamental and interesting principal. Wherever you look, no matter which country you are in, or which people group you associate with, man has this need to worship, or desire for "a god"; the "atheist" is a very small and recent phenomena.

The fact that we need a god to worship is often considered to be the element that produces religion. My thesis concluded the reverse. My point was that religion is man's way of trying to find God, and of course he may not succeed. The reality is that God is not into religion, He is into revelation and, ultimately, relationships. I have no intention of being unkind about different religions, but I do think that sometimes man worships the most bizarre gods, which seem to me to be more the stuff of fairy tale and legend than anything to do with the rationality of God. I did ask in one country why the god that many people were praying to was in a box, I was told that if the god wasn't kept in the box he would get dirty!

In our search for God we need more than religion, we need revelation. We need God to say, "Here I am. This is what I am like, and this is what I am doing in my world. This is how I see you, and this is what I am looking for from you, and with you." From my perspective, this is what happened when Jesus came, the Word of God, became flesh (a man), and the Word (Jesus) said, "If you have seen me, you have seen the Father (God)." He also said, "I don't do my own will, but the will of the Father (God) who sent me." In other words if we want to know what God is like, we need look no further than Jesus.

Jesus shows us how, "The God who is there," deals with sin, sickness and most importantly, broken relationships. Ultimately, Christianity, if you want to use that word, is not about religion, but about relationships and those that are broken and who cause us pain.

[215]

The vital relationship that is broken is the one between man and, "The God who is there." This relationship is fractured because sin, and especially the sin of rebellion. We wanted to be in charge of ourselves, no matter what mess we might make. We wanted to be god. That is why we end up making gods in our own image, rather than looking at what has been revealed by the Word, Jesus. We also need to be careful not to make Jesus into who we think he is, rather than who he truly is.

In the beginning, it is obvious from scripture that God was in very close communion with mankind, talking, walking, and being in relationship with him. Rebellion said, "I want to do it my own way." Thus the unique bond was broken. But God was desperate to mend the fracture, and so he took drastic action. The restoration of that relationship required the death of God Himself.

Ultimately, "Real Christianity," is as far removed from religion as the east is from the west. The reality is that it's *all* about relationship, a restored relationship with "The God who is there," making us aware that he is not far away, and can be within us, listening to us, interested in us, talking with us, guiding us and, most humbling of all, asking us for our opinion! He says to us, "What do you think?" Because the relationship has been broken for so long it takes time to get to know him again. Just as any broken friendship takes time to be repaired. The amazing thing is that as that key relationship is restored with Him, He then helps us to restore relationships with other people.

God extends his grace (undeserved favour) to us. That means He is constantly reaching out to us with forgiveness and blessing, often crediting us for our intentions rather than what we actually delivered. We, in turn, need to learn how to pass on grace to others.

My conclusion of a first principal about relationships is knowing that, "The God who is there," is all about relationship and very little about religion. It's about knowing Him, talking with Him, being with Him, and of course, being with His friends. I like being one of God's friends!

Principle in Action

We have established that being a Christian is not at all the same as being religious. How does that work out in practice, or at least how should it work?

One of the major problems is that over the centuries we have made Christianity much like a religion. Perhaps it was Constantine's fault as much as anybody's. However, we cannot lay all the blame at his door. It's time for us to think for ourselves, and if necessary, to change. And if possible, influence others to change. It is vital that we do not accept the "norm," that we don't maintain the status quo. Rather let us be alternative.

Jesus said, "This is how everyone will recognize that you are my disciples—*when they see the love you have for each other*." (John 13:35 TM)

The word, "love," has some strange connotations in western culture, and especially its use in the English language. We love each other, we love our children, we love our boyfriend or girlfriend, and we love tomato ketchup. We use the same word for all of it. When marriage breaks down, we say we have "fallen out of love," whatever that means.

The bible talks about the fact that Jesus loved us enough to die for us, "while we were still sinners." In other words, while we did not like Him, know Him or love Him, in fact, while we were actively rebellious against Him, He loved us enough to die for us. That is amazing and real love!

Love, of course, has its emotional element, but ultimately, real love is an act of the will. The love that God has for us, and the way that he wants us to love each other is a love that is consistent and unwavering. It is a love that keeps on loving even when that love is not returned. That is how God loves us. "That's hard," I hear you cry! Yes, I agree. That's why we need that kind of love to be put into us by God. We are not very good at that type of love are we?

But we are very good at the namby pamby sort of love that falls away when the emotions fade, the type of love that when tough times come, pops like a soap bubble.

The love that God has for us keeps on flowing even when it is not returned. Let me be clear: that does not mean that in our loving relationships nothing is questioned or challenged. That's the namby pamby type of love. Real love challenges and does not accept wrong. It does not say in a friendship, "Because you are my friend, and I love you, I will bless you whatever you do or say, always going along with anything and everything you say and do." The Bible says that, "You are blessed when you receive wounds in the house of your friends." That is a strange saying that means friends who truly love you will tell you the truth, and will let you know when they see you going off track. They love you enough to help you get back on the right path.

That's the theology - the theory - but how does that work out in practice? People often say to me, "I have real problems at work, or college, or school (you fill in the blank) because I am a Christian." But I think to myself, "Actually, that is not the case at all. The truth is, you are an awkward person, someone who is very difficult to get along with." I rarely voice that, but nonetheless I think it. From experience, I know that voicing it can often make matters much worse. I do try to be a little more tactful.

These same people will also say, in the presence of others they perceive to be Christians, "God has accepted me as I am, so you must too!" In these instances I usually do have something to say. Something like, "Sure! God loved you while you were rebellious and not even liking him. However, because He loves you so much He does not want to leave you like He found you. His plan is to change you. Actually, his ultimate plan is to make you like his unique son Jesus. And to do that He uses your friends as well as His Holy Spirit. These change elements, over time, will rub off your rough edges, and I will not let you cop our by trying to stay as difficult as you are at the moment."

If we are going to have real love in our relationships, then we will carefully correct each other, giving and receiving advice and guidance in love.

But this correction tactic is to be used gently and wisely and not as a weapon. Sometimes, when a so-called friend says, "I love you but ..." you know it's time to swiftly don that hard hat! We must earn the right to speak. Before we can speak, we need to know that person, understand the path they are walking, recognise their struggles and avoid a judgmental heart at all costs. Our example is Jesus. He showed us He loved us long before he brought about any change. That showing must come before the telling!

We need that "70 x 7" approach to forgiveness that Jesus speaks about.

I also think we need faith. It's odd how much easier it is to have faith for stuff like money, cars, jobs and events - but so very hard to have faith that people can change and be different. However, we need to have that expectant faith, that God can and will do new things in our friends, as much as we need to have faith that God can change us.

That's all it takes. Let's start having God's love in our relationships. Let our love for others be so clear that no-one will be in any doubt that we are his followers.

The Principle of Judgment

I am sure you must have often heard that frequently quoted phrase; "You mustn't judge!" When questioned, people will quote the bible verse saying, "Judge not, or you will be judged." Actually it does not say that. What is says is, "Be careful of your judgments, of how you judge, because the way that you judge others will be the way that you are judged." It goes on to say, "How can you take a speck of dust out of someone's eye when you have a great big plank of wood jutting out of yours."

The fact is, we all have weaknesses and strengths, and in the body of Christ it is good to collectively use each other's strengths. We must also help each other in our various weaknesses, and to some extent that will involve judgement on what is weak, what is strong, what is good and what is bad. I am not talking here about sin. That is rebellion. I believe if we love God we don't really want to live in rebellion. However, we do make mistakes.

[219]

We do have weak areas, some of which are simply practical things. For example, if you are trying to book an appointment with me, I will often ask you to speak to my wife. I don't know why it is, but booking dates is one of my weaknesses. I can book myself into meetings on three continents, with only 10 minutes between appointments and often see no conflict. It's not helpful to say, "That's a weakness. I don't do that." I need to protect those who are booking appointments, but I also need to try and improve that area, and I am - trying that is.

Often we are guilty of judging others by their actions and ourselves by our intentions. We give ourselves credit when things go wrong by saying, "At least my intentions were good." The fact that we didn't achieve what we were attempting to do is passed over because we, "had good intentions." The flip side is that we often do not extend the same kind judgement to others. Instead, we judge the action, or the outcome of the action, and never bring intentions into the equation. Funny that, don't you think!

Some years ago, our leadership team set up a meeting with a group of people because we wanted to discuss with them their situation. They were people we wanted to help. However, we were unsure about how to do this. They had ongoing problems which usually led them into bad situations. We were honest with them. We told them we wanted to help, but did not know what to do next. Some of them got mad with us. They said they didn't have a problem. One or two of them broke down in tears and said, "Please tell us what to do. We want to change." Guess who got the best out of that situation.

Real relationships, real friendships must mean that we tell each other the truth, not because we want to hurt or destroy, but because we want the best for each other.
 We want our friends to succeed and to reach their potential. Dr. Donald Howard said, "'Discipline is not something you do **to** someone, it is something you do **for** someone." In the words of scripture, Father God says that he only discipline those he loves, lack of discipline indicates lack of love.

That's all very well. Nevertheless, I am sure, like me, you have been in those situations when someone approaches you and tells you that they need to talk to you, and you can tell from their tone and their body language that they are going to put you right, which they do, and for good measure. They tell you that they are only doing this because they love you. But you don't feel loved. And perhaps, like me, you wish you had metaphorically reached for your hard-hat and bullet-proof vest, because you know you are about to, "get it." The truth is, we need to get to know someone - really know them, as a true friend, in a real relationship before this type of conversation can be effective, fruitful and as pain free as possible. It is only within real and loving relationships that we can properly hear those hard things, and even then, it's not easy.

I know my wife loves me, but if she wants to, "put me right," then I have to swallow hard and listen, then agree that, yes, she is right, and something needs to change. But I am more likely to try to change because the words have come from someone with whom I have a real relationship, rather than someone who smothers their correcting punch with the pretence of doing it in love. The basic problem is that even if they are correct in their judgement, because I am not in loving friendship relationship with them, or them with me, it is going to be very hard for me to receive it.

I like to think of it in this way, that we, "earn the right to speak." Many years ago I lived in the north of England. In the church community there was a lady who was very hard to get on with. She was quite gruff in her approach to almost everyone. As I got to know her, I discovered she had a soft heart inside and a willingness to try to help make my life easy in whatever way she could. She was still gruff, but looking past that gruffness I discovered her heart and her intentions. Many times people said to me, "Why do you listen to her? You even try to do what she asks. She is such a difficult person. Why do you do that?" My response was always the same. "I know her. I know that she really cares. That's what makes the difference. I know she wants the best for me, and that's what counts." We had formed a real relationship, she had earned the right to speak and because of our friendship, I could hear what she said.

God loves us too much to want to leave us as we are. He plans change for our lives. To activate that change He uses our collectiveness to bring it about, our love for one another, our good judgement of one another, our willingness to care for each other. As we care for others, we also care how we affect others, and we want to change bad habits and wrong directions. But for this to work effectively, there must be real friendship and real love. "This is how people will know you are my disciples; because you have *Love for one another!"*

The Principle of First priority

We have talked about meetings and the reason for them. Now let's now take a look at what I call the "Principal of First Priority." What is the most important command for people who follow Jesus? We have discussed other commands, for example the need to love one another. But what is the first priority, or primary command? It is that we, "Seek first the Kingdom of God and his righteousness." With this command is a reward. God says, I know that you need lots of other things, but seek me first, and everything else will follow on.
I used to think that there was no difference between the Kingdom and the church. I have strongly changed by views on that issue. Seeking the Kingdom is not the same as seeking church. Someone recently said, *"The Kingdom is a dynamic greater than the church. If you pursue the church you won't find the Kingdom, but if you pursue the Kingdom you will find the church."* (Simon Markham with adaptations from Howard Snyder) God is at work in his world. The Kingdom has come, although not yet in its fullness, but it *is* here, and has broken into this time-space world. We have the ability to pull down handfuls of his Kingdom that can impact and change situations.

I appreciate that is a bold statement, that we can grab a handful of the Kingdom. Let me give you a couple of examples to help you understand what I mean. Sometime ago one of our leadership team came home very tired. We were due to go to a meeting together that evening, but when I looked at him closely I could see he had had a bad day. I asked about his day. Had it been tough? He told me it had been terrible. One of his colleagues had been sacked and blamed for not completing a task for an important project. I asked, innocently if he believed that his colleague was at fault.

[222]

My friend told me, "No! It was not his fault at all." I asked "Did you speak up for him?" He told me, "You don't understand. If I had done that, perhaps I would have been blamed, and I would have lost my job." My response was blunt. "You missed out on doing what we are supposed to do as first priority: Seek first the Kingdom of God."

My friend was not happy with my response, but I needed to say what I believed to be right. I needed to state where it's at!
What we know as The Lord's Prayer gives us a clue to what the Kingdom looks like. That is helpful, as we need to know what we are seeking. The prayer says, "Your Kingdom come. Your will be done on earth as it is in heaven." From my perspective, heaven, or where the rule of the Kingdom of God is, will be a place where there is justice, righteousness, peace, love, goodness and wholeness. Therefore, it follows, that if we see those things missing on earth, we need to "Seek the Kingdom." My friend could have grabbed a handful of Kingdom. He could then have sprinkled justice and righteousness into the meeting, but he was afraid.

Here is another example. For many years my wife and I fostered children. One of the young ladies we fostered had, due to her lies, caused much trouble for Social Workers. Some had even been dismissed. In one of the meetings that regularly take place with Social Services when you are a foster career, I became convinced that the young lady was on the same tack. I strongly believed that she was on a campaign to get the current Social Worker dismissed, or at the very least, in serious trouble. I was also convinced that what she was saying was untrue.

During the meeting, out of the blue, my wife said to the young lady, "Does your boyfriend ever do anything wrong?" "Yes, of course!" she responded quickly. "And do you forgive him?" my wife asked. "Of course I do. He's my boyfriend." My wife then put the young lady on the spot. "Could you, on this occasion, forgive your Social Worker?" The girl fidgeted, aware that she had been cornered. She then looked at the Social Worker. "Yes. I could forgive you." At that the meeting concluded, although I couldn't help but notice a queue of people lining up to ask my wife about this new method of conflict resolution. However, the truth is that it is not a new method. It is just bringing the Kingdom of God into our space time world.

[223]

How does this story fit into a series of articles on relationships? It troubles me that there are those who think relationships are the be all and end all. Everything hinges on being together, so a lovely shared dinner, in a cosy environment, is the sum total of life. We meet because we meet and that is all there is, that is the point of everything.

I believe relationships are incredibly important, perhaps the most important thing of all in life. Nevertheless, surely we ought to be together for something? What about mission? Shouldn't our relationships be about doing something, seeking The Kingdom? Then we would come together to equip each other, and support each other as we mutually seek The Kingdom. I can already hear some of you retorting, "Oh how task orientated! How terrible! We just need to chill! We need to learn to be. We are who we are not what we do." Yes, and No. Who we are often leads on to what we do, and what we do together. If you can, imagine a couple who meet every night, but never do anything together. Very boring! And I strongly feel the relationship would flounder.
I think we are in this God relationship for a purpose - His purpose. I think all our other relationships also need purpose - His purpose, which ultimately becomes "our" purpose.

And that purpose? To be doers, not just hearers of His words. To be Kingdom seekers in relationship with God and each other.

The Principle of the collective

We have looked at the first principals of relationship. Now we need to look at how that should work out in practice. Let us look more closely at the issue of collectivism; the coming together of the followers of Jesus. This subject, for some at least, looms large and is discussed widely. It is the whole action of meeting.

I hear some crazy discussions about meetings which are not sound arguments. They are reactionary and emotive, and not based on solid reasoning and good understanding. One phrase I frequently hear is, "I love God. I am a Christian, *but* there is no need for meeting with other Christians."

[224]

A very strange and unhealthy comment which is diametrically opposed to what the bible says, which is "Let us not give up meeting together, as some are in the habit of doing." (Heb 10:24 NIV)

At the opposite end of the scale of the "Meeting" debate is the feeling that we have ended up with "meeting-itus," or "meeting for meetings sake." Meetings have become the standard mark of "spirituality." If you are not at the meeting then you can't be truly spiritual, whatever that means.

What is the purpose of meetings? To comfort preachers who need to see lots of 'bums of seats'? To make sure that the offering is taken? I also hear people say, "I love God, but I hate church." I find this hard to swallow, simply because the Bible says that, "Christ loved the church and gave himself up for her" (Eph 5:25 NIV). Although I do have sympathy with some of these expressions and feelings, I don't think that they are well thought through.

So yes, I do have sympathy for those who get tired of pointless meetings, but another friend of mine has this simple quote with which I wholeheartedly agree: "The answer to wrong use is not, "no use," but, "right use!""

The other problem is our perception of church, which is not the building, but of course, you know that don't you? But then we announce, "I am going to church." How can you do that? You *are* church. Christians, singly and collectively, are the body of Christ, or church. So you can't "go to church," you can only *be* church. That, of course, does not mean that you don't need to meet!

Why do we need to meet? Quite simply because one cannot form real, long term relationships via Face Book or My Space (although I am sure there are some that think we can.). I am reminded of the little child who wanted her mother to stay with her at bedtime until sleep arrived. The mother said "I can't stay. I have lots of work to do. But don't worry, God is with you all the time." The wise child replied, "I know that, but at the moment I want someone with skin on!"

Real relationships require contact; real contact between real people, and that includes all of us, with our hang ups, foibles, peculiarities, difficulties and awkwardness, as well as the positive aspects that we all have of being, "just lovely."

The development of real love requires that we connect with each other physically, not just over the ether via our favourite social networking site, but with our skin on, in real time. We need to get to know each other, to explore each other's needs and to benefit from the gifts that God gives to each of us individually. These gifts strengthen and develope the church, that is, us. Certainly the videos, the blogs, the books, the CDs all have their place, but nothing can totally replace that personal contact, and you cannot get that without meeting.

The final question is: What kind of meeting should it be? The answer is very broad, from a formal meeting with a timetable, to an informal, "Let's see what happens" meeting when we worship and pray together. There are, "learn together," meetings, "share our stories," meetings, and meetings when we just want to be together and provoke one another to LOVE. Then there are the meetings when we just hang out together and have fun.
Whatever we do, we don't want to be meeting just to have a "meeting," i.e. the, "Hymn-prayer sandwich," type meeting, the "meeting I must go to in order to look spiritual meeting." All the other meetings I have mentioned have a purpose. But no one was proposing anything else - were they?

S is for Sex

Sex and the Robbery that takes place in our Culture

How to write this? It's not an easy one, realising as I write that to say what I believe to be going on, in terms of robbery, will be both counter cultural, and it will also put the backs up of those who think themselves to be "scientifically superior," to other mortals.

Let me start by saying that what is being taught educationally, and absorbed without too much question by the general population, perhaps even unknowingly absorbed, helps us to act in such a way that we are robbed.

What am I talking about? Educationally, there is a strong push that would have us believe that we are, "just an animal," and when we take that on board, it becomes, "normal," to act like one. Therefore **robbery number one** takes place. We are robbed of what should really be human sexuality and its richness, and taught to settle for something a lot less valuable. And the **robbery** does not end there. Another line that we are sold, educationally, is that we are all just part of "the great machine," and therefore all sexual acts are really just the machine in process. It causes one to wonder why we should take any responsibility for any action we make, doesn't it? It is just the brain firing neurons that gives us the reactions, "ultimately no meaning," "just part of the machine," "luck," "the accident of nature," "somewhat of a bad joke," or, as they say, just an add-on of the "goldilocks theory." Again, serious **robbery** takes place if your sexuality is only understood like this, even if you have not thought it through, but are subconsciously acting as if this were the case.

Within our current culture it is a trend to think that sex is fun, (which it is of course) and therefore, does not need to be taken seriously. It encourages the belief that, "If I have lots of one night stands and take precautions, then that should be fine." **Robbery** is taking place at this point, and the whole of sexuality has been devalued. You are by these means, **robbed**.

[227]

In saying that it does not take into account all the STDs that are on the increase, and for females, there are even some that do not seem to have very clear symptoms, yet could carry infertility and heartache up the road. Yes we do know that these STDs are there, and if we look, we know that they are on the increase in our society. Yet, are we taking this seriously? The statistics suggest that we are not! **Robbed again!** This is probably, because we just do not take note.

So are we on the right track? Is sex just an animalistic or mechanical function ... one that does not really matter? Or are we, by acting in accordance with our cultural leanings, namely, "Everyone is doing it," being seriously **robbed**?

My thesis is this. Sex is for marriage, and it should be fun! When it takes place outside of marriage, and in terms of the mechanical or animalistic "fun" approach for a night out, then all sorts of other things are taking place. Never mind the risk of STDs (according to the statistics which I quote below). What happens is quite strange. First of all there is the creation of what I call "brain DVD's" which have the power to impinge on future sexual relationships, often detrimentally.

Then there is the **real robbery. W**hat I call the terrible devaluation of sexual relationships. Sex, you see, is much, much more than a physical act. Interestingly, Biblical scripture likens the act to the relationship that is created between Christ and the Church, and pushes it up to an extraordinary high level. In another part of scripture it talks about our physical bodies being linked into Christ. Why would we then like to link that to a prostitute, male or female? 1 Corinthians 6:15 *"Do you not know that your bodies are members of Christ himself? Shall I then take the members of Christ and unite them with a **prostitute**? Never!"* I hope that you can see that the level of sexual relationships is being ratcheted up. It's not simply a physical act. It's not simply a mechanical act. Within the act is a high level mystery that has eternal symmetry, and it has clever typology built into it. There is spirituality here that, when sex is treated lightly, robbery is taking place. What is said in the Bible, is that sex has a soul element to it?

[228]

My observation is that when used correctly, lovingly and, of course, with imagination and fun, sex in permanent, committed relationships has the ability to draw a couple together in stronger bonds of understanding and development. It goes beyond the physical act to a soul connection, which can be much more satisfying and exciting. When used wrongly, I note that, what frequently happens, this act causes division, and often hatred in those who use it that way. **Robbed!**

So I am probably not being very culturally correct, or even politically correct, but what do you think? Is **robbery** taking place? Are you being **robbed**? If so, there is a better protection. There is a better way of believing. There is a better value system. And there is a better way.

*1. Goldilocks Theory of the Universe.
The **Goldilocks principle** states that something must fall within certain margins, as opposed to reaching extremes. When the effects of the principle are observed, it is known as the **Goldilocks effect**.

The thesis is this: the Universe as we know it shows a multitude of features that makes it ideal for life. As such, is mentioned the structure of atoms and molecules, the force of gravity which is neither too great nor too small, the quantities of vital elements like oxygen and carbon which are found in exactly the right amounts, the ready combination of oxygen and hydrogen to make water with its unique properties, and several others. It looks, almost as if the Universe had been especially designed for life. At this point, there should be an interruption, to ask if that was not then the logical assumption to make. Perhaps it had indeed been designed? The reply from the clever scientists though is, "Ah! No! You cannot allow the idea of a Designer into your thinking, because that is unscientific. Also, it merely moves the problem of the Universe back a stage. After all, who designed the Designer?"

*2 STD statistics from Avert

Over the past decade there has been a substantial increase in diagnoses of sexually transmitted diseases (STDs) in the UK, particularly among young people.

[229]

Since 1999 the number of annual cases of chlamydia has more than doubled. In 2008 there were 123,018 new diagnoses of chlamydia in GUM (genito-urinary medicine) clinics – a record number. Chlamydia can have serious side effects, one of which is Pelvic Inflammatory Disease (PID), which can lead to infertility in women. Chlamydia can have no symptoms and therefore many people do not come forward for testing, even though the infection can be easily diagnosed and effectively treated. Cases of gonhorrea rose steadily from 1999. The number of diagnoses of syphilis has risen substantially in the past decade in the UK. In 2008 there were 11 times the number of primary and secondary diagnoses in GUM clinics, than 1999. This rise has been attributed to a number of local outbreaks, the largest of which was in London between 2001 and 2004. During 2008, 7,220 people were diagnosed with in the UK. Although this represents a decline from the previous three years, the number of new HIV diagnoses has more than doubled since 1999. Between 2005 and 2006 the largest increases in new diagnoses of genital herpes were among men aged 35 - 44 (15%) and 45 - 64 (18%) and among women aged 16 -19 (16%) and 20 - 24 (11%). London had the highest rates of diagnoses per 100,000 population, followed by the North West, and Yorkshire and the Humber. In 2008 a record number of people (28,957) were diagnosed with genital herpes in GUM clinics in the UK. Just over 60 percent of these diagnoses were among women. (Source: http://www.avert.org/std-statistics-uk.htm)

Rochdale Sex Scandal

Listening to the news coming out of Rochdale, everyone is saying, that this is not the end of the story. For my readers who follow what is happening in the British news, or those that don't watch the news, there has come to light the fact that some 1,000 plus young people have been abused, prostituted and beaten, giving them, of course, lifelong problems. Yet they were under the care of the authorities and had allocated Social Workers "caring" for them. Police were also aware, but no one did anything to help, in case political correctness was interrupted or their carers where put in jeopardy.

When I look at the regulations governing Social Work, fostering and the care of young people in the UK, so much of it is good.

[230]

Meaning good regulations, good intentions with an emphasis on good practise. However, it's not so much the regulations that are at fault, rather the culture. A culture that from many Social Workers is a culture of, "I must protect my back at all costs. I must make sure, that if something goes wrong, then I don't get the blame. And if it does go wrong, how I can make sure I do not take any responsibility? I must protect my career and my income, my salary and my job!"

I have some sympathy with the approach - not a lot, but some. I know that Social Workers are often criticised for doing as well as being criticised for not doing. It's a no win situation. But, there is a huge cost to that culture, and who pays that cost? As we can see, in Rochdale, it is, of course, vulnerable young people and children that pay the price, the very people that the Social Workers and the system is there to look after and protect.

I wonder if it's the training that puts this culture into the system. Or is it Mrs Thatcher's fault with her, "Look after number one," philosophy that was promoted in the 1980's? Or, is it that we fail to think in terms of good and bad? Even the word, "evil," has become politically incorrect.

Often, I will say to people, when in those difficult situations, "We need to ask, "what is right,' and not, "what protects me or defends me and my interests."" It can be that I lose out by doing what is right. It is still wrong not to do it.

I'm also sympathetic to the, "whistle blowers." Don't tell me that they will be fine, legislations assures them that they will be protected. It is too clandestine and, "under the carpet," for that. I still think they need to blow the whistle, even if being right puts them in the wrong place. I do know what this means. We had a case, whereby I encouraged a young person to take a particular authority to court for the wrongs being done to them. The authority used our service. I did think they woild not use us after this (i.e. encouraging the young person to take them to court). The young person won the case, and rightly so. The local authority has not used our services since. Caan I prove that it was because of this case? Of course not! It's just one of those things. Would I do it again?

[231]

Unfortunately, yes. I say, "Unfortunately," because the moral imperative is more important than the consequences that I might suffer.

What do we need to do in going forward? Maybe, to start with, we should make sure that "would be" Social Workers actually foster for a year before being approved. However, what is really needed is a change of culture and that is not easy. Usually it means a change of heart, and many people don't think that is possible, and certainly don't know how it can be achieved.

T is for Thinking

THINKING...

When I first started a Christian school, some 30 years ago, I was part of a denomination. Having got the operation off the ground very quickly, some 160 children being educated with us, I was naive enough to believe that if I could do this, lots of other ministers and churches would too. My thinking was that if little old me, who only has a Road Safety colouring certificate, can do this, "What could others who are clever than me do?"

Picture my horror when I discovered that my biggest critics where my "supposed Christian friends," and colleges.

One national Christian leader said to me, "How foolish of you, to THINK that you can have Christian Maths or Christian grammar in English!"

The problem for me, was that I had a foster child who had moved from our Christian school at 16 to do English Grammar at a local college. She showed me her homework one night. Innocuously enough, she had to punctuate and put capital letters in some sentences. The first unpunctuated sentence read, "on arriving home I was disappointed to find that my boy friend was in bed with another girl – correct the sentence." Never, never underestimate that hidden curriculum!

How Wise are we that call ourselves Christians?

Luke 16:8 says, *"The master commended the dishonest manager because he had acted shrewdly. For the people of this world are more shrewd in dealing with their own kind than are the people of the light!"*

I continue to hear the comment that I am sure many of you that run Christian schools hear: "You are brain washing them." – and everyone else is, of course, Amoral, and has no agenda! "You are not making them aware of the real world." – which is just the same as the Genesis statement "you will know good and evil."

[233]

Your children should be salt and light in school." – just like you were when you were young? "You will produce hot house children." – and of course we should allow our 3 year olds to cross the road by themselves? And other such nonsense, phrases that I hear, actually, more from Christians than those who do not follow Jesus.

What we fail to understand is where the battle is joined. Some love to sing those songs of victory, like, "Onward Christian soldiers." But where are we going to fight? What is it that God uses, and asks us to use to make us different?

He tells us how to change. Whenever I ask folks as to how we should change I hear all sorts of things like, "love," "repent," "read the Bible," and, "go to meetings regularly." They might help. But that is not what Scripture tells us to do. The Bible says to put on the mind of Christ. Renew your thinking. Whatsoever things are good, honest of a good report, think on these things.

In other words: THE BATTLE IS IN THE MIND FOR THE MIND.

Those who sought the overthrow of what was formally Rhodesia understood this principle very well. What did they attack in the country to force the change? Where did they take the fight? I know. I lost a friend who was clubbed to death in the struggle. I very rarely get a correct answer to this question when I ask people for their opinion. Actually the soldiers attacked the schools. They took the children across the border into what was called the front line states, for, as they called it, "re- education." They understood that to win a generation, and change the future, one has to change the minds of the current generation and keep them thinking. I want to put good thinking into the minds of the children that I can influence.

The Battle is for the Mind, and I want people to be in their Right mind!

Culture – challenge – change - conform
One of the things that I ask audiences who say that they are Christians is, "If you are one, have you changed? If you have changed, what methodology do you think, you or God uses to change you?

I get lots of answers. Usually things like:

- The Bible
- Prayer
- The Holy Spirit
- Meeting with other Christians
- Love
- And others sometime a bit more obscure

Of course, all of those things have a bearing on change. If change is necessary, however, these aspects of the Christian life are not, actually, the prime means of how we change. In fact, the Bible does tell us what the method of change is, and more than that, it tells us how to maintain and continue with the relevant and vital changes that are needed to become a new kind of person. The Book of Romans starts us off ...12:2 *"Don't be conformed to this world (allow the world to squeeze you into its mould), but be transformed by the renewing of your mind, so that you may prove what is the good, well-pleasing, and perfect will of God."*

Thinking is what changes us. What and how we think transforms us into what we think. So often we don't – think, that is. When I was a teenager I used to hang out in what was euphemistically called "Coffee bars," the place where young people could legitimately go and hang out. One went there before going out, and came back there after you had been out, if you see what I mean. It was the place you met your date, before you went on the date… a bit more like a house front room with frothy coffee, and the very required juke box.

One of the things I noticed, and that hasn't changed much in 50 years, was that the music had to be very, very loud. In fact, it had to be so loud that one couldn't think. I asked a few of my friends back then, why they liked the music so loud. Most of them answered the same, "It saves me from having to think!"!

The trouble was and is, that there are many times that we think we are thinking, but we are not. Rather, I would say we are conforming.

We conform to our culture, our peers, those we feel we need to impress, to be the same as, to want them to like us, to feel a part of

[235]

the crowd, and to be accepted. All of those things are going on inside of us, but often without much thought.

I have been to a lot of parties of late. Most of which, I have to say, were not for folks in my age group. However, even when occasionally it was my age group, I noted that the attempt to conform to the group mentality was very strong. Our culture, the bits of it that we don't think about,puts us into a box where we act, do and be, just like everyone else but without much thinking.

Let's be honest it's hard to change culture. Not that we shouldn't try, particularly when culture has it wrong, which often it has. When you change your thinking you can change your behaviour. However, changing the thinking of others is not that easy, even if your thinking is right and theirs is wrong. Think about Ignaz Semmelweiss. You mean you don't know him? Well, in 1847, he discovered that if doctors washed their hands before attending women in childbirth, it dramatically reduced deaths from puerperal fever. His views were ridiculed and eventually drove him insane – not that he was wrong - but it took some 15 years for Pasteur and Lister to develope their germ theory of disease, which explained why Semmelweiss was correct.

Going back to those parties; why is it that we have to have so much Alcohol? So much, "same" music? So much, "same dress style?" So much "conformity?" Are we thinking, or just culturally conforming? And, if we are just conforming to peer pressure, are we right to do so? Are we that different to my coffee bar era, "well - it saves me from having to think?"

To quote Richard Wilkinson and Kate Pickett in, "The Spirit level," they said, "It is a remarkable paradox that, at the pinnacle of human material and technical achievement, we find ourselves anxiety-ridden, prone to depression, worried about how others see us, unsure of our friendships, driven to consume and with little or no community life.

Lacking the relaxed social contact and emotional satisfaction we all need, we seek comfort in over-eating, obsessive shopping and spending, or becoming prey to excessive alcohol, psychoactive medicines and illegal drugs.

So why am I going on? Because I want to provoke you to THINK! Think what about? Things like:

- Why are you here in this world?
- What is it that needs changing?
- What is it that you could do to effect change?
- Why are you just being one of the crowd?
- Where are you going anyway?
- When are you going to do something constructive?

Sometime the problem starts by what you think about yourself. Again, to quote the Bible, it says in Proverbs 23:7, paraphrasing, *"As you think in your heart so you are."* So, what do you think about you? Are you insecure? Unsure? Do you think of yourself as not so good? To start with, that would need to change if you are to tackle the thinking that answers the questions above. And, of course, it can and should change.

What should you be doing? Shouldn't you be the person to change things, by first of all changing your own thinking? Why be a, "same-ee?" Why not be a change agent? You could be a world changer. But first, you yourself, probably have to change. Personally, I do that by firstly becoming a follower of Jesus, then trying hard to, "not conform," and putting on the mind of Christ, thinking about good things rather than bad. In fact seeking to renew my mind covers everything. Not got there yet, but trying and am on the way.

How about you? Wouldn't you rather be here to change things, rather than just be one of the crowd? Think about it! There's a challenge!

U is for Unexpected

Car Smasher Builds Garage

From wrecking cars in London to building a garage for mechanics in Kenya

ROEHAMPTON, ENGLAND/KENYA, AFRICA (ANS)

REGENERATE is a ministry formed in 2000 out of a realization of the social and spiritual needs of young and old on a British housing estate.

That realization led to dreams of a changed community, "where the gospel was demonstrated as well as spoken about," according to its ministry website.

"The needs were huge. Being one of London's largest estates, the Alton estate was high in deprivation, child poverty, street crime and drug addictions," the site states.

Over the years REGENERATE'S work has developed. It has run projects for both young and old including -- mentoring schemes, football clubs, outings, children's church, lunch club for the elderly, a visiting service to isolated elderly, drop-in youth centre, residentials and trips overseas.

Now REGENERATE is in the process of building a car mechanics garage on the outskirts of Nakuru, Kenya, in the heart of Africa. The garage will provide opportunities for up to 35 young people to learn a trade and gain employment, helping them out of the poverty trap.

The vision for the garage came from Luke Clifford who first visited Kenya with a group of young people from Roehampton in 2005. The trip changed his life and he came back with the idea to build the garage. He has since raised over £6,000 GBP ($12,000 USD) for the project, and been back three times to help with the project.

On the next trip in February 2008 the garage will have its official opening, with Luke being able to see the dream become reality.

[238]

"It took me some time to persuade my friend Andy Smith to visit Kenya with me, as I felt his church needed a third world focus as well as the great work he was already doing in the Roehampton Estate, which is one of the larges council estates in Europe," says Adrian Hawkes the London-based leader of a ministry that plants churches, works with asylum seekers, and provides aid to children in Sri Lanka.

"Andy was a little squeamish about coming with me to Africa, even though some of the stories he told me concerning the work on the (Roehampton) estate made me somewhat careful. Things like the fact that if you want home delivery Pizza then you have to phone and arrange to meet the delivery man on the other side of the main road -- they won't deliver on the estate because they lose their delivery bike, money and pizzas. Great place to live in it seemed to me. Give me Africa any day. Andy took to Kenya like a duck to water so to speak," Hawkes said in an interview with ASSIST News.
That was in 2004. The following year (2005) Andy decided to go again, this time with some of the young people from Roehampton including Luke Clifford, who was famous on the estate -- or rather infamous -- not only because he had dropped in to the Regenerate club but also because he took a liking to stealing Andy's car and rolling it down hills into brick walls.

"Just for fun you know. Seemed a bit surprising to me that Andy was still willing to take him with him, but he did," said Hawkes.

Kenya turned Luke Clifford's life around, along with giving him a vision for a garage, the trip changed his life and he came back with the idea to build the garage to help people by supplying work. He has since raised over £6,000 GBP ($12,000 USD) for the project, and been back three times to help with the construction.

Hawkes continued: "He came back from that first visit and told us he had found God, more than that he was determined to help young people there. From his own small wages he gave Andy money each week and made it quickly possible to buy land and prepare for his dream of building a garage for the youngsters there."

[239]

Last February, Luke won the Anthony Walker Memorial Prize, the top Champions of Respect award from the Evangelical Alliance in the United Kingdom. Luke was honored for initiating the garage project in Kenya.

Local press and Premier Christian Radio in London have all picked up on Luke's story, and some have even donated money for the project.

Back in Roehampton, Luke has now stopped trashing Andy's car and is helping to facilitate all the other good work on the estate there, such as the Juice bar, drop-in site, the Bus program, and the many, many other things to change the people's thinking on the estate.

Angry young men

For me, understanding the principals of the Kingdom of God was a bit like Paul's Damascus Road experience. I fell off my donkey and a bright light came on. The only difference was that I fell off the donkey very slowly and the light came on very gradually. Rather like slowly turning up a dimmer switch.

I had grown up with the idea that the Kingdom of God and the church where one and the same thing, now I understand that the Kingdom of God is not the church and the church's job is to seek the Kingdom, while God worries about the building of the church, though I doubt very much that He worries about it.

As a member of the church it stands to reason that my job, also, is to seek the Kingdom of God. Not seek church or denomination or even conversions, but to make seeking that kingdom my number one priority.
I had paid lip service to the fact the Christ will build His church, but then I got on with building a local church community, thinking that the job had somehow been delegated to me, although I am not sure when that happened!

I guess that is the mission, and that is what I want to write about. I recognise now that the kingdom needs to be everywhere in God's big wide world.

We are to seek it in the church and also outside of the church. I believe that if you seek the church, you might not find the kingdom. If you seek the kingdom you will find the church.

Salt purifies and preserves. Light eliminates darkness and gives direction. We seek the kingdom by being salt and light influencers, in all the pillars that hold up and mould society; the culture, the politics, the business, the education, the media and arts.

An interesting analogy can be seen in the Old Testament scripture. When the kingdom of David was at its height it had influence on all the surrounding nations. It constructed a David fortress in each of those territories, although it did not take them over or rule them. I assume the local countries did not want to offend this rather strong neighbouring kingdom, and when they wanted to pass a new law or make a decision, although they were free to do so, they felt it was a good idea not to offend this rather strong king and kingdom, and would first check with the local influencers at the David Fort.

Let me tell you two stories that illustrate what I mean by seeking the kingdom. But first, let me ask you a question. What does the Kingdom of God look like? The Lord's Prayer gives us an indication. "Your kingdom come. Your will be done on earth as it is in heaven," says Jesus, as recorded in scripture. What is God's kingdom like? From scripture we can deduce that it is a place of justice, righteousness, peace and joy plus many more good things. If we find these things on earth we will have found a piece of the kingdom. When Jesus was on earth, and He put a wrong right He would say, "The Kingdom of God is amongst you." That must mean he had brought the Kingdom of God to the earth.

One evening, when I was running a youth club in the north of England, a crowd of disruptive lads came in and began causing a ruckus. They bullied the young people who were already at the club, then they started throwing chairs around, and smashing anything they could lay their hands on. It was all getting rather dangerous. In the middle of the mayhem I walked in and swiftly became very angry and made it clear that they should leave. They moved out of the club and onto the street, with me in hot pursuit. I singled out their leader, a very tall young man, and marched up to him to give him a piece of my mind.

He was head and shoulders taller than me, accompanied by a pack of his feral mates. If they had turned on me I would not have stood a chance, but I was annoyed and perhaps not thinking straight. I looked him in the eye and berated him about what he and his mates had just done to the club, and then, I have no idea why, I said "Are you afraid of me?"

He sneered at me, looked around at his mates for support then announced, "No way!" I then said, "OK! In that case, you won't be afraid if I pray for you will you?" He looked at me as if I was stark raving mad and said, "I ain't afraid of you, or anything you can do, including praying."

I took his hand and without closing my eyes began to pray. "Lord Jesus, this young man does not know that you are with me and that you are strong and powerful and that you actually want to do something in his life …" I didn't get any further. I saw that he had tears streaming down his face. He snatched his hand from mine and ran away as fast as he could. The rest of the gang looked at me as if to say, "What have you done to our boss?" and they all ran after him.

I never saw him or his gang again. We rarely know exactly what to say in these situations, but all we need to know is the Kingdom of God is amongst us. Those of us who know God can find his kingdom in the strangest of places, even in the middle of the street surrounded by a gang. We just need to seek.

Recently, at our office in north London, a young Pakistani Muslim guy came in to speak to one of our staff. He was very angry. He was so angry that the staff member was afraid and asked another staff member to come and sit in on the meeting for support. Gradually, as he raged on, it emerged that he had been at the airport, on his way to catch a flight to go and visit his sick mother, when the police arrested him as a suspected terrorist.

For some strange reason, his mates had suggested he should come and see us, telling him that we would be able to help. As the staff listened they became more afraid. For all they knew, he could have been a terrorist, and they had no idea how they could help him. In desperation, one of the staff members offered to pray for him.

She didn't know what else they could do. At this suggestion he became even angrier and shouted, "I have already been to the mosque today and prayed, there is no point in praying, do something else!"

The staff members apologised and said they didn't know what else to do. The only thing they could do was to offer. Eventually, they persuaded him and grudgingly he agreed.

Both members of staff shut their eyes tight, not out of reverence but out of fear, and they began to pray. They prayed and they prayed. They didn't want to stop because they didn't want to open their eyes and look at the angry young man. Eventually they did stop and when they opened their eyes they saw a very calm and peaceful young man, who smiled and said "I don't know what you just did, but thank you! I have never experienced anything like that before." And with that he left.

He returned twice more and was very keen to express his thanks. "I don't know how you did it, but everything is sorted. I am flying to see my sick mother. Thank you, thank you, thank you!'

What we want to do is find that kingdom everywhere on God's earth. That then is mission. Seeking his kingdom here on earth.

Beer and Bandits in Ruddington Nottinghamshire

The team of young people known as Ribbons of Faith (RoF) with whom I was working in the sixties, were getting known further afield. We began to get invites to work with different churches who thought we may be able to help. Perhaps we did, perhaps we didn't, I don't know.

One day we received an invitation from a church in the small town of Ruddington in, Nottinghamshire. They wanted us to lead a series of meetings. They had been praying for "revival," whatever that is, and they believed that we could be the answer to their prayers. The members of the church community were getting older and older. They began to realise that they would all eventually die, and with them, the Christian community. They decided they had better do something about it.

[243]

We were that something.

We were scheduled to spend a week of evenings in the area, and as usual we were not sure what to do. Part of the RoF team included a band - very sixties, guitars, drums, a trio of girl singers called The Ribbonettes. Alright, I know it's cheesy but that's what they were called. There was not much to do for young people in Ruddington. We found lots of teens hanging out of street corners, arguing and making a noise. They had no money in their pockets, so when handed a leaflet advertising a free band and the inevitable cup of tea, they were more than willing to come along and hear what we had to say.

We discovered that just across the road from the church building there was a working man's club. We also found out that the band they had booked for the evening's entertainment had done a no-show. One of our crowd offered our band as a stand in. A problem arose, not for us, but for the local church community. They felt great concern that we should go into such an "evil place." Apparently they drank beer in there. Worse was to follow, on the evening when the band was playing, one of our girls was watching one of the guys play the one arm bandit. "Hey love," said the guy. "You come and pull the handle for me. I'm sure you'll bring me good luck." She grinned at him and innocently pulled the handle. The machine whirred and three apples slowly slotted into a matching row. The machine began pumping out the jackpot. Needless to say the rest of the time while we were there, our crew were in great demand on the one arm bandits, especially that particular young lady. But this only made things worse with the church community, now we were gambling in this den of iniquity.

Being a small town, word spread quickly about these strange 'Brummies' who were invading their community. Soon, there were loads of young people drinking tea, listening to the band and chatting. I was impressed with what they talked about, they asked serious questions about God, the meaning of life and where they were going. They were also keen to know what they needed to do to find out if the Maker had any designs for their lives.

More problems were in store for us. The chatting went on and on. Some of them truly wanted to know the living God.

[244]

One of the first young people to make a commitment to Christ was the daughter of the owner of the Working Man's Club. He was not at all happy about this and began to regret having met our band.

The leader of the church was an old man, although he was only 21. Even at this tender age everyone called him the Pastor. He opened up the building each evening and looked completely out of his depth, surrounded by all these unchurched youngsters. He also looked strained, waiting for us to leave each evening so that he could lock up and go home to bed. It was all a bit too much for him, even though he only lived in the next street. Whereas, our mini-bus convoy often didn't arrive back in Birmingham until the early hours.

As we were getting on so well with this great crowd of youngsters and did not want to curtail their serious conversations, I asked the team to stay a little later on Friday evening. The 21 year old Pastor said that this would be impossible, as it was a Friday. I pushed him a little, explaining I knew it was Friday. I wanted to understand why this was such a problem. Then he dropped the bombshell. "I always wash my hair on Friday night, so I need to lock the building early." Oh Dear! Help!

During the conversation, he had also told me that the people in the church were very unhappy about the way the building was being used and how the youngsters that were coming along were not showing respect. As for me, I had found them to be intelligent, articulate and open hearted. As far as I was aware, nothing had been broken and they seemed very polite. I was concerned to find out if I had been missing something. Had something happened, about which I was unaware. He went on to explain that the, "church," people were upset because the young people didn't sit on their chairs correctly. He saw my bemused face and said, "They turn the chairs round, and straddle them so they can lean forwards on the back of the chair when they talk to you. This is very disrespectful." I didn't say anything. However, in my head I was yelling. Help! Oh help! Help! Help!

It was a tough learning experience; some of those young people had a real encounter with the God who is there. But the local, "church," was not ready for them.

They were totally unwilling to come alongside them, or reach out to them. Rather like new wine in an old skin perhaps.

When we were originally invited to Ruddington by the church community, they said that they had been praying for God to send them loads of young people. God did. However, they didn't like who God sent. I guess we should be careful what we pray for, or perhaps, when we pray, we should be more open minded and allow God to answer our prayers His way and be a little less prescriptive. If we are not open, we may well miss out on all that he could or wants to do.

V is for Vision

VISION
A true pioneer of multi-racial churches around the world
By Dan Wooding

LONDON, UK (ANS) -- I first met Adrian Hawkes back in the mid-sixties in Birmingham, England, when he brought his Ribbons of Faith outreach team to my father's little church, the Sparkbrook Mission, in Birmingham, England.

The female members of his team seemed rather glamorous for this rather dour area of England's second city, wearing colorful sashes and singing modern songs, and then Adrian brought a challenge for our church to start going out into the community with the Gospel.

We were so stirred up by his sermon that soon my sister Ruth and I started The Messengers, which grew very quickly to about 60 members. We would go out each Saturday night to the local pubs and coffee bars with the Good News of Jesus Christ, and soon we partnered with the Ribbons of Faith, and other groups in Birmingham, to start the Late Night Special in the Lloyds Bank Building each Saturday night.

Then Canon Bryan Green, a liberal evangelical who was sometimes described as "the Anglican Billy Graham," invited us to start a Sunday night outreach in St. Martin's Church in the Bull Ring, Birmingham.

When Adrian married Pauline, his lovely wife, he asked me to be best man at this wedding and, of course, I agreed.

Not long afterwards, Norma and myself, had become involved in working with drug addicts at All Saints Hospital in Winson Green, and this developed, with the help of some local businessmen, into the start of Hill Farm, Europe's first drug rehabilitation farm. We were Hill Farm's first wardens.

[247]

After we left the farm, our family moved to London where I became the chief reporter with The Christian, Billy Graham's newspaper there and shortly afterwards, Adrian and Pauline moved to Middleborough to run an Elim Church there. Then, in 1974 he and Pauline moved to north London where they took over the famous rock venue, The Rainbow, to establish a unique church there. The Rainbow had hosted hundreds of shows, including several of the Beatles Christmas concerts, and also had David Bowie performing as Ziggy Stardust, as well as Queen, Cat Stevens and Jimi Hendrix, to name just a few of scores of rock luminaries who performed there.

In June, 1982, Norma, myself, and our two boys, Andrew and Peter, moved to Southern California, but Adrian stayed in London to pioneer a unique series of ministries, including those to asylum seekers in the capital city.

In a recent e-mail interview, Adrian Hawkes talked about his work with what is called Rainbow Church.

"At one time, we had some 41 nationalities working as one church," he said. "Out of that multinational congregation came a natural interest from many in the affairs of their home countries.

"Rainbow church is part of an international network of churches called Pioneer, and for a long time I worked with Pioneer on their international program, however I became very aware that one of the good things that needed to happen was to see people of different nationalities working in teams together so that people would see different cultures working, and caring alongside each other.

"It does of course happen. One can see it working as you look at things like Youth With A Mission and Operation Mobilization, but it was not happening in my neck of the woods.

"So, three years ago I decided to do something about it. Collecting all my connections around the world, I invited them to a meeting in Zurich Switzerland. Many said they didn't really know why they came, except that they knew me.

"The outcome of the meeting was that a church in Norway began to support a church in Paris with their international TV broadcast. The Tamil churches in Switzerland and France worked with the Norwegian church to try and plant a new Tamil congregation in Oslo Norway.

"A further outcome of our time in Zurich was that everyone wanted to meet again, so we decided to go for the next year to Norway. This was again a good time together and from that teams of Norwegian and UK young people went together to Kenya. Canadians and Norwegians worked together in Switzerland with the Tamil churches and young people went to Norway with Norwegians to play snowballs and ski."

He went on to say, "Again, after our time in Norway, everyone wanted to meet again and so the next point of call became Paris France and next year it will be the UK

.

"The whole point of the exercise is to continue to encourage different nationalities to pull together for international work. We need to demonstrate that Christians can, and do, function across nationalities and cultures. Often times (at least in Britain) we are encouraged to be tolerant of each other's culture. If followers of Jesus cannot do it then no one can."

Adrian then spoke about the Paris gathering:

"For the third year running a group of people from various countries met this time in Paris France, to see what we have done together and what we could do and what we are going to do.

"Some of the good things that were done together were in Switzerland and Norway with UK teams and Norwegian teams. This year there are plans for the Norwegians the UK and Canada to all join and help out with the big Swiss Conference of Tamil churches young people joining in from all those countries and from France as well; it sounds like it is going to be great.

"During the year the group at the 'happening' had been in touch with some 21 countries. We had updates reports on the work in Norway, Sri Lanka, Brazil, Kenya, Qatar, Germany, Zambia, UK, South Africa and the USA, to name just a few.

[249]

"All who attended felt that this was a profitable yearly event, and we all agreed to meet again next year at the same time that was Friday 1st May 2009 until Sunday 3rd May 2009 with arrangements for any who want to come a bit earlier or stay a little later.

"Our delegation was a little smaller this year because one of our team, Jenny Sinnadurai had experienced the sad loss of her mother who had died and many attended the funeral in Sri Lanka from Switzerland, Canada, New Zealand, France and the UK. On top of that we missed Kenyan Sammy Nawali who, this time, had visa problems for France, which was strange as he had successfully attended Switzerland, Norway, USA, and UK events recently."

Adrian Hawkes and his ministry are a perfect example of what a World Christian should be. After all, the Body of Christ is made up of people from all parts of the world and he is doing his part in bringing them together under a banner of God's Love.

To find out more about the Rainbow Churches, go to www.rainbowinternational.org.

Pioneers or Settlers

I wish that I had thought of this title but if memory serves me correctly it was first used by Gerald Coates in a book of the same name, and he certainly used the phrase often.

The reality is that as we get older even those of us who have wanted to pioneer and seek out fresh lands, we opt for settling.

When I was the tender age of 19, I was part of a team of young people who were pioneers, trying to make a difference. We were saying to anyone who would listen, "Hey, we're followers of the way. We've met a great Person who is our friend, and we would like to introduce you to him." We had found a new Kingdom, and we wanted to bring it down to earth and make the world a better place. We wanted to change the world. And I still do.

As is usual with people of that age, they started getting married, buying cars, having children, and worst of all, they took on mortgages!

When I tried to encourage them to continue in the pioneering path of excitement and challenge, to bring about change in the world, this was their response, "We're married now. We have a car and a mortgage. When you get these things you will understand, you will have to settle down." Jesus replied: "A certain man was preparing a great banquet and invited many guests. At the time of the banquet he sent his servant to tell those who had been invited, "Come, for everything is now ready."' Luke 14: tells the story of their excuses.

So what happened? I got married. I had children, and much, much later, I took on a mortgage too. To my delight, I discovered that one doesn't have to settle, not if you don't want to, and not if you have excitement about the future, relish what is new and realise the best is yet come. Life is still out there to be discovered. The worst enemy of better is very good!

I also found out that one doesn't have to maintain the status quo and always do what is expected. Let me demonstrate. I thought it would be good for my two month old baby, my wife Pauline and I to go out and celebrate one evening, by going out for a meal. Pauline said, "We can't go out this late in the evening, surely the baby should be in bed." Unconvinced, I suggested we put her to bed in her carry cot and take her along, where she slept peacefully under the table. Nobody even knew she was there until she let out a loud yelp in her sleep, and made the rest of the diners jump. I know that people perhaps do this a lot now, but then it was frowned on. It was "just not done."

As time moved on, I grew older, but even my growing family of three children did not deter me. I still wanted to push those boundaries even though doing that often involved hard work and late nights. I came home one morning at 2:30am and said, "Hello," to my drowsy wife, who did not appreciate being woken up and was complaining about the noise. As I climbed into bed I teased her. "You are getting old and boring." That was a big mistake! She threw back the covers, switched on the main light and started to get dressed.

"What's going on?" I asked. "We're going out to celebrate!" she declared as she yanked me out of bed. "Celebrate what?" I groaned. "Celebrate the fact that I am not old or boring!" As we lived in London we had no difficulty at finding a place serving good food at 3:00am. But I have never again accused my wife of being a boring settler.

Scripture describes it this way: If we are a follower of the way we are in a race, and there is no point in starting a race if we don't complete it. "Do you not know that in a race all the runners run, but only one gets the prize? Run in such a way as to get the prize." 1 Corinthians 9:24. It's great to start. It is better to continue. But it is best to finish. Be a passionate pioneer, not a sedentary settler!

Vegetable soup

Birmingham at St Martins in the Bullring

In the late sixties I was living in Birmingham and trying very hard to have an effect on young people. At that time we were running an event each Sunday night at my local church. It was attracting hundreds of youngsters, including, "Rockers," on their motor bikes, which did not make us particularly popular with our neighbours or the "nice'" leadership people who had permitted us to use the building.

After the demise of the, "9 o clock special," due to the arsonist attack, which subsequently led to the leaderships refusal of permission to continue our use of the hall, because they did not want "nasty unchristian, non-churched people in their building," I was left wondering, "What next?"

Fortunately we were working with another local team, who were friendly and supportive. This was headed up by Dan Wooding, who as it happens, was best man at my wedding. Dan and I and a few others were invited to meet with Canon Brian Green, the rector of St. Martins in the Bull Ring, a city centre church. He was quite a pioneer being one of the prime movers of the first visit to the UK by Billy Graham. Cannon Green had just overseen the completion of a large 500 seat hall attached to St. Martins and was seeking to make an impression on the young people in Birmingham.

The outcome of the meeting was that we were given the opportunity to re-launch the "9 o clock special." We used the same format of very loud music, a testimony and a 10 minute talk followed by tea, biscuits and chat. All over bar the shouting - and there was often a lot of shouting - in three quarters of an hour. We launched with a large team of 100 plus and attracted capacity crowds. They were not exactly polite and they knew nothing of church etiquette, but they came nonetheless.

People prayed, dished out invitations on the streets, gave their money and their time. Canon Green also offered us financial support, meeting any shortfall on our weekly costs. He did this faithfully, every time we had a need. The average donation he made on many occasions was £50. You may think that is a drop in a bucket these days, but if you take inflation into consideration, then that is in the region of £745 per donation in today's money. (http://www.thisismoney.co.uk/historic-inflation-calculator)

As I mentioned, the youngsters who came were not polite. Couple this with the fact that the building we used was right next to the fruit and vegetable market. By the time we kicked-off on a Sunday night at 9:00 pm, there were always many stray vegetables lying around on the street. These became useful missiles if the crowd didn't like the band or the speaker. On nights when the crowd considered the speaker poor, the post meeting hall clean up could produce enough veg to make a large and hearty soup!

I cannot now remember how many years we ran the, "9 o clock special," in the city centre, but I do remember that many young people had encounters with the living God, and many went on to become history makers and bringers of change, introducing still more people to The Way.

One day many years later, when I was leading a church in Grangetown, Middlesbrough some young lads from Birmingham contacted me and offered to come and help with work we were doing on a nearby estate. Four or five of them showed up one day and knocked on my door in Wilton Way. One of them seemed familiar. "Don't I know you?" I asked, he simply laughed.

[253]

Later in the evening, over coffee and sandwiches, I said to him again that I was sure I knew him from somewhere. He again found this amusing, and when he had finished laughing this was the story he told me.

"I used to come to the late night specials at St. Martins in the Bullring and I made a commitment to Christ. You said that you would pick me up each Sunday and spend time talking more about what my commitment meant. You came every week, and every week I would hide behind the curtains and tell my mum to tell you I was out. I couldn't believe that you didn't give up, that you kept on coming week after week, that's why I was laughing. Years later I strolled into another meeting in central Birmingham and the guys who were talking were saying the same stuff that you had said. I finally realised that this is life. From then on I have never looked back, but that first encounter made the initial impression and put the spark in me."

When I look back on what we did and how we did it, I feel as though we were blundering around. However, maybe God honours our blundering commitment and love for Him and His world. Later on we were privileged to have small glimpses of what he was doing in people lives as a result of his blessing on our blunderings. We don't always get to see what we want to see, and we don't always get it right, but if the love of God is in us, it definitely has an effect.

To quote Gerald Coates, the founder of Pioneer, *'Often God is doing more behind our backs that he is in front of our face, but every so often we get to laugh at the success he has brought from something we did that we hadn't even dreamt was possible and actually maybe what wasn't even that good.'* Perhaps that's mission?

You in your small corner and I in Mine

When I was around 5 years old, I went to Sunday School. I liked the people and I liked the other kids, but what I remember most is one song that they always sang. I must have sung it too as I can still remember all the words. Maybe you know it too. It starts off with, "Jesus Bids Us Shine," and ends with the line, "You in your small corner and I in Mine." I hated that line. I still don't like it now.

I don't think I liked corners and particularly not small ones. I certainly did not want to be in one.

When I was 11 years old I made my first trip, as the Brits say, "overseas." I went to France with my school for a week. We travelled third class, as you could in those days, on a ferry across the channel to St Malo. Third class meant that you could not go inside the ferry. Third Class passengers had to stay on deck come rain or shine. They did, however, give you a blanket and you could snuggle up to the funnel to keep warm.

It was great fun in a hotel in Dinard with loads of school friends. However, I remember thinking, even way back then, how different France was. Not just the scenery and the language, but everyone seemed to be much more aware that there was a big world out there. There were other countries that spoke different languages, and many of the young people spoke French, Breton, and English. Some, it seemed, spoke German and Dutch too. It struck me then, at 11 years old, that I lived on an island, and these people lived on a continent. In a sense, I was in a corner, and these people were more aware of the world than I was.

Recently, I have again been made aware of the small corner thinking that is around me. I talk to supposedly well educated people who, when asked, who is the new Labour leader of the opposition in the Westminster Parliament, they do not know. I listened to my wife talking to a full hairdresser's salon about the abduction of people by terrorists, and discovered she was the only one there who knew anything about it. They were shocked to discover from her that such terrible things are going on in our world. Do they not have TV's or ever see a newspaper, I ask myself.

What is it that makes us want to live in a corner? What is it that gives us this disinterest in the rest of the world? Is it selfishness? Is it a complete lack of concern for our fellow human beings? Maybe we are just hard hearted? Why do we not take an interest in our world?

As a follower of Jesus, and I know many people who read what I write say are Christians, we need to know that Scripture commands us to do things *in* the world. He never told us to live in a corner, rather we are told to care for strangers.

[255]

So what is going on? We are not stupid, are we? Are we really that uninformed? Could we really not care about how we are governed? Don't we want to know what is happening in the rest of the world?

Do we really not know that we, the world, are facing the largest displacement of human beings ever? Do we not know that this will affect us all? Do we have no response?

Do you live in your corner? Do you like it there?

W is for World

An article by Dan Wooding of Assist News of our work in Sri Lanka.

The History of the work in Sri Lanka

VANNI, SRI LANKA (ANS) -- An outreach of the church in Sri Lanka has been approached by the government there to help provide assistance to Internally Displaced Persons (IDP) as a result of the long-running conflict which recently ended in a government victory over the rebel Tamil Tigers.

According to an e-mail report, obtained by ASSIST News, from Karen Dey who heads up New Living Ministries International: "In March our church ministry team in Jaffna had a desire to provide aid into the IDP camps (Internally Displaced People Camps) in Jaffna, but at that time the Sri Lankan Government was not allowing anyone to visit the camps. In March there were just four camps in Jaffna, but as the conflict was increasing, the amount of people fleeing from the conflict zone increased."

Dey says that by April the camps in Jaffna "were not able to cope with this sudden influx of the large amounts of people arriving.

"We were contacted by the local authorities in charge of the camps requesting urgent assistance into the camps. There are now 12 camps with between 200 - 1,700 people in each camp," she said.

"We began taking teams of seven people from our church ministry team into each camp. On visiting the camps we were requested by the army and the people in the camp to provide essential items that the army was not able to provide for them.

"Many of these people have been hiding in bunkers for months and are traumatized, exhausted and severely malnourished. The camps are severely overcrowded and unable to meet the basic food and shelter needs of those who are arriving. Most of the camps are without decent water and sanitation facilities. Those detained in these camps, which are surrounded by barbed-wire fences, are denied their liberty or freedom.

[257]

They are not allowed to leave the camps, and visiting is severely restricted. By God's Grace our church has been able to enter many of these camps now."

Dey goes on to say that many children have witnessed terrible scenes as they escaped to safety.
"Some saw their parents killed or were separated from them during the journey. These children will need intensive counselling in the near future. The sense of fear amongst those in the camp is strong, unsure of what the future holds," she said.

"For the past month we have been visiting the camps on a weekly basis providing families with such items as baby's milk bottles, milk powder, flasks for hot water, Nestamalt build-up for children, supplementary food items, medications, milk powder for adults, soap, babies' and children's clothing, sarongs for men and saris and dresses for ladies."

Dey says that many war victims are also in the Jaffna teaching hospital and other local hospitals in Jaffna.

"Most are suffering from severe burns, bullet and shrapnel wounds. Our teams have been visiting these hospitals and providing the patients affected by the war with meals, and any medications requested by the hospital. We have also assisted to provide to the hospitals with such things as vitamins and food supplements, waterbeds for burns patients, burns clothing, colostomy bags, replacement glass eyes, and Jaipur Limbs."

Dey said that New Living Ministries International is at present working with two children in the Jaffna hospital, Mythili, a 9-year-old girl, and Subashkaran, an 11-year-old boy, who have no parents or guardians.

"When they were escaping out of the Vanni area their family was catching a boat together when shelling started. The children were pulled into the boat but their parents were left behind. We are not sure if their parents are alive, so have requested that these children be released to our care once they are discharged from hospital. Both are being treated for bullet and shrapnel wounds."

Dey explained that the A9, the only road into Jaffna, remains closed to private vehicles.

"So the only way to provide these essential items to the camps and hospital is by purchasing them from the shops in Jaffna. Each time we visit a camp we need around £800GBP ($1,295USD) to purchase the necessary goods to distribute to the camp people.

"To date we have managed to do this thanks to donations from our own churches in Sri Lanka, and abroad, but we are now seeking financial help from other sources so that we can continue this work into the IDP camps and hospitals in Jaffna."

POLITICS

I don't usually write anything about Politics, but the recent elections at which I did vote, seem to me to be setting a trend that require lots of us who, maybe think differently, to say something.

An Iraqi friend of mine recently said to me, "Maybe there is a problem with democracy in that stupid people get to vote. Perhaps we should have an exam before people are given the franchise?"

Recently listening to the debate in a ladies hairdressers, waiting for my wife, who had just commented on the problems for the kidnapped girls in Nigeria, I was staggered to discover from about 10 plus people there, she was the only one who knew that girls had been kidnapped. They moved on in conversation to various other world shattering events, but it seemed to me that my wife was the only one who had a TV that showed any news programmes. The world affairs, local and national politics seemed at such a low level of interest to them I wanted to scream. Aargh…!

It isn't that this stuff isn't out there it is, but most of the main three political parties are not telling it as it is. Perhaps that is because they shy away from the real facts to try and be popular to those who don't listen to them anyway.

The big issue over the UK and many other European countries, has been "Immigration! Immigration! Immigration!

[259]

There has been lots of rhetoric but not many facts - facts that are easily findable, such as:

London, one of the most prosperous European Cities, owes much of its prosperity to the fact that it is such an international, diverse city due to immigration.

When questioned about what percentage of immigrants that go to make up the UK population, people had wildly wrong numbers, usually way too high. In fact out of the 15.4 million refugees in the world currently, due to war, bad government and the like, in 2012 the UK only had 193,510 of these people in the countries that go to make up the union and that represents just 0.33% of our population. Did you know that?

Over a quarter of our NHS Doctors are immigrants. I did not hear that fact quoted. Maybe it was and I missed it. Did you know that? I wonder where we would be if they all downed tools?

When talking about immigration we don't talk about emigration do we? Yet something like 5.5 million British people permanently live in other countries other than the UK. I wonder how those countries responded to those immigrants?

Nasty one here, immigrants are 60% less likely to claim benefits than a UK born person. Oh dear! What shall we do about benefit tourism?

Oh, and about those pesky EU immigrants, taking all our funds - did you know that between 1995 and 2011 EU immigrants made a net contribution of £8.8 Billion more than they gained from being here.

It seems for all the cries, most studies suggest that immigration has little or no effect on overall employment or British workers unemployment. I am pretty sure that often immigrants are job creators rather than job takers, and that they often end up creating wealth and employment on a grand scale. Think about companies started by immigrants, like Marks and Spencer's, Burtons, Mumtaz Khan. Akbar turnover £85 million, James Caan turnover £250 million (James Caan is seen regularly in Dragon's Den on British TV.).

Sir Anwar Pervez who set up his first corner shop in London in 1963, expanding to ten convenience stores by the early 1970s and now head of Bestway which has the second highest turnover of any cash-and-carry in the UK.

14% of start-up businesses in the UK were founded by immigrant entrepreneurs, according to a newly released report. The report says that there are 456,073 immigrant entrepreneurs working in the UK who have founded 464,527 businesses which employ 8.3m people.
http://www.workpermit.com/news/2014-03-14/

And just for fun have you ever been to an ODEON cinema? Very British! Why call it ODEON I wonder? Actually the creator's immigrant name didn't seem to have the right ring, so he thought up the acronym ODEON. In case you are wondering what it's an acronym for, it stands for Oscar Duetsch who wonderfully entertains our nation. Very English!

Enough already I hear your cry! But if we are going to have this debate lets have the other positive side of what makes places like London so prosperous. Yes there are problems of immigration, I have some solutions to that too if you do not want the people to come and make us richer, but that's for another day.

Socialism
I think its good we all get to know this stuff, but I am particularly thinking of my American Cousins as I write. Particularly the Christian Right wing so called.

> The term socialism was first introduced by Henri de Saint-Simon
> (1760-1825), the French social theorist also credited with the advent
> of Christian socialism and what would later become labelled as
> "utopian socialism." The term itself refers to a collective mode of
> production and political economy.

Socialism's roots go far back beyond Marx's works. Church's actually led the first socialist movements. The US gave birth too many of Socialism's key concepts.
The original Socialistic concepts date back to 1700s and influenced even the founding fathers of the US. You find many of them embedded in the
[261]

Constitution and in laws passed over the years. Prisons for example were one of the first major socialist contributions to society. Before prisons came about, people generally were publicly punished with physical punishments, financially punished or executed. There was not much in between.

The first prisons date back many years. Socialists in the early 1800s made major penal reforms in the US which quickly spread to the rest of the world completely redefining crime and punishment. That is an example of early Socialism in the US and its predating Marx.

There are things that puzzle me about my American Cousins, and I love the USA. But from a Jesus Follower perspective, I want things that are good for people so I cannot understand why as a Jesus follower I would not want to promote Health Care for everyone at the point of deliver, I want people to be as healthy as possible, whether they can afford it or not.

Then again, another area, I want people to be housed, I don't want them to be homeless, even if they cannot afford it. How can we help them?

Yes I know that when it comes to government enforcing these things that where the problems start, why is that, well much as people don't like to hear it we are as people not intrinsically good, rather we are selfish, self-serving, and we tend to look after number one, us!

If you look at History when Christians are in control of the levers of government we have not done very well, but does that mean I should forget Biblical commands to Love Justice, (Matt 12:18 Luke 11:42 Gal 5:22:23.) If government of whatever ilk try's to put in place things that do good, help people, give justice, welcomes strangers amongst us (Exd 22 and Exd 23.) Surely as a follow of Jesus I would want to support such action. Likewise when people are being unjustly treated, marginalised, poor and denied the means to help themselves by government policy should I not cry out against such things?

The problem is we like to read the parts of Scripture that we like. So we would like to put things on one side such as (Matt 19:24) concerning the rich man, or (Acts 4:34 on, having all thing in common) and I often hear

Christians say such things as well that was then, this is now, you cannot do things like that now. Why not, is that part of scripture we don't like?

I often hear people say, why should we support free loaders, or as my Mother in law used to say why those people don't get a job. Sorry but that really is uneducated. On frequent visits to Kenya, another country I love, I have often asked leaders what do you need. They will say things like more crusades, more meetings, and more preachers.

I look around and think no, what you need is more jobs. I see loads of people who want to work, need to work, would work hard, sitting waiting trying to find work, are they free loaders. We need to understand that often the way society is structured means that the opportunities you are given are not just or righteous, the poor are often not poor because they are lazy or free loaders, or unwilling.

Please there is a lot of other reasons way beyond their control that put them in such positions. And if the follower of Jesus can change their position for the better be that by influencing government policy, or direct action to help, then God calls us to do it.

To quote Jim Wallis – A Budget is a moral document. And a bit more Wallis to end The Biblical prophets do hold their rulers, courts, judges, landowners and employer accountable to the values of fairness justice and even mercy, evil and sin is in the concentration of power, politics and economics need to be held accountable to Justice especially in the protection of the poor. Fair outcomes not necessarily equality should be the goal of governments.

Socialist or whatever, let those who follow Jesus cry out for His values in His world.
https://uk.answers.yahoo.com/question/index?qid=20061214083112AArAIeF
http://www.faithstreet.com/onfaith/2011/08/12/from-jesus-socialism-to-capitalistic-christianity/10731
https://sojo.net/articles/caring-poor-governments-biblical-role

Paalam International School - Building Project

Paalam International School

was opened in September 2003 with the purpose of providing children from underprivileged families from the Wattala district with an opportunity to study.
Many children in this area do not attend school. They are instead sent out to work so as to help their families to meet the needs of day to day living. Most of the children's parents are in the very low income earning bracket. Some children's parents are drug addicts or alcoholics and so spend all their income on their habits leaving the families with little finance to live off. In the school we are not only looking at the children's educational needs but we are also overseeing many children with food assistance, medical care, provision of uniforms and shoes, transport, and social assistance.

The Paalam Project has also built new housing for five of the children's families who were previously living in shacks made from cardboard boxes, plastic and anything that they could find to provide shelter.

The school has a total of 145 children ranging from the ages of 5 – 17years. Twenty five of these children are fully sponsored into the school. We currently have 14 full time teachers all of whom were previously unemployed.

For the past six years the Paalam International School has been using the New Living Flame church building to operate the school in. The school has grown so big that we no longer have enough places for any further classrooms.

The Project and church owns some land adjoining the Wattala site and we are now desperately seeking help to build a new school building.
Applications to various organisations for grants to assist with the building work have so far been unsuccessful, due to the past war situation in Sri Lanka. However the war has now ceased giving us a great opportunity to construct the much needed school building.

Without building a new building we remain very restricted in how many children we can take into the school and with the activities that we can provide for them.

We are presently working on an architectural drawing with a local architect and once this is completed will be seeking a quotation from local contractors.

The new building will be three stories high and provide us with a further 6 classrooms, space for a library, computer room, store rooms and a medical room. We estimate that this new building will cost approximately £99,000.

If you or your organisation would be willing to assist us to construct this new school building which would help the lives of many young children and provide them with an opportunity to change their future and the future of their families please do contact us. We would greatly value all contributions towards the Paalam International School building Project.
We are seeking 100 Business people to Donate £1,000 each!
This will enable the Paalam Project to raise £100,000 to build the new school building!

Jaffna Internally Displaced People Camp

From March we received funding from numerous donors to assist the Paalam Project with aid into the Welfare Camps in the Jaffna District. Our aim was to assist the Kopay Camp in particular, as the Paalam Project and New Living Flame Church has its main base in Kopay. In the Kopay camp we have been assisting the 200 families consisting of 483 individuals on a weekly basis.

Thanks to the funding from our donors we were able to provide bed sheets and towels to every person in the Kopay camp. We were also able to purchase clothing for each of the babies in the camp and clothes for the children and teenagers.

We are also working into the Kodikamam Camp, where there are 389 families and 1,176 individuals whom we have provided sheets and towels for, along with clothing for the babies in the camp.

On our initial visits to the camps, it had been very difficult to get permission to take teams into the campus. We had to write letters to the Government Agent (GA) at the main City Council office (Katcheri) in Jaffna and once we received their approval we had to take this to the Ministry of Defence for a clearance signature from the Brigadier. This was very time consuming and difficult with our requests often being turned down.

After we received the funding from our donors we went to the Kopay camp with all our permission letters. Still we were told we could not distribute the goods needed in the camp. So we asked to speak to the person in charge of the camp. At first they were not willing, but, after much persuasion, the officers put us through and our senior Pastor, Jenny Sinnadurai, spoke to the Colonel in charge of the camp explaining that his staff were not permitting us to enter the camp despite having received permission letters. The Colonel arranged with us to come back to the camp in two day's time. That Tuesday we returned to the Camp, where we were met by the Colonel who escorted our vehicle and team into the camp.
The goods were checked by the army, and then we were able to prepare to distribute them. Prior to this we had requested to have a small service.

We had with us a team of 13 people consisting of two youths from our church in Switzerland, two youths from our church in Colombo, myself from New Zealand and others from our church in Kopay. We sang two songs in Tamil & Sinhala and then Jenny our Pastor spoke to the crowd that had gathered.
We had an opportunity to pray and speak to those who wanted prayer, which turned out to be most of the camp people. It was such an amazing opportunity for us to share the love of God and the gospel with those in need. We were able to give 30 bibles to families upon their request.

Following the service we distributed sheets and towels to each person in the camp. The Colonel also assisted us in doing this. Some of our youth gave out sweets to the children, which was a real treat for them

Here is an experiential account of how God is helping us in our work in Sri Lanka:

Normally we are not allowed to take photos in the camps, but this day the Colonel requested that we take photos as he needed some for his records, and as he didn't own a camera, would we take photos with our camera and give them to him? We requested also to use the photos to send to those funding the work and he agreed for this. By God's grace we were able to take as many photos as we wanted.

Since this first encounter with the Colonel he has been in constant contact with us. We no longer need permission letters to enter his camps. He will call us on a weekly basis to inform us what is needed in the camps and then he will meet us at the camps and escort us into the camps. We are no longer checked and the goods are no longer checked. We are able to freely run services on each visit to the camps and we are also permitted now to speak to individuals, pray for them and counsel them as requested. God has given us an open door into these camps. Really, we have been amazed at God's grace in granting us the privilege of entering these camps so freely.

Since we began working in Kopay camp we have been praying for the release of the people back to their relatives or their own land. In the last two weeks 72 people have been released from the Kopay camp back to their relative's homes in the Jaffna area.

And yet another testimony to God's grace:

From the Nelliyady Camp, one elderly couple and their daughter have been cleared to leave, but as they had nowhere to go to, they refused to leave. The Colonel contacted us regarding this family and we offered to provide the daughter with employment at Paalam Children's Home if the Colonel would provide accommodation for them out of Neliyady. This family has now been resettled in a house outside of the camp and their daughter is working full time for us. This family is now attending the New Living Flame Church each Sunday. The opportunity to work with the Ministry Of Defence to assist such families could only have come through doors that God has opened to us.

Neliyady Camp Family outside the house provided by the army.

Spiritual Impact:

Our ministry teams are visiting the Kopay Camp, each week and the Kodikamam and Nelliyady Camps monthly. At each visit we are running a 20 – 30 minute service where we give song sheets to those attending and encourage them to take part in the singing of songs in Tamil and Sinhala. The children really enjoy this time taking the opportunity to sing at the top of their voices. Ninety percent of the people in the camps attend these services. We have had the opportunity to pray for almost all people in the camps. Most are Hindus or Catholics.

In the Kodikamam camp there is a Pastor who is running a church in the camp. Initially he had 20 people attending services. After we started to visit the camp and pray with people and distribute Bibles his congregation has grown to around 40 people. We have been able to support his work by providing him with tracts and Bibles in Tamil & Sinhala, along with a tambourine and bongos for the services.

Many seeds are being sown in the lives of those living in the camps that we are visiting. Our ministry team is able to talk with, counsel and pray for people on a weekly basis and we believe that as people are released from the camps that they will seek churches to continue to receive this input into their lives.

We have taken the opportunity to expressly share with people about the need to forgive and forget the past and move ahead into a new future of hope. We believe that by planting these seeds of peace, people will not desire to go back to their old ways of war.

Alternative

It's a sad fact of life, the majority opinion is not always correct. Not that I dislike democracy, I think it is probably the best way to be governed, and greatly preferred to some very dark alternatives. Which is why I think a good democracy must have laws and ways to protect the minorities, even though that is sometimes irksome to the majority.

During my life I have had the privilege of working in many different areas, and had the opportunity to observing a great deal. I am more than ever convinced that the corporate majority way of 'being' just does not cut it, even though; sadly, that is often where we end up.

Some of the corporate organisations that I have observed include church, business, social services and education; regularly the 'company man' will tell me how I should do it and why my way of doing it is wrong. I look at what is being done in the name of the establishment and it frequently causes me to let out a load groan. They seem not to notice that what is being done is inefficient, usually lacking heart and passion, often controlled by Mr. Jobsworth. If sense is common, then I don't see that, as it seems to be regularly lacking in practice. Corporations have become large, impersonal and dehumanised as anyone will know who has sat on the end of an interminable telephone answering system, stabbing at menu choice after menu choice as the tension mounts.

I look at Social services and think; this is just too big. If it was smaller, more personal, with more manageable units and real accountability, surely that would work better.

I am involved in education, running small schools, but often get told 'that won't work', usually by people who have been trained 'in the system'. 30 years of doing this has shown me that actually, it does work, and works very well!

Church is another area of involvement. When I first moved to London I took charge of a couple of congregations, their leadership at the time asked my why I was changing certain things, my answer was to try to do what I believed 'church' was supposed to do. Their response 'do you know if what you are doing will work?' I was honest and told them I did not know. They got very upset and said, 'if you don't know if it will work or not, but you are changing it, that's a bad thing to do, why are you doing that?' I responded without hesitation, 'we already know that what is being done at the moment doesn't work don't we.'

As Anthony Robbins says, (he is a self-help author and motivational speaker) "If you always do what you've always done, you'll always get what you've always got".

In the business arena people talk to me 'who know' and tell me how to do it successfully. And usually it is not the way that I am doing it. I don't think I have failed yet, it may depend on the measuring rod I am using, but what I am doing looks successful to me even though I am not doing it your way.

These advisers often tell me that what I plan to do 'can't be done'. But I am a stubborn curmudgeon and don't understand the word 'can't'. In many instances, what they tell me can't be done, I have already done successfully. But I save my breath because even if I did tell you I don't think you would hear me.

Where am I going with this? What I am saying is be careful about throwing away, dismissing, casting cold water and poo pooing that 'alternative' idea, plan or operation.
It might just be the answer we have all been looking for, just because it challenges your training, gets you out of your comfort zone or is not how it has always been done. Having no experience does not mean it will be a non-starter, be daring, be bold, be alternative!

X is for Xenophobia

XENOPHOBIA and the Good Samaritan

Some time ago, before the tribal troubles in Kenya I was speaking at a conference there. I was using for my talk the story of the Good Samaritan. Knowing a little about the tensions of the area, I used as my illustration, one of the tribes who in the area where I was, was not very popular to say the least. I chose this least popular tribe and used the tribal name instead of "a Samaritan." At the end of my talk, and the meeting over, I was taken on one side and told how dangerous it was to speak thus. "It would be much better to tell the story with the Samaritan as the good neighbour, as I did not understand the culture of tribal enmity and by putting one of the 'despised' tribes in place of the Samaritan, I was living dangerously and people would not like it.

I wondered how we might tell the story today, maybe in the streets of London, or New York perhaps, where some poor Christian guy has been mugged and beaten and is lying in the gutter. Along comes a good Charismatic Pastor, who, knowing that he has to preach to his good congregation, hurries by on the other side of the Road. He must protect himself to deliver his sermon.

Then along came worship leader par excellence, boxed instruments over the shoulder, ready to lead the people in Praise and Worship. However, it was very necessary for him to be on time to tune his instrument and do a sound check. "1,2, 1,2, 1,2. It's a shame for the man in the gutter, but there are people to lead, to stand, to raise holy hands." It was very important that he was there early to get it all ready.

However, a young Muslim guy saw the guy from his nice new car. He stopped and lifted the mugged young Christian and put him, dirt and all, on the back seat of his new car and drove very quickly to the nearest hospital, phoning the police on his mobile. He then visited the poor guy every day while he was in hospital until he was well again.

Which one I wonder was the man's neighbour?

You can read the original story in Luke 10:25-37 I have put some of it here for you from the New International Version (NIV).
Jesus answered, "'Love the Lord your God with all your heart and with all your soul and with all your strength and with all your mind 'and, 'Love your neighbour as yourself.' [28] "You have answered correctly," Jesus replied. "Do this and you will live." [29] But he wanted to justify himself, so he asked Jesus, "And who is my neighbour?" [30] In reply Jesus said: "A man was going down from Jerusalem to Jericho, when he was attacked by robbers. They stripped him of his clothes, beat him and went away, leaving him half dead. [31] A priest happened to be going down the same road, and when he saw the man, he passed by on the other side. [32] So too, a Levite, when he came to the place and saw him, passed by on the other side. [33] But a Samaritan, as he travelled, came where the man was; and when he saw him, he took pity on him. [34] He went to him and bandaged his wounds, pouring on oil and wine. Then he put the man on his own donkey, brought him to an inn and took care of him. [35] The next day he took out two denarii and gave them to the innkeeper. "Look after him,' he said, 'and when I return, I will reimburse you for any extra expense you may have."

[36] "Which of these three do you think was a neighbour to the man who fell into the hands of robbers?"
[37] The expert in the law replied, "The one who had mercy on him." Jesus told him, "Go and do likewise."

Y is for Youthful

YOUTHFUL

The students are coming….

I went to a college in a place called Capel, in Surrey, in Southern England. It's just between Horsham and Dorking.

I used to come home to Birmingham during the holidays. If I couldn't cadge a ride off one of the other students going in my direction, I would hitch-hike as I never had any money.

I had been at college a year and was home in the summer holiday. As usual, I visited my home church to say hi to everyone. The leader of the church at the time was George Canty. He pulled me to one side. "Let's have a chat in my office," he said. I knew George well as I had worked with him in Port Talbot, Wales when he was running some meetings there. I sat down in his office expecting a friendly chat, when he said, "I think you have had a very lazy year. You have had nice theological conversations, drunk lots of coffee, talked with friends and pontificated about all sorts of things. There is a world to change and you have wasted a whole year. I'm expecting you to go back for your second year and use your time more." I looked at him amazed and wondered which wardrobe he had been hiding in and under which bed he had been secreted. His summary was terribly accurate.

At the start of the next academic year I pulled some of my college friends together and said, "Hey guys! I got chewed up during the holiday period. I've come back to college with the intention of turning over a new leaf. We need to change the world so who is with me? I want to start with Dorking."

We set to with a vengeance. I'm sure the exams suffered a little. On top of that we lost a lot of sleep working on the mission to Dorking and trying to study at the same time. But it was profitable, not least for Dorking as well as for us. We learned a lot.

First of all, we pulled together those students with graphic art and advertising skills.

The Students were a mixed bunch from all walks of life. Then we hit the town with a subliminal advertising flyer; *"Look out the students are coming,"* is all it said. No address. No dates. Nothing else. It even took the police three or four weeks to track it back to our college. They were worried and sent a delegation to interrogate us. Did we intend to invade this small town? What were we planning? Good question! Hard to answer because we didn't know. We were making it up as we went along.

The college principal got wind of developments and he also wanted to know what was going on. He wanted to know how it might affect exams and I wasn't sure I wanted to enlighten him on that one.

We approached the town with a, "Let's try everything," attitude. We set up a bookstall in the market which was on each weekend. My future wife, Pauline, got the job of selling the books. We were not really interested in selling books; this was just an excuse to talk with people about the good news.

We discovered that the local paper was often short of copy to fill the pages, and they loved it when someone else did the work. Each week David Butcher was commissioned to produce a relevant photo, and we would then produce copy and post it off to the editor. Every week, almost, the paper contained an article about, "Those students,' and the fact that they were indeed coming!

Quite a few of the students were musical, so we formed a band, "Contacts International." Two members were from the UK and two from the USA. Each weekend we stood them on a street corner with instructions to sing a few songs. This gave us the opportunity to chat to passers-by and answer questions about why the students were coming.

We talked to the kids in the town. We ran fun events for them and told them, "The students were coming with good news."

Finally, after many months of this razzmatazz, we booked the Dorking Halls and invited the townspeople to come and meet us.

We even managed to get a big American band called the Forerunners to come and perform. The hall was packed. The town came. Some of the local religious people were incensed by the terrible music. Why is it that religious people always get so incensed?

The conclusion of all these actions was that people found Christ. We opened a small community church and before the year was over, we borrowed a building that had a tank in it (that's one that holds water not one that shoots shells) and in it we baptised many of the local people on their heartfelt declarations of their new found faith in Christ.

Would I do it all the same way again? Probably not. Do I think the time was wasted? I doubt it, but I guess only eternity will clarify that point.

Tea, biscuits and rockers

I am always puzzled by what people mean when they used the word mission. Do they mean sharing good news? Or something else? Claire Smith, from "ourlab" blog fame, has asked me to write some stories about mission. So, stories I will write. Are they about mission? You decide.

Very early Birmingham

I grew up in Brum and at around 19 years old, somehow God had got hold of me and a group of other young people. For me, it was one of those 'blinding light' revelations. I was in a coffee bar with a guy called Tony Stone, when he commanded me to go and talk to some young people about Jesus. My pulse was racing, and my breathing was shallow as, carefully carrying one of those frothy coffees that had had just come on the market, I approached their table and hesitantly asked if I could join them.

Much later, as I walked out of the coffee bar and the cold air hit my face, the light of revelation also hit me. I knew the reality of a relationship with the living God.

During the evening, as more and more people had crowded round the table, listening to my quiet conversation about Jesus, I realised they were not anti; they just didn't know anything about Him.

Yet, the fact that they stayed, and listened, surely meant they were interested. I knew God. They didn't. But they were keen to hear. For you, perhaps, that is not so profound. However, I wanted to fall off my donkey and lie on the ground in awe. Please note: I didn't actually have a donkey, and the pavement looked hard and cold. Nevertheless the light had flashed down on me.

I was so turned on by this experience that I gathered a group of like-minded young people and we decided we would "Evangelise." We didn't know what to do, and for many of us our extended church background did not prepare us to engage with the real world. But we were keen to do something. We decided to ask the church leadership if we could borrow the building in order to hold some, "Special meetings." Their response was confusing and disappointing. "You might bring some nasty people into the place." I thought that Jesus came for the sick and needy, not the healthy and secure? Our youthful enthusiasm was not thwarted, and we kept on nagging. Eventually, they agreed to let us use the building on a Sunday evening, at 9:00 pm, after all the nice people had gone home!"

Looking back, it now seems very old fashioned, unsophisticated and perhaps a tad crazy, but we did what we knew. We printed some flyers and dished them out to local young people. The flyer heading was, "Nine O Clock Special." printed upside down, beneath this the text read; "In this upside down world, 9 o clock special is a must. Tea and biscuits." This was the early sixties!
The programme ran as follows: For 15 minutes our musicians played hymns, very, very fast. Next, someone gave their testimony. Lastly, to wind it up, a preacher, who had strict instruction to speak for no more than 10 minutes. It was all over by 9:45 except for the tea, biscuits and chat.

To my amazement, the place was packed Sunday night after Sunday night, 52 weeks a year.

Hundreds of young people came through the doors and due to the fact that some of our clientele were rockers, lined up outside the church building were rows of gleaming motor bikes. At the end of the evening, the rockers usually all left at the same time, each one firing up their bike and waiting until everyone was ready, the deep throated machines revving in unison. Finally, they peeled off one by one, in a cacophony of sound, up the Walford Road. This did not make us popular with the neighbours.

One of the regular speakers made a lasting impression on me. He was the oldest guy in the church. Mr. Holt was his name and he must have been in his late seventies. He spoke in authorised version Bible English, and I am convinced to this day no-one understood a word he was saying. However, he loved the young people and wanted them to know his God. The impact he had, no other speaker could replicate. When he came, more people than ever wanted to make a connection with Jesus. The fact that he loved God, followed Jesus and so obviously cared for his audience was communicated despite his words.

These strange meetings, at least when I look back they seem strange to me, went on for many years. People were inspired to become church leaders. Lives were changed. The effect of those meetings echoed and re-echoed. Years after they had ceased, I was still meeting people who told me that the "9 o clock special." was where they had their first encounter with the living God, where Jesus first became their friend.

The end came early one Monday morning. The phone jolted me awake and I was summoned to the building by one of the church leaders. I was greeted by a swathe of fire engines, police cars and disgruntled church leaders. In the middle of the night an arsonist had broken into the building and used our advertising materials to set fire to the back hall, the one we had been using to hold the meetings. The leader's attitude was, "We told you so. We knew if you invited nasty people into our sanctuary something terrible would happen."

Once the insurance had paid up, the renovation and redecoration was complete, and everything was looking better than ever, I was summoned before the church leaders.

As I listened to the case they made against me, it felt a little as if I had organised the fire. They left me in no doubt that I would never again be permitted to use the, "Sanctuary."

And that was the end of the story, or at least, this part of the story. Jesus, or rather His people, were not interested in rockers or ruffians. They only wanted nice people, in a nice tidy building.

Do you want Grass with that bacon"?

The wind was blowing hard, the canvas snapped and strained as the rain beat down. I was half asleep listening to the howling wind when I heard a loud crack. The canvas went slack and began billowing wildly. I struggled out of my sleeping bag, "Mark! Mark!" I yelled, "One of the ropes has gone!" It was 3am. We returned half an hour later, soaked to the skin and sat there drinking hot chocolate to warm us up before we climbed back into our sleeping bags. It was 1967. Mark Drew and I were living in a marquee, pitched in a car park underneath a motorway flyover.

Living like that for three month had its challenges, one of them being that Mark was self-appointed chef, and every time he dropped anything on the floor, like the breakfast bacon, it was always my bacon sandwich that had the grass and gravel in it, never Mark's!

The aim of this strange living arrangement was to be the security personnel as well as general dog's bodies for a mission organised by George Canty. The mission had two aims, to introduce the people of Port Talbot, Wales, to the living God and to establish a community of believers in the area.

George had a very interesting process of gaining people's attention. I thought that a huge marquee positioned in a car park would be an obvious draw to the crowds, but this was not enough for George. He produced a flyer in the style of a single sheet of newspaper. After he had written the copy, he would sit there pouring over it for hours, eliminating every word or phrase that was in the least bit religious or churchy. He wanted the language to be the kind that normal people used every day. He was striving for a, "Red top," newspaper style of advertising.

[278]

Stage two was to print and distribute the advertising newspaper. Mark and I blitzed the place, pushing them through doors, handing them out on the street and talking to anyone we met about the mission. There was already considerable interest since the marquee had appeared. People were curious to know what it was all about. All they knew, so far, was that it was in the car park and a couple of young lads were sleeping there. I say "sleeping," but that was a euphemism, bearing in mind we were underneath a busy motorway, in a huge draughty tent, in Wales, where it rains a lot! If we weren't shivering in our sleeping bags, we were running round in our pyjamas tightening guy ropes in the dark and generally keeping the meeting place from blowing away.

The evenings developed a pattern. Hundreds of people turned up each night. Mark and I showed them to their seats and George stood at the front beside an easel with a large white blank canvas placed on it. As George spoke, he produced an oil painting from scratch. He was the Van Gogh of the mission circuit. When it was finished, the painting would be awarded to the person who had brought the most people that evening. After he had chatted to the crowd about how good God is, he would then offer to pray for anyone who was sick.

George came in for a lot of flack from the religious people in the area. The accusation levelled at him was that to give away an oil painting each night to the person who brought the most people was a "gimmick" and not in the least bit "spiritual." I asked George how he would deal with this criticism. His astute and sharp response still sticks in my mind. "One person's gimmick is another person's good idea!" It reminds me of a similar quip from General Booth, when someone said to him, "I hate the way that you evangelise!" Booth responded, "Yes, and I don't like it much either. How do you do it?" The truth of the matter was that the critic was not doing anything to share should the good news.

During the three month period in Wales with George, I saw some amazing things. One night, a lady who was deaf came forward for prayer. I had showed her to her seat earlier in the evening and had been almost hoarse trying to make her hear, she was so deaf. She did not ask for prayer for her hearing, but for her sore throat. George, in his inimitable maverick style, ignored the request about the sore throat, stuck his fingers in her ears and prayed that the gifts of healing that God gives to his followers would be granted, and that she would hear again. He then moved to the opposite side of the marquee and began to have a conversation with this, "deaf lady." He spoke in a very low, ordinary tone. "Where do you live?" he asked her. "About three streets away," she replied. "How long have you been deaf?" "He enquired. "About 25 years." She responded. "How much can you hear?" he asked, "I can't hear anything at all. I am pretty much stone deaf," she answered efficiently. George continued this conversation with her for some time. The audience began to giggle sporadically, and then, as the conversation progressed, the whole place was falling about laughing. Gradually, she became aware of the merriment. She looked at the laughing crowd, then back at George. "How come I can hear you and answer all your questions?" She said, her face a picture of curiosity and astonishment.

Another lady had a very badly twisted leg. She couldn't straighten it and therefore was badly incapacitated. God healed her. Her leg became straight and she was able to walk again. I went to visit her at her home and asked if she would like to come to one of our church community meetings. She told me in no uncertain terms that she wasn't interested in such things, all she had wanted was for her leg to be straight and now it was and she was happy with that. She bid me good bye and closed the door on me. I was reminded of the words of Jesus when he said, and I paraphrase; "It's not really me or my message that you are interested in, you come and follow me because you have heard about food and you love to eat bread and fish."

When the three months of mission was concluded, a small church community had been established. Mark and I stayed on for another three months to help it become established. Not, I hasten to add, living in the marquee!

Z is for ZEITGEIST

Zeitgeist

I have thought about this a lot. It is one of those words that the English have borrowed from the Germans, but which, in its usual dictionary explanation, does not express all that the word implies. Some words are just like that, aren't they?

The dictionary definition of the term is, "The spirit of the times and general trend of thought, or, the feeling characteristic of a particular period of time."

The thing is, when you go into the background of the word from a German perspective, it has many layers to it. This is perhaps why we don't have a good feel of its translation, or its common English usage. The word in German carries the idea of being in a fog. It means that the, "spirit of the age," is not recognised by you or me, because we are so influenced, affected, controlled by, engulfed by our eyes being covered by the fog of the "spirit of the age" so that we do not know there is such a spirit, nor can we see any alternative.

From a German perspective, one can only assess zeitgeist in retrospect, looking back, or, better translated, "the ghost of the age or ages past." Then we can see what it was and know where they went wrong, or how they could have done better. Hindsight is a wonderful thing.
I often think it's funny as politicians seek to correct history, and pardon this or that from the past, or say how the government was so wrong seventy or a hundred years ago. Then they suggest that as their party got it wrong then, let's put it right today. As if we can put what we see now into history, and make it different to what it was they saw and understood. I think that process is daft.

Why am I going on about this? Well one of the reasons, is that I teach a class of senior students in our school and am talking them about entrepreneurs, and how to be one. As I have talked with the class, I am very aware of how often, both in history and in the present day, people cannot see certain things. Clever people like Albert Einstein, who said in 1932 that there could never be atomic energy.

[281]

Or Thomas Watson, the head of IBM, who said in 1943 that he could only see the need for about 5 computers in the world. Even funnier, to our mindset today, was the president of the digital equipment corporation as late as 1977, who said, "There is no reason anyone would want a computer in their home!" In 1927, H.M. Warner of Warner Brothers quipped, "Who the hell wants to hear an actor speak?" as the possibility of, "Talking movies," were coming on stream. David Sarnoff's associates, in response to his urgings for investment in the radio in the 1920 said of Radio "It has no commercial use and will not catch on." Sir William Preece, Chief engineer of the British Post office, said of the invention of the telephone, "Americans have need of it. But we British do not. We have plenty of messenger boys." Why did they say such things? Is it zeitgeist?

I have often spoken to audiences about the problems Moses had with the children of Israel after they left Egypt. The thing is, if one's next door neighbour is a slave, and one's friend across the Road is a slave, and in fact everyone one knows is a slave, one's vision of 'freedom' is a nonstarter. Zeitgeist has you. Sadly, you don't want this, "freedom," thing. What you want is more onions, leeks and cucumbers (The Bible, Numbers 11:4-6). Can you blame them for the conceptual perception of fog?

So are we suffering from zeitgeist now? I think we are. But how do we know? How do we break out? How do we change the future? Cairine Reay Mackay Wilson (February 4, 1885 – March 3, 1962) was one of those people who broke zeitgeist. She wanted to become a senator in the Canadian parliament. The problem was that the zeitgeist of the time held that woman were counted as a "non-person." Therefore one could only have a make person as a senator. For that reason, a woman could not do the job. From the point of view of the zeitgeist this was obvious.
Cairine did not accept the obvious. She appealed to the UK Privy Council, Canada's highest court. The ruling given changed the very "nature," of a woman's person-hood and Cairine became the first Canadian female senator.

So are we in the fog of our own zeitgeist?

I think we probably are. There are things we should see, things we could do, a better way to live, a better way to be, a different paradigm to be in. What we need is to listen to the seers, and see what they see.

Maybe we need someone from the other side to come and tell us that there is a better way to live and be, and then we should listen to them. Oh yes! Of course! He has already spoken.

Words

I like words. Trying to speak French gives me great frustrations, as I know my vocabulary is incredibly small, which it is not in English. I remember telling a story to a young lady in French. At the end of the story, I asked if she understood me. "Yes," she replied. So I enquired, "Then why are you laughing?" She answered, "Because it's like listening to a five year old!"

I used to think that words where just how you expressed things, and so I got irritated by those in the, "Equality lobby," who wanted to change expressions like, "Chairman," to "Chair Person," or "Man-hole," to "Person-hole." It seemed to me to be picky, petty and stupid. I no longer think that way. I recognise that our words come from our thinking, and actually re-enforces our actions. So, if we are sexist, using sexist expressions just enhances our bias.

For those of us who are followers of Jesus, language is such an important element. Words are important. The great thing is that John, in his book in the New Testament part of the Bible, in the very early verses, says a very interesting thing about words. He says, "The Word, became Flesh, and dwelt amongst us" (John 1:14). He is of course talking about Jesus, and powerfully presenting the fact that God puts his words into action, in flesh and bones, so that we can really understand what is being said by a physical being in a historical setting in our time/space world.

So then we as followers of this Word go on using words wrongly. And though we profess to say we think or believe something we, usually because it's easier, use words that say the opposite. Let me give you some examples:

[283]

We say we believe in "The Priesthood of all believers." Yet, we then refer to clergy and laity, which sort of, in fact, quite explicitly holds to the opposite to what we have just said we believe.

We say, "I am going to church, "implying that church is a place or building. But we profess to believe that we, as people of faith, are the body of Christ, i.e. the church. I know it easy shorthand, but it is actually, in action, saying something opposite to what we say we believe.

People get irritated with me when they ask where do you go to church, and I reply, "You can do that?" Then, with puzzled look, they ask, "What do you mean?" I answer, "One can't **go to** church. One can only **BE** church – sure lots of the church can gather together. But one cannot go somewhere when you are the very place you say you are going to."
A friend used to ask me with a smile when I used to ask, "What time is the Service?" He would mischievously ask, "Do you mean for the car? Or do you need a service station?" What do we think, "Divine service" is anyway? I guess, if it is as scripture would have it, "Present your body as a living sacrifice," then I can understand?

Of course, we use words, in language, to cover up the seemingly unacceptable don't we. So we have, "Collateral damage," and "Friendly fire," when what we are really talking about is "Dead people." "People who have been killed." But that sounds a bit harsh doesn't it?
Words are important. Let's try and say what we mean and mean what we say

MY FRIEND THE CAR SMASHER

Car Smasher builds garage

It took me some time to persuade my friend Andy Smith to visit Kenya with me, as I felt his church needed a third world focus as well as the great work he was already doing in the Rohampton Estate, which is one of the larges council estates in Europe.

Andy was a little squeamish about coming with me to Africa, even though some of the storeys he told me concerning the work on the estate made me somewhat careful, things like the fact that if you want home deliver Pizza then you have to phone and arrange to meet the delivery man on the other side of the main road, they won't deliver on the estate because they lose their deliver bike, money and pizzas. Great place to live it seemed to me, give me Africa any day. Andy took to Kenya like a duck to water so to speak.

The following year 2005 he decided to go again this time with some of the young people from Roehampton including Luke, Luke was famous on the estate or rather infamous, he had dropped in to the Regenerate club but also took a liking to stealing Andy's car and rolling it down hills into brick walls. Just for fun you know. Seemed a bit surprising to me that Andy was still willing to take him with him, but he did.

Kenya turned Luke Clifford's life around, along with giving him a vision for a garage the trip changed his life and he came back with the idea to build the garage to help people by supplying work. He has since raised over £6000 for the project, and been back 3 times to help with the project.

He came back from that first visit and told us he had found God, more than that he was determined to help young people there, from his own small wages he gave Andy money each week and made it quickly possible to buy land and prepare for his dream of building a garage for the youngsters there.

Last February 2007 Luke won the Anthony Walker Memorial Prize, the top Champions of Respect award from the Evangelical Alliance. Luke was honoured for initiating the garage project in Kenya. Click here to see Luke receiving his award.

Local press, Premier Radio, have all picked up this story, and some have even donated money for the project.

Back in Roehampton Luke, has now stopped trashing Andy's car and is helping to facilitate all the other good work on the estate there such as the Juice bar drop in site the Bus programme; and the many, many other things to change the thinking really to Regenerate. If you want to know more have a look at the web site. www.regenerateuk.co.uk

Other Books by Adrian Hawkes:

adrianhawkes@phoenixcommunity.co.uk

website/blog links:
www.adrianhawkes.blogspot.com
www.adrianhawkes.co.uk

Other Books by Adrian Hawkes from (Amazon etc) and all good books shops:

You might have to put in By Adrian Hawkes if you are using Amazon

Leadership And…

Spanish edition of Leadership And...
Lidezago y...

Jacob a Fatherless generation

Hello is that you God?

Attracting Training Releasing Youth

Culture Clash

Icejacked

Printed in Great Britain
by Amazon

79170977R00169